Return to Nisa

Return to Nisa

Marjorie Shostak

Harvard University Press

Cambridge, Massachusetts · London, England · 2000

Library of Congress Cataloging-in-Publication Data

Shostak, Marjorie, 1945–
Return to Nisa / Marjorie Shostak.
p.   cm.
Includes index.
ISBN 0-674-00323-3 (alk. paper)
1. Nisa.   2. Women, !Kung—Biography.
3. Women, !Kung—Social life and customs.   I. Title.
DT1058.K86 N577 2000
305.48′896106883—dc21   00-33462

for Lois Kasper
in loving memory

Contents

Return to Nisa

Africa!

Towering beside them, I sit awkwardly in the circle of small-boned !Kung San women, shifting often, my body unused to the cross-legged position. The quarter moon drops toward the horizon, and the stars brighten as it descends. The sounds of a healing dance flood the air. Complex clapped rhythms drive the women's songs, fragments of undulating and overlapping melodies. Each woman tilts her head toward her shoulder, trapping sound near her ear, the better to hear her part. The women's knees and legs, loosely describing a circle, fall carelessly against one another—an intertwining of bodies and song.

In the center of the circle, a fire flares as it is stoked and whipped by human breath, soon to ebb again into glowing coals. Beyond the circle, men and boys-almost-men, their taut upper bodies hardly visible in the darkness, pound the cool sand with bare feet, blending new rhythms into the song. So forcefully do they dance that a deep circle forms in the sand beneath them, enclosing us, separating us from the profane, protecting us from the unknown.

Beyond, in the dark, the spirits of the ancestors are said to sit, drawn to the event to watch, possibly to stir mischief. A trancer screams at the spirits, warning them not to cause trouble, not to inflict harm. He weaves among the seated women, laying on hands to heal those who are sick and to ward off illness from others. Hands reach out to steady his trembling legs and body, to protect his feet from the burning coals as he nears the fire.

My own hands tire of clapping and drop to my lap, easing the tension bound up in following along. The melodies of !Kung traditional songs swirl around me, familiar and soothing. My attention moves off, beyond the healing dance, beyond the village with its small groups of traditional grass huts and more contemporary mud ones, beyond the half-dozen villages that use the same local well, to the vast Kalahari landscape, immensely quiet and immensely broad. The intense human

3

drama enacted on the sand would go unnoticed from a plane flying above the dark, mysterious land.

A lull in the singing brings me back, to the sounds of small talk and the distant ringing of donkey bells carried on the wind. The healing dance slowly builds again, layers of song and movement both strange and familiar to me. I savor a strong feeling of well-being and peace, a sense of rest in the midst of a long and difficult journey.

꽈꽈꽈 In June 1989, I left my home in Atlanta to spend a month in a remote area in northwestern Botswana, on the northern edge of the Kalahari desert. I had lived and worked in the area twice before, but had not been back in fourteen years.

My first sojourn with the !Kung San, or Bushmen,* began in 1969. Then the people were still part-time hunters and gatherers, although their traditional ways had begun to change. They were trying to emulate the herding and agricultural ways of life of their Bantu-speaking neighbors, the Herero and Tswana.

During that first stay of nearly two years, I learned to speak the !Kung language—replete with clicks, glottal flaps, glottal stops, pressed vowels, and tones—well enough to pursue my research on the personal lives of !Kung women. Using the format of the life history narrative, I asked women about their childhoods, marriages, sexuality, friendships, and dreams, delving into their experiences and feelings as only an outsider might do.

Of eight women I interviewed, one stood out. More open than the others and more willing to articulate the intimacies of her life, she had a striking gift for verbal expression. She was about fifty years old at the time. We completed fifteen interviews during my first field trip and another six when I returned in 1975: about twenty-five hours of tape-recorded talk. She knew I hoped to write about her, and together we chose a pseudonym to protect her privacy. The name we selected was Nisa. I translated and edited the interviews, and in 1981 Harvard University Press published my chronological rendering of her story, *Nisa: The Life and Words of a !Kung Woman.*

Now, fourteen years after my last trip, I was on my way back, in-

* They call themselves the *Zhun/twasi*, "the real people." Referred to in the past as the Sonquas and in Botswana as the Basarwa, they are also known as the !Kung Bushmen, the !Kung San, or simply the !Kung.

fused with a particular sense of urgency. Nisa was now about sixty-eight years old, far beyond the usual !Kung life expectancy of fifty-five. And my own life had taken a distressing turn toward early mortality. A year earlier I had learned I had breast cancer. Although my odds were favorable and a majority of women with my prognosis survived, I was terrifyingly aware that many women lost their lives to the disease. My future had been cast into deep, threatening shadow; the present turned in on itself as my daily experience acquired a brutal, slashing edge.

〰〰〰 A week after my mastectomy I had a visitor: an unnervingly cheerful, I've-been-there-myself woman a bit younger than my forty-two years. Having experienced no recurrence of breast cancer for five years, she had entered the fortunate statistical category of cancer survivor. She bubbled as she told me of the changes she had made in her life. She had always wanted to go to nursing school, she said, but had never followed through. Once diagnosed with cancer, however, she had no longer felt she could keep putting off her dream. She had successfully balanced the demands of school with raising two small sons, and proudly announced her impending graduation.

I was usually wary of people who addressed somber subjects with unremitting cheer, and this woman proved the rule. She spoke of her experience with cancer with only the barest hint of emotional pain—or, to put it more generously, perhaps she spoke from the other side of the pain. In my thoughts I dubbed her "Miss Chirpy." And yet, in the end, her visit served me very well. At some point during the following year, a year of endless doctor's appointments, blood tests, chemotherapy, chest X-rays, bone scans, fear, and paralyzing depression, I asked myself the same question she had asked herself: "What can I no longer afford to put off?" And a voice in my brain shouted: "Africa!"

〰〰〰 Thursday evening, June 22, 1989: Almost time to board a flight from Atlanta to London, en route to Botswana. The scope of my gesture felt overwhelming. I, "Mommy" to three small children, wife to a concerned husband, was about to leave, to be gone a month, after having been distracted for weeks.

The exchanges in the airport bristled with an air of unreality: words spoken of departure and separation, of coping and managing, for the family and for myself. Each of my actions was a step toward removing me from the children who had sprung from my body, who were part of my soul, whose presence bolstered my flagging spirits. And from my husband, my companion and friend.

The children were on edge, wary of the impending change, unsure of how to say goodbye. With the last travel details completed, we had half an hour: to talk, to connect, and then to let go. I had tried to prepare my youngest child, Sarah, for my leaving, but at age two and a half, what did she understand of "Africa" or of a month without her mother? We ate sweets, took pictures in a concession booth, and read goodbye cards.

Finally it was time. Holding Sarah on my hip, I hugged my eldest daughter, Susanna, my son, Adam, and then my husband, Mel. Slowly, reluctantly, I transferred Sarah from my hip to Mel's. They waved as I turned and walked through the "international passengers only" security checkpoint. A few steps later I looked back at the tightly knit group receding down the terminal, already working out their new alliances, discussing dinner and treats, reassurances of continuity in the face of disorienting change. When they were no longer in view, I passed through to the gate. I was alone. I was on my way.

The decision to go had preceded the practical, starting with a need, the need to return: to see, to taste, to smell, to experience again, perhaps even to heal. I yearned to be surrounded by the landscape that had etched itself upon my young, impressionable soul twenty years before, that had initiated me into the beauty of its sparse, wild, and independent rhythms. And I wanted to see Nisa again, the woman whose views about life had infused my own during my years of writing and thinking about her. I had heard periodically that she was alive, the latest report received only months before. I wanted to connect with her again before her life ended, and, for reasons that were not entirely clear to me, I wanted her to know that my life was threatened.

Thinking of returning to that stark world filled me with longing. For years, bearing and raising children, teaching at a university, doing research, and writing a second book had edged out most serious thoughts of a return. Then, without warning, my life had changed, and my priorities had as well.

The voice calling me back to Africa, which had been lost in the clutter of those other concerns, became audible, then compelling. As it gained strength, to my grateful surprise, it displaced my despair. Gradually it garnered a powerful alliance of internal forces that enabled me to leave my family—my support and my charge—to travel around the globe on this personal quest. If my life did end prematurely, at least I would have confronted again one of its most intense and mysterious chapters.

Determined to make the trip no matter the financial and emotional cost, I was delighted to learn that two other anthropologists, Dick Katz and his wife, Verna St. Denis, would be in the area. Dick, knowing of my illness and sympathetic to my desire to return, offered help: I could live at the camp where he and Verna were working. They would drive me to Dobe, Nisa's village, and we could take her back to their camp—or I could stay in Dobe, and they would pick me up at the end of my visit. Neither option was ideal. I wanted to see Nisa in her own world, but to be without a truck of my own—for transport and for emergencies—would be foolhardy.

Then I was awarded grants that would cover most of my expenses. In exchange for my collecting, drying, and documenting plants the !Kung used as food, a pharmaceutical company interested in the level of vitamin E in the "natural human diet" paid my airfare. And the dean of Emory University—with which I was affiliated—provided funds for most of my other expenses, affirming the work I had done and might yet do. At last I was able to see my way clear: I would rent a truck, hire a driver, outfit myself, and live at Dobe.

As the plane sat on the runway, the drone of its engines enveloped me and fears suppressed for days clamored to the surface. Going alone to the wilds of Africa—was it a mistake? Would I face death in that remote land? Would something happen to me so that I would never see my family again? Would something happen to them that would alter our lives forever? If something went seriously wrong, could I live with the responsibility?

My anxiety staked in deeper. Would I see Nisa? Might not administrative red tape, tribal warfare, mechanical problems, or some simple practical limitation undermine my journey? Would I be safe? A strange thought, because in the past year "safe" had changed its meaning: nothing had protected my body from invasion, and nowhere did I feel safe.

My fingers moved to a sore spot on my elbow, probing at an unexplained pain, one similar to others I had watched and worried over until they, fortunately, had disappeared. Would this one be different? Was my body harboring a second, lethal round of dread disease? Was this departure from my family a dress rehearsal for my more dramatic, final leave-taking?

Breaking into my reverie came the sudden firing of engines as the plane took off. Rain beat against the windows. Now I truly was on my way. What would I be staying for, after all: for more fear, more depression, more despondency? Whatever lay ahead, it would be hard to rival the pain of that previous year. I looked around the cabin, at other faces caught in reverie, and as the plane lifted from the earth, excitement rose within me. Ahead was adventure.

In London, with almost a full day's layover, I groggily headed toward a hotel to sleep before the next twelve-hour flight. I woke with the alarm for a phone call home, prearranged to reach the children before the older ones left for day camp. Ready to be touched and filled with yearning, I was surprised by my impatience and by how little I had to give. I conversed with all three, yet was eager to go back to sleep so as to wake in time for a few hours of exploring London before my evening flight. As we spoke, my son spilled hot coffee on himself, hurting his arm. I said the right words, yet, knowing that his father was there, I was only marginally engaged.

That evening, at the British Airlines check-in counter, excitement surged again as I spoke the words "Gaborone, Botswana" to the clerk. I peered at others waiting in line—blacks and whites on their way to Africa—searching for something of my past, straining to identify an accent or the look of a face. My eyes moved among the dark-skinned men in business suits and women in multicolored dresses, then rested on a woman with closely cropped hair and high cheekbones, her face so reminiscent of !Kung San physiognomy that I was tempted to greet her in the !Kung language. With three days' travel ahead before I would reach their world, I nevertheless felt kinship with those who made Africa their home. I wanted to embrace them, to tell them of my love for their land, to share my longing after fourteen years of separation.

Around me, passengers slept restlessly as the DC10 moved south over the vast African continent. It would take twelve hours to reach Lusaka, Zambia, our first stop. A woman across the aisle nursed her four-week-old infant; sounds of satisfaction, too soft to be heard over the hum of the engine, reverberated in my thoughts. My chest ached as I recalled the tenderness and sensuality of nursing and the anguish of weaning fifteen-month-old Sarah in one day, a wrenching deprivation necessitated by the diagnosis of cancer.

That Monday morning a little over a year before, I had been concerned but not terrified: a small hardness in my breast would surely be diagnosed as a clogged milk duct. I had refused my husband's offer to cancel his classes to go with me to the doctor but had asked my parents, who were passing through town, to bring my daughter along: she would drain my breast of milk before the examination. My concern intensified, however, when the doctor proposed a needle biopsy: with local anesthesia, he withdrew cells from the breast and sent them to a lab. As I dressed, his voice rang out from the phone in his office, speaking to a radiologist who was my friend, medical advisor, and colleague. "Boyd," he said, "I'm sending Marjorie over to you for a mammogram. No, I don't think it's cancer."

The needle biopsy came back positive, and the mammogram showed a sizable tumor with spread into the milk ducts. Boyd broke the news to me in the mammography room where I had been waiting. Not only was it cancer, but because it had spread beyond the initial mass, he couldn't tell how pervasive it was. The next day, Tuesday, a radioactive bone scan and a tomogram—a sci-fi–vintage robot whirling above me taking multiple-exposure chest X-rays—gave me my first good news: no detection of cancer in my bones or chest. On Wednesday, I had a mastectomy.

My daughter slept with a close family friend the night she was weaned, the night before the operation, when my body still retained radioactivity from the day's procedure. I didn't see her again for four days, until I returned from the hospital. It was the first time we had been apart for more than a few hours.

When I got home from the hospital, it seemed as if years had passed. Wary of a mother who had disappeared so suddenly, Sarah remained aloof, although interested. She stayed beside her father, her support. Only much later did she nestle in my arms again, a healing for both of us. Drinking from a bottle, she searched for the skin of my neck with her hand, stroking it gently, a reminder of the tender warmth of our former bond.

𝖪𝖪𝖪𝖪𝖪 "I guess I need this time away," I wrote while on the plane. "Time not to be available to others, not to answer to anyone but myself. The intensity is powerful, at times overwhelming. It's beyond anything I remember feeling before. Sheer pleasure, to be so self-involved, so self-contained."

Restless and uncomfortable, I eventually slipped into sleep. I woke as we descended below the clouds in Zambia, with its brown fields and scattered leafless trees. My heart pounded as we touched down on that winter landscape, dispelling the daze of forty-three hours of travel. Then my senses dulled again; I was grateful not to have to disembark.

The DC10 took two hours to reach Gaborone, the capital of Botswana, where I went through customs and immigration. Then I boarded a flight on Botswana Airlines that would take me to Maun, a dusty town with the feel of the American Wild West, on the banks of a marshy, crocodile-infested river.

Sadness and pride mingled with anticipation as I traveled farther and farther from family, friends, all that was easily familiar. The plane's shadow traversed the barren land below. Like relics of an ancient millennium, flat salt pans stretched endlessly beneath us, only the faintest of trails suggesting human or animal passage.

As we approached Maun, the land sported settlements, isolated at the farthest fringes, with cattle fences mere pencil lines across the vast undifferentiated canvas of sand. Rising from the flat land, round thatched homes clustered together as if on a game board: a simple tilt of the land seemed enough to rid the baked earth of this human presence. Yet the compounds survived, a testimony to human ingenuity and stamina. Nearer to the town, green vegetation followed the river's course, and the land was thick with human settlement. Rondavels and thatched huts, earthen in color, spoke distinctly of Africa.

𝖪𝖪𝖪𝖪𝖪 In Maun, the town that had served as my reentry into "civilization" years before, I headed for the hotel, still called Riley's but recently remodeled. I tipped the porters, bought a four-ounce can of soda water, and went to my room: a broad bed with starched sheets, thatch and wood beams rising high on the lofted ceiling. Jet-lagged and exhausted, I craved sleep, but first placed a call to my family and then took a shower, one of a precious few I would have in the coming month.

The phone rang: my call to the United States had gone through. This time it was different. The two older children, excited that I was in Africa, insisted I call again as soon as I knew the color of my truck. The youngest had cried for me that morning, I was told, but had accepted her father's comfort. Keeping me somewhat distant, she asked me to send kisses to and talk to her doll, and I did, speaking words of endearment meant for them all. I hung up, happy and suddenly energetic—not sad or even guilty. Having both the connection and the independence was exhilarating.

Wanting to eat before I slept, I headed to the newly refurbished dining room, complete with imitation-lace vinyl table coverings and bouquets of plastic pink and blue roses. At the table I reviewed a message I had received at the airport: Dick and Verna planned to arrive in town that day or the next. That was good news! I had worried about traveling—ten or more hours into the wilderness—with a driver I knew nothing about. But with Dick and Verna in town, we could drive to their camp in convoy, and then my driver and I could take off together for Dobe; by that time I would know whether I felt comfortable with him.

As I picked through the thin bones of the local bream fish that was my dinner, Dick and Verna arrived and joined me. They told of their experiences in the bush, and I shared some of the pain that had led to my sitting alone at a table in Riley's. We discussed the best ways to outfit my trip, and they generously offered to help. The next morning we would begin by renting my truck.

After a fretful sleep, I woke, keenly alert to my new surroundings. Outside was bright sunlight, a gentle breeze. Shifting shadows played along a path luxuriant with tropical plants. A man with a thick broom was clearing away debris from the previous night's drinking and socializing. The patio and walkway beside the office and bar were being waxed with a thick red paste, its color and odor familiar even after fourteen years.

Leaving the shelter of the tall trees near the parking lot, Dick, Verna, and I drove out into the bright world and onto the only paved road in town. As we headed away from the center, sand colors and shades of brown were everywhere: little vegetation grew in the compounds of mud huts and thatched roofs, where children played and their elders sat and talked. Trucks passing on the right side of the road threw dust onto our window as we drove to the edge of town, where a truck was reserved for me through Avis.

Helena, an articulate Tswana woman who had spent some time in the United States, was the manager of the Avis office. She greeted me with a friendly smile. After the papers were signed she gestured toward a truck resting in the shade of an open-sided hangar: a blue Toyota Land Cruiser. It had a closed cab in front and an open back with two high safari-style viewing seats crossing from one side to the other.

I opened the right (driver's-side) door, got behind the wheel, and carefully reviewed the shifting pattern. My left hand moved to a knob on the floor that controlled high and low four-wheel drive, setting off memories from years before: harrowing driving experiences through mud and sand. I started the engine and inched out slowly from under the hangar, keeping an eye on a parked truck to my left and on the rear and side mirrors. Then I started to turn. My confidence surged as the heavy engine followed my command.

Then *scrunch!*—the sound of metal grinding against metal filled my ears. Unbelieving, I got out of the cab. The massive front right bumper was hooked tightly around one of the poles supporting the hangar. Shame displaced my elation as Dick, Verna, and Helena looked on sympathetically.

Our repeated attempts to dislodge the bumper inflicted even more damage. Finally, by roping Dick's truck to mine and pulling sideways, we freed the reluctant metal. Helena assured me that the damage was essentially cosmetic and could be repaired after I returned the truck. The deductible, however, was so high that my insurance wouldn't pay for the repairs. I asked Dick to drive back to the hotel; I wasn't ready to tackle driving on the left side of the road just then.

〰〰〰〰 Dick and Verna told disquieting stories of life in the !Kung villages where they worked. Drinking was widespread, as was accompanying violence, and people were depending more and more on government handouts for food rather than procuring it for themselves. Dick and Verna also gave me the troubling news that the army, the Botswana Defense Force, had an outpost near Dobe.

Concerned about the military presence, I arranged to meet with an army colonel before I left Maun. With only a tourist visa in hand, I told him I had taken a leave of absence from my university to visit people in Dobe whom I hadn't seen in fourteen years, including a woman about whom I had written a book. This was not considered actual research—which would have required administrative approval with advance notice of at least six months, approval that I might or might not have received—but was more like a working holiday. I said I was worried about being a single woman in the bush and asked if I could count on the army if I needed help. The colonel assured me that I could. He gave me the names of three officers who were stationed in the Dobe area, and promised to send a communiqué to let them know I was coming.

꧁꧁꧁꧁꧁ "!Kung San Works," read the fading sign outside the low whitewashed building. After hours of shopping for staples to take to the field, I stepped through the portal of the shop, going back in time. Piled on the desk, hanging from the walls, overflowing from boxes were San bows and arrows, beadwork, decorated skins and bags, mortars and pestles. The familiar aroma of San perfume—pressed from the branches of the *sa* plant—surrounded me.

Dick and Verna introduced me to Kxau, an office worker also known as Royal—one of a handful of San who had gone through primary school and who spoke English. Words pouring from my mouth in uncontrolled enthusiasm, I attempted to resurrect a language I hadn't spoken in fourteen years. My tongue moved heavily among the clicks used in words of greeting; the sounds stuck to the roof of my mouth. Crimson-faced, I labored on, unwilling to resort to English.

I managed—perhaps because Royal was being polite and tolerant of my awkward phrasing—to convey greetings from Richard Lee, another anthropologist Royal had worked with. I learned that Hwantla, the woman who had given me my !Kung name, had been seriously ill but was getting better. I even teased Royal about his having children by two different women—a !Kung San woman and a Herero woman, neither formally married to him—and asked why the Herero hadn't killed him. (At least, that's what I thought I said.)

What a thrill to speak again a language whose sounds and thought patterns I had learned to love, a language that had been difficult to master, that I had used as a reference in my daily life long after I left Africa, that had remained dormant in me for years. And to speak it with someone with whom I could stop in mid-sentence, ask what a word meant, and have it translated on the spot into English! I begged Royal to take time off from his job at the tourist shop to work with me at Dobe. He could help me learn and relearn subtleties of the language after years of disuse.

He couldn't tell me for sure, Royal said, because he had agreed to take an American tourist to Dobe, a man who had heard about him from Richard Lee. But it was long past the time when the man had planned to arrive. Tempted by my offer, Royal decided he would wait another week. Then, if the man still hadn't come, he would find transport and meet me at Dobe.

Maun's fresh food market was our last stop before leaving. Sacks of potatoes, onions, apples, and other foods that could withstand the journey were piled under the tarp in the back of the truck, on top of the jerry cans of gasoline and water and the trunks filled with canned and dried foods. Baitsenke Habana, the driver I had hired, now took the wheel. Following in the dust behind Dick and Verna's truck, we headed out of town.

Helena had vouched for Baitsenke's trustworthiness, and my own impression of him, from a day of packing the truck and driving around town, was quite favorable. We talked of cameras and film and of his ambition to become a proficient photographer. I asked about the tiered social system in which have-nots herded the cows of the wealthy, and we touched on local and national politics. He was pleasant and responsive in conversation but not especially talkative, and we soon lapsed into comfortable silence as he expertly maneuvered the vehicle along the ridged road surface, swerving to avoid deep holes and sand pits.

The sun was strong, the air pleasant through the open windows. Within minutes of town, settlements became sparse. A thick mantle of dust, gritty in my mouth and coating my skin, robbed the trees nearest the road of color, graying their graceful hanging branches as if with age. Goats, singly or in small herds, rummaged in the underbrush, searching the overgrazed, denuded earth for food. The road stretched forward, a wide ribbon, rising and falling with the land.

Baitsenke drove on, and soon the vigilance with which I was soaking in each detail of the landscape eased. I thought of my family, and of our last phone call two days before. Once again it had been difficult. Susanna told me that she missed me, a sad gentleness in her tone. Adam said he was doing all right, but my husband told me Adam was falling asleep every night to the sound of my voice singing lullabies—a tape I had recorded before I left. Sarah, the youngest and the one I most worried about, was distant, rotely saying she loved me.

Now, as I withdrew from any possibility of telephone contact, a longing rose to hold Sarah's tender body against mine, and to be with the others—the most intense longing for the family I had felt since I left. Yet the harried sound of my husband's voice—weighed down by the responsibilities of car pools, piano lessons, soccer practice, camp schedules, dance lessons—had seemed a mirror of all the days of my life. And from my end of the phone line, the image in the mirror was unappealing. Was that the only way to be a good parent? Had I perhaps given up too much, lost too much of myself in trying to meet their needs? Did I have to travel nine thousand miles to learn about balance?

Fear surged in me at the immensity of this journey and its power to transform my life. Fear, and with it, exhilaration. And yearning. But this time the yearning was for years of life: to experience fully the last drop of my youth, to bask in the concerns of middle age, and to live to be old. Living to be old, taken for granted only a year ago, now seemed an extraordinary luxury.

Dick and Verna stopped their truck at a town with a handful of rondavels and a small one-room store, and Baitsenke and I pulled in behind them. At the store we bought sodas and snacks. We were still two hours from where the road to Dobe would split off from this one, which led south to the village where Dick and Verna were working. In two hours I would have to decide whether to follow them or to go off alone with Baitsenke.

When the time came, I took the plunge. At the fork in the road, Baitsenke and I turned toward Dobe.

⧩⧩⧩⧩⧩⧩ Night fell quickly, as it does near the equator, and without moonlight it was an impenetrable black by the time we reached one of the permanent water holes making up the Dobe area. Cows, caught in the headlights, ambled toward the safety of the darkness, looking back as if unsure whether to contest the right of way. Far from human habitation, trees cut down when the road had been widened to two spoors still lay along the roadsides. Excellent as firewood, they had long since disappeared nearer the villages. We broke off some branches and piled them onto the truck.

A wrong turn took us to a compound shrouded in darkness, barely discernible in the glare of the headlights—a fence, the outline of a thatched roof, a voice responding within. Baitsenke spoke Setswana (one of the official languages of Botswana, the other being English) from the truck, and soon we had hired someone to guide us to Dobe. Retracing our route, we found the turn we had missed, and by ten o'clock we passed the first of the six villages at Dobe.

This homecoming was different from others I remembered. Where were the people lining the road to see who was in the truck? Twenty years before, we had had to stop at each village along the road—the deep hum of the engine having carried ahead for miles—so eager had the people been to see who was traveling and to get news from the outside world.

Perhaps it was just too late at night for people to come out to the road. But what were those other tire marks? The tracks seemed unsurprising at the outermost villages where transport was more common, but what were they doing closer to Dobe, the last village before the border with Namibia? Whose tracks were they? A chilling thought: Could it be other researchers? Would I have to share my time in Dobe with onlookers? Had I come all this distance to sit around the fire dealing with a world I was desperately trying to leave behind?

⧩⧩⧩⧩⧩⧩ Baitsenke stopped the truck, leaving the headlights on, and told me we had reached the village where Hwantla, my namesake, lived. I stepped out onto the cool night sand to a strange quiet.

People must have been sleeping, for it took some time before figures cloaked in blankets slowly emerged from the shadows to see who we were. Hwantla's husband recognized me and, smiling, greeted me as his wife—acknowledging my name relationship with Hwantla. I greeted "my husband" and asked after my namesake. Then Hwantla herself walked toward me, her blanket pulled tight against the cold. Her voice was barely audible as she greeted me; then a cough consumed her small frame.

We talked a little, but it was late and everyone was tired. Hwantla soon went back to her hut. Baitsenke and I set up camp at the site where Richard Lee had most recently stayed. That made it "right," not appearing partial to any one group. With the help of others, Baitsenke pitched my tent beside a leafless tree, whose bare branches might provide a modicum of shade in the heat of the day. He placed his own tent at a respectful distance. A fire was lit, and soon we handed around tea heavy with sugar and a fistful of raisins to the men who had helped. When the moment seemed right, I asked about Nisa, and was told she was well and lived nearby.

Later, inside my tent, with a flashlight propped against my shoe, I put on my nightgown, applied some mosquito repellent, and crawled into bed—an inch-and-a-half-thick pad over which lay my rented sleeping bag topped by three blankets folded in half to provide double the warmth.

Donkey bells rang in the distance; a bird chattered shrilly. All those days of planning and dreaming, of traveling and preparing—and here I was at Dobe. Feeling at home, already healing. Fourteen years ago might have been yesterday. Like those old piano-lesson songs still in my fingers after thirty years, the ruts in the road, the spindly trees, the thatched roofs and mud houses—all this was etched so deeply that time had barely touched it. This wasn't new learning, or even learning something over again; this was just acknowledging what I already knew.

Voices in Dobe

I woke to the sound of four or five people talking at once. They were waiting to greet me, to ask for a pipe of tobacco, perhaps to be offered a cup of sweet tea. Gathered around the fire, they spoke in soft tones. I listened carefully for the raspy cadence of Nisa, but the lone female voice was not hers. Disappointed, I pulled the covers close, still chilled from the night, exhausted from a restless sleep, and sore at the shoulder and hip from the hard ground. The deep rumble of a truck sounded nearby, then faded and was gone. I lay quietly, relishing the stillness; I would wait a little longer before stepping out into the bright sunshine.

𝕂𝕂𝕂𝕂 Dick and Verna had been right—the Botswana Defense Force was certainly present near Dobe. That first morning, and almost every morning of my stay, they paid me a visit. I was talking with people at the fire when they appeared: two trucks crowded with uniformed soldiers, rifles in hand, with ammunition belts crisscrossing their chests.

I knew that the neighboring country, Namibia, would soon hold free elections—for the first time since South Africa had seized the government and imposed its illegal apartheid regime more than forty years before. Tensions about the elections were affecting people in Botswana, especially those living near the border: the Herero and the !Kung. And Dobe was only a mile from the border.

The border between the two countries was first fenced in the early 1960s, cutting the !Kung community in half. When the height of the fence was doubled to eight feet in the 1970s, a stile was built that allowed the !Kung free access to either side. Nevertheless, the !Kung in Botswana and the !Kung in Namibia, while sharing a common language and culture, began separating their histories in the mid-1960s. In Botswana, the !Kung lived in contact with the Bantu-speaking Herero and Tswana people, who had moved into the area in the 1920s and whose numbers had been steadily increasing. Tending cattle and goats and planting crops, they moved onto traditional !Kung land. From the grazing of their herds, the land near the water holes soon became depleted of edible plants, and wild animals could be found only at greater distances. Unable to sustain themselves by hunting and gathering as in the past, many !Kung worked as low-paid laborers in Bantu villages, herding livestock and tending fields.

Across the border in Namibia, the !Kung had their own homeland, or Bantustan, a separate area for the "Bushmen" in the apartheid system. Free of competition from Bantu-speaking people, they nevertheless suffered the political consequences of South African rule. As they were encouraged, and then required, to leave their original water holes and live in a settlement called Chum!kwe, their traditional values and way of life started to erode.

The idea behind aggregating nomadic !Kung groups into a central area had been benign enough: it would allow the government to better serve the !Kung as they moved into the modern world. Salaried jobs would be created; agriculture and animal husbandry would be taught; medical services would be made available; and schooling (in Afrikaans) would be provided. But in practice, it didn't turn out benign at all.

Not that there weren't rags-to-riches stories circulating among the Botswana !Kung about Chum!kwe. "People are given goats and cattle," they would tell the anthropologists, their tone envious. "People have jobs and are paid good wages." "Food is distributed." "Children are learning to read." "There is a medical clinic with a nurse."

But there were also descriptions of squalor, violence, drunkenness, and promiscuity; of people who had traditionally shared their wealth now hoarding it; of those without paid jobs becoming dependent upon those who had them; of lassitude and hopelessness; of the dissolution of a previously viable culture. Overall mortality rose because of crowded living conditions, illness, poor nutrition, and violence. In 1978 !Kung men were conscripted into the army, to patrol the border and to fight in Angola—on the side of the South Africans.

Now, with elections scheduled in Namibia in November, the Botswana government was fearful that political turmoil might cross the border. Hence the presence of the army near Dobe and the border.

The Botswana government was also aware that the end of South African rule might encourage the Herero, whose roots were in Namibia, to return to the land of their ancestors. In the early twentieth century, a campaign of extermination by German colonists drove hundreds of thousands of Herero from their homes. Most of them died at the hands of the Germans or in their escape to the desert. Others were fortunate enough to reach Botswana—then called Bechuanaland—and settled there.

Although they prospered in Botswana, many Herero yearned for their homeland. The government of Botswana, eager to retain so large and vital a population, did allow them to repatriate—but only if they did so legally, within the guidelines of international law. For the Herero living in the Dobe area, that meant driving their cattle hundreds of miles—to one of a handful of legal border crossings—getting the necessary paperwork approved, crossing the border, then driving the herd back again, to end up a few miles from where they started. When cuts in the border fence were discovered and Herero cattle from Botswana were seen grazing in Namibia, the Botswana army was sent in.

For years, while the Bantu-speaking populations had not been permitted to cross the border, the !Kung had been allowed free access by both governments, as long as they did not take livestock with them. A month before my arrival, when the !Kung were first told that the border was closed, they had found it hard to believe. People visiting relatives and friends in either country were stranded, forbidden to return home; babies were born, people got sick or injured, first menstrual ceremonies were celebrated—all without the support and care of family members who lived on the other side of the border.

&&&&&&& I rose from my seat beside the fire to shake hands with a pleasant-looking officer who spoke impeccable English. Dick and Verna had told me about this man, whose fiancée was working for them, and he also knew about me.

I asked him if the colonel in Maun had sent a communiqué about my visit. Yes, he said, there had been a communiqué. I offered tea, but he declined, leaving the air tense with expectation. After these perfunctory pleasantries, he got to the point. "Exactly why have you come here? What do you plan to do?"

As I had with the colonel, I avoided calling my trip "research," which would have required approval from various government agencies. My tourist visa allowed me access to any nonrestricted area in the country for thirty days, and this included Dobe. I said I had received travel funds from my university and had decided to update my information on the !Kung, with whom I had last worked fourteen years before. I also said I hoped to take a group of people to the bush for a few days to camp and to hunt and gather.

"This trip," the officer asked, "when would you do this? Where exactly would you go?"

Years ago, I told him, we had camped five or ten miles to the north, close to the border road in the groves of mongongo nut trees. If possible, I hoped to go there again. But I didn't want to expose myself or the people to danger. Was there anything I should know? Were there problems along the border that might make a bush trip dangerous?

It didn't take long to see that information flowed in only one direction: from me to the soldiers. I learned little about the army's presence or activities, or about anything else of consequence in the area. Fortunately, however, they readily agreed to the trip to the bush.

Only one piece of information did they relay, and it was one I already knew: the border was no longer open to the !Kung crossing between Namibia and Botswana. "This is an international border," the officer told me, "and it has to be respected like any border between two countries." Stepping toward his vehicle, he went on: "The people will adjust. After all, this border is no different from the one between the United States and Canada, or that of any other modern nations."

If I wanted to be of help, he said, I should make it absolutely clear to the !Kung that the border was closed. This was deadly important: anyone disobeying the command would be shot.

As the noise of the army trucks faded into the distance, the air filled again with the sounds of people living simply. At last I could return to the fire, to welcome my visitors, to offer tea, and to share news.

I noticed Bo, Nisa's husband, sitting among the small group that had gathered. Seeing me scan the faces around the fire, he told me Nisa had been waiting for the soldiers to leave; she was on her way.

I wasn't sure from a distance, but as she approached—colorful scarf covering her hair, bright shawl crossing her right shoulder, eyes riveted upon me—I had no doubt.

"My aunt, it's you," I greeted her.

"Eh, hey. Niece, my niece, my little niece."

We hugged, somewhat awkwardly. "Nisa," I asked, "how is it that you are still young? Look at me, your niece, my youth has left me. My hair now has gray." But, seeing her questioning look, I added, "My tongue is heavy, no longer lithe. Perhaps you do not understand me."

In the less than twenty-four hours since my arrival, I had become painfully aware how much of the language I had lost in fourteen years. I could still understand the spoken language well enough, and could even communicate simple things, but a complex thought—even one I had felt some confidence in expressing—often prompted people to rush in to fill an awkward silence, to rephrase my ungrammatical constructions, to try to string my somewhat off-the-mark word assemblages into something comprehensible.

Animated debates and conflicting interpretations of what I was trying to say sometimes followed. The substance of my ideas would usually come across, but not necessarily in the right sequence or with proper colloquial nuance. When we were really stumped, we would try to find someone of proven ability, someone with the necessary imagination to crack the code. Fortunately, I could recognize the correct construction when I heard it. "That's it, that's it!" I would shout, beaming gratefully at my astute translator, relieved to be understood at last.

⟨⟨⟨⟨⟨⟨⟨⟨ Nisa and I walked to the fire, joining the others. I had so many questions: What was her life like? Why had she moved to Dobe? How was she earning a living? Was she healthy? Was she getting along with Bo? Was she still close to her older and younger brothers? What about the two nieces she had helped raise?

I also wanted to know how the publication of *Nisa,* the book based on her life, had affected her, especially through the cows she had bought with money from me (with the help of Richard Lee, who was then working at Dobe) five years before. Those cows had fulfilled a promise I had made to Nisa when we were last together: if I finished writing our story, and if it was published as a book, and if people liked the book and bought it, I would buy cows for her. When Richard returned from the field, he reported that Nisa had bought five pregnant cows. When Richard went back to Dobe a few years later, I again sent money, and he again returned with news: Nisa was doing well; her cows had multiplied; and with the additional money she had bought a branding iron.

I had other questions as well, many concerning the life story Nisa had so generously shared years before. Had time changed her perspective? If I asked her to tell her story again, would it be similar to the one in the book? If not, what kinds of differences might I find?

For help with these questions before my trip, I had turned to Ulrich Neisser, a professor of psychology at Emory University and a scholar of memory research. He had recommended that I choose a number of stories Nisa had told in the past and ask her to tell them again. The stories about her early life, he suggested, might still be close to the published account; having happened so far in the past, they might be less susceptible to reinterpretation. The later ones, especially those involving people with whom Nisa was still in contact, might reveal more change, incorporating more of her current perceptions of herself and those around her. Our discussion helped clarify questions I wished to explore, and Ulrich's unstinting enthusiasm for my project convinced me it was well worth the try.

I had one more set of questions. Closer to my heart, and less clearly formulated, these were the ones that had propelled me back to Nisa. What was our relationship? What would our conversations be like this time? Would we still have rapport? Would she talk as freely about herself as she once had? What about sex? Did she think about it differently now? Or aging? Or death? Especially death. Had she come to terms with mortality, bearing down on her as it was on me? Would she have insight that would help me? And would she be interested in what was happening to me?

What I finally said out loud, or at least tried to say, was that I hoped she would be willing to talk to me later, when it was just the two of us, alone. Then we might pick up our talks where we had left off years before. Now, on my first day and with everyone around, it was awkward—we should wait until things were quieter.

"You want to talk with me again as we did in the past?" Nisa asked, to be sure she understood my fumbling words. Even as I nodded in agreement, she did the same, saying, "Yes, when there are fewer people, we will begin our talk."

I responded, speaking softly, "Even so. You and Bo are welcome guests at my camp. Whenever you visit, you will be fed. You are my people, after all, my family here."

My approach to anthropological interviews had always been direct. I had asked Nisa, "Tell me what it is to be a woman." Her answers became her published narrative. Our conversations went where I led them as often as where Nisa did. I interrupted frequently, asking for detail and clarification. The book portrayed a feisty, highly sexual, independent-thinking Nisa.

Not long after *Nisa* was published, a professor at Harvard invited me to lecture to her class. Another anthropologist, who had written a book about an East African woman, was also invited. Our techniques for collecting data couldn't have been more different.

The other anthropologist's approach had been indirect. She understood that anything she said to the woman could influence what the woman said back to her. Therefore, she tried, like a psychoanalyst, to present herself as a "blank slate." She initiated no conversations, and responded, when necessary, with neutral remarks. Whatever the woman said, she recorded. Sitting there for hours, day after day, the African woman eventually spoke about the trials of living in her in-laws' village and her fears of witchcraft. In the anthropologist's book, the woman was portrayed as fearful, isolated, miserable, accepting, and repressed.

Underlying the differences in our techniques were differences in our personalities. I was somewhat unconventional, rebellious, at ease talking about intimate matters, enthusiastic, and direct. The other anthropologist, who had a glorious English accent, was proper, genteel, and cool in manner.

After the two of us presented our approaches and talked about our books, the professor spoke, her eyes twinkling. "How would Nisa have sounded if an anthropologist had recorded only what Nisa chose to talk about? And how would the other woman's story have sounded if an anthropologist like Marjorie had asked her what it meant to be a woman?"

〰〰〰 Nisa joined the others at the fire. Tuma, whom I had hired as a helper, served Nisa and Bo and other "honored" guests with large portions of cornmeal porridge with reconstituted milk and tea with milk and sugar; smaller portions were shared by other visitors, as was customary. Having brought only a minimal amount of tobacco—a gift highly favored by the !Kung—I handed around enough for a few pipefuls, saying it was in short supply.

Then I remembered the tape. Before leaving home I had taught my two eldest children a few words in the !Kung language: the expression

"Tchum-o," meaning "Greetings!"; the sentence "My name is . . ." with the blank filled in with each child's !Kung name; and "You are my big namesake; I am your little namesake."

⚞⚟⚞⚟ Years before, at the beginning of my first stay in the area, women had vied with one another to touch me, to shake my hand in greeting. Pointing to themselves and to me, they poured forth a torrent of animated words I couldn't understand. The anthropologist driving my husband and me, whose charge was to introduce us to the people and to the area, explained that each woman was asking me to accept her Bushman name.

The "name relationship" was an important one: it established kinship ties with the community, even for an outsider. Once you accepted a name, you in essence adopted your namesake's position, greeting others as she would. Her brother was your brother, her mother your mother; you couldn't joke casually with those whom she was expected to treat with respect.

It wasn't primarily the unique connection between namesakes that made the women offer me their names; it was the hope that this relationship would pay off: that the outsider, with seemingly unlimited resources, would apportion more gifts, more truck rides, and more favors to a namesake. The anthropologist cautioned me to get to know the women before accepting anyone's name.

Pressure to choose mounted immediately. The main contenders were Nai, a very old woman and the senior wife of a patriarch in one of the villages, and Hwantla, a dynamic, forceful woman in her mid-thirties, married to a Bantu man. Though I feared insulting the older woman and starting my stay undiplomatically, my heart went out to Hwantla. She visited our camp regularly, sang tender songs (her own compositions) about being unable to have children, and tried (albeit somewhat impatiently) to help me with the language. While both women often spoke of the gifts I would give them, and neither hesitated to ask me for things, the decision was made when Hwantla gave *me* a present—a beaded leather covering. I accepted her name on the spot.

⚞⚟⚞⚟ When my husband and I had children, it was inevitable that we would give them !Kung names. Our eldest, Susanna, had been given Nisa's name soon after birth. Although it was not filed legally or marked by a ceremony, either in America or in Africa, Susanna nevertheless had a !Kung name: Nisa-ma, or Little Nisa. Nisa had instructed me years before that my first child (the one "by my forehead," an expression used while tapping the forehead just above the eyes, designating the firstborn child, no matter the sex or whether the child survives), if a girl, was to be named Nisa. This would ensure continuity in Nisa's relationship to my family, as it would connect the "child of my forehead" to Nisa in a close and immediate way.

To believe that Nisa's request did not involve self-interest would be extremely naive. But the name-relationship to Nisa would give my daughter a direct connection to the !Kung world through a powerful !Kung tradition. Unfortunately, Nisa had no offspring to carry on this and other relationships forged throughout her life: the most coveted kind of inheritance for people with little material wealth to pass on. If one day Susanna wants to explore her namesake's world, the one that riveted her mother, her !Kung name will be of only marginal help—unless, of course, Nisa is still alive.

Adam, our second child, had been given the name Kxoma-ma, Little Kxoma, after a man who had befriended Mel and me years before, a man of humor and wisdom, a natural leader. Fluent in Setswana and Sehen, the languages of Bantu-speaking people in the area, Kxoma was a model for the future: he believed in self-reliance and hard work; he helped his village be among the first to receive permits to plant fields; he encouraged the villagers to herd goats and the occasional cow; and he used money gained from selling crafts to further their "modern" style of life. His intelligence and equanimity made him a favorite at government meetings and in the regional courts, and he quickly became the spokesman for !Kung who had to deal with the Tswana legal system. Although Nisa had instructed us that if we had a son we should name him Bo, after her husband, Kxoma had won our hearts. If Adam one day partook of Kxoma's wisdom and dignity—not to mention the physical prowess and courage he demonstrated in hunting—we would be proud.

For our youngest child, Sarah, we had been less certain what !Kung name to choose, although many women would have coveted the connection. We finally gave her the name Tasa-ma, after two women named Tasa, each with characteristics we admired. Tasa Nxam or Old Tasa was the matriarch of a huge family, kin to people at Dobe and beyond; life in her village, and in others nearby, seemed to revolve around her. In her sixties, she gathered food for her dependent children, coddled and helped care for her many grandchildren, actively traded with a wide network of people, and was influential in decisions that affected herself and the group.

The second Tasa, the younger sister of my own namesake, Hwantla, was part of an interview study I conducted on women's moods and the menstrual cycle. In her late twenties at the time, she was a woman of great beauty and grace. (Hers was the face on the cover of the book *Nisa*.) Tasa usually greeted me with a smile and brought me close, telling me things simply and from the heart. Commenting on her husband, she said, "He is like my father, my mother. My mother has gone visiting and I sit with him." Tasa never knew we had named our child after her; a few years before I returned to Africa, I heard that she had died.

Nisa, Kxoma, and Tasa; Susanna, Adam, and Sarah. Susanna was now ten years old, Adam seven, Sarah two and a half. On my last evening in Atlanta I had recorded Susanna and Adam's voices, and now, by the fire in Dobe, I played the tape. "Tchum-o," Adam greeted his namesake, Kxoma, pronouncing it as the !Kung do, with a loud popping click at the start. Then, coached by me, he continued in !Kung: "You are my big namesake, Big Kxoma. I am your little namesake, Little Kxoma. Tchum-o!"

Kxoma himself was not present—he was away in the bush on a hunt—but others gathered around to listen, excitedly praising Adam's clarity of speech, along with his ability to make the click in his name and in the words for "big name" and "little name" resonate just as the !Kung themselves did—a feat that, despite years of working in the language, forever eluded me. Next came Susanna's message for Nisa, essentially identical in content to Adam's. Everyone listened as Susanna greeted Nisa, her namesake, and Nisa, clearly pleased, spoke a return greeting into the air.

〰〰〰 Later that day Baitsenke drove the truck to Kangwa, a village an hour and a half away, where we could fill our empty drums with clear water pumped from deep in the ground. People from Dobe had vied for seats in the truck, offered first to those seeking medical help from the clinic; any additional seats were grabbed by those who wanted to buy provisions in the small shops, to visit, to trade, or just to drink the local home brew, a flourishing business at Kangwa.

Nisa didn't want to go and asked Hwantla to go in her stead. While Baitsenke drove, Hwantla and I sat next to him in the cab of the truck, our voices carrying over the drone of the engine, talking about the years I had been away.

She had been sick and nearly died, Hwantla told me, but Megan Biesele—an anthropologist who had once lived at Dobe but who was now working with the !Kung of Namibia—had saved her life. Megan had taken Hwantla to a clinic where they nursed her back to life with medicine for tuberculosis. Only recently had she felt well enough to come home to Dobe, although she was still weak. Showing me a vial of pills, she said she had to take them until they were finished.

We talked of the death of Hwantla's younger sister, Tasa, sharing words of grief over the loss of so vital and well-loved a woman, a woman with whom I had spent hours talking about love and life, sickness and death. We spoke of Hwantla's tumultuous marriage to her Tswana husband, and the large family he had managed to have with his mistress at Kangwa while Hwantla remained barren at Dobe. We talked of others, and then I told her about myself. She listened sympathetically, not saying much. But then, as our conversation had made clear, stories of illness were not unusual out there.

Spirit Travel

Music resonated through the darkness: syncopated rhythms, sinuous melodies, the voice of the drum, the occasional cry of a healer in trance. It came from the direction of Kumsa's village, named after Kumsa-the-Hunter, Tasa's widower. He lived there with his two daughters, their husbands, and their children, each family occupying a separate hut. Following the sound to the village, I was surprised to find the two women continuing the song far into the night without help from others. Their young beauty, so reminiscent of their mother, Tasa, glowed in the firelight as they sat, their heads tilted in song, carrying on where their mother had left off.

The healing was over when I arrived; Kumsa was resting, having already laid hands on his grandchild, who had been ill. His daughters and the drummer, the younger of his sons-in-law, went on exploring songs, first one, then another, dictated by their mood. I sat transfixed, enveloped by the sounds and rhythms.

Then, in a lull between songs, something from far off caught my attention: faint music rising and falling with the wind, the unmistakable strains of another dance. Leaving the intimacy of Kumsa's world behind—"Eh, hey. Thank you all for your hospitality. Stay well"—I walked off in search of the other drums sounding in the night.

Flashlight in hand, tape recorder and camera bags bouncing at my side, I followed well-worn trails in the sand through high and low thorn bush, constantly orienting myself toward the music about half a mile away. The blackness was so dense I only knew I had arrived by the powerful vibrations of the drums, urgent and loud, and by the immediacy of the song. Slowly I distinguished the dark shapes of women standing in a circle, shoulder to shoulder, around a dim fire, pouring out their song. Light from the embers rested momentarily on the intense, passionate faces of the drummers, at opposite ends of the circle, in rhythmic conversation with each other even as they responded to the women's intricate clapped counterpoints.

35

Two men were in trance in the tight space between the fire and the women. Theirs was the trance of advanced age, low in energy and internal, almost private. Yet each was still considered potent, and each laid on hands around the circle, intermediating with the world of the spirits on behalf of people: a gift given by God to those who heal. One was Kasupe, Old Tasa's husband. The other was Kantla, Nisa's longtime lover. Kantla seemed frail and did not look well. I worried that he might not survive much longer, and I wondered what Nisa would have to say about him.

But something more was on my mind, or rather, in my heart. It had been hard to admit as I planned my trip, but one of the attractions of returning to Africa was the chance to be healed by !Kung healers. The wish embarrassed me, and I didn't talk about it even to friends. But I felt it nevertheless.

It wasn't that I subscribed to the !Kung belief that illness was sent by the spirit world. Nor did I share their belief that, by eliciting the cooperation of the spirits, a healer in trance could extract sickness and make people well. But the power of the tradition was breathtaking, and its drama had captivated me years before. A person in trance sets out alone to battle the unknown, the chaos lurking beneath the mundane, the disorder and darkness at the edge of our consciousness, all propelled by forces beyond human understanding. When successful, the healer wrests some measure of control over human suffering and pain, averts tragedy, reverses misfortune.

These benefits come at great cost to the healer. Out in the dark, according to !Kung belief, just beyond the circle of those attending the trance dance, sit the spirits of the dead, having come to watch, to be entertained, or to cause mischief. These spirits are partially responsible for human misery. Only those in trance, imbued with the power to heal, can see them. Calling out into the shadows, the healers argue, moralize, and plead with these vindictive, mean, or merely bored spirits that wreak so much havoc among the living. At other times they do battle, throwing sticks while they scream at the spirits to cease their wrongdoing.

In the process, the healers risk their lives. They may enter a trance state that is so profound, so deep and coma-like, that their own spirits, which are said to have left their bodies, may not return. Death can be averted only by the efforts of other healers in trance, who lay on hands, rub the unconscious body, and sing plaintive melodies appealing to the spirit of the animals of the wild, and to the Great God, the most power-ful and compassionate of all.* Their efforts are rewarded by the return of the healer's spirit. Sound from the deepest recesses of the healer's soul rises up, a tentative moan building in strength and finally erupting into a full cry: the cascading wail of the healer in trance.

The men and women who embark on this journey are true warriors, heroes, travelers in Dante's Inferno. They are Pamina and Tamino in *The Magic Flute* willingly facing the terrors of the dark side. With cour-age and daring, they teeter at the precipice and open their eyes—and the mysteries they discover bring comfort and relief of suffering to those who remain behind.

How? By a complex process. First, they "withdraw" illness from those they heal. Inside the bodies of healers is believed to reside a spe-cial substance or medicine, called *n/um*. With vigorous dancing, this healing power heats up, getting hotter and hotter. When it starts to boil ("boiling energy," it has been called), the healer achieves a fully altered state of consciousness: a trance. The body trembles, behavior becomes erratic, the mind is disoriented, speech becomes slurred or nonsensical.

At one dance I remember, Kxoma, my son Adam's namesake, having finished laying on hands in trance, stood with his knees slightly bent, his arms stretched out and open, plaintively calling, "My arms . . . my arms." His wife rubbed his arms and told him they were fine. He re-peated, in an almost childlike whimper, "No, no . . . my arms . . . my arms." Again she attended to him, touching his arms, assuring him there was nothing wrong with them. This scene was repeated over and over again. Only much later did Kxoma sit down. The next morning I asked him what had been wrong with his arms. He said, somewhat em-barrassed, that it had been his legs: he had been unable to bend them to sit down, but the only words that would come from his mouth were "My arms . . . my arms."

Disorientation characterizes the early stages of trance for many heal-ers. For novices, it may even be the primary experience. But a skilled trance requires fiercely focused concentration. The healer peers into the "patient" to the very core, in order to locate the source of ill-ness and discover its cause. By laying on hands, the healer dislodges the sickness he has "seen," or "pulls" it into his own body, where it is ejected through the top of the spinal column and rendered harmless.

---

* The !Kung believe in a number of supernatural beings, one of which is said to rule over the others. This being, called Kauha, I have translated as "God" or "the Great God." The various other spirits are called Ilganwasi.

The "cure" is strengthened by the transfer of *n/um* from the healer into the patient.

~~~~~~ I am not going to argue that the !Kung approach to healing is comparable to penicillin or anti-malarials, or that it can substitute for the ionized fluids needed by a child dying of dehydration. But there is more to bolstering the human immune system than finding the right chemical key for a given disease. There is the patient's cooperation, and the will to live, and, perhaps most important, the belief that a cure can be effective.

This is not the place to review the vast literature on healing. But a look at best-selling books over the last few years, many written by doctors, should make it clear that many in our society, professionals and laypersons alike, believe that the psyche influences both our getting sick and our getting better. Even the *Merck Manual,* the bible of medical information for fieldworkers, concedes that a large percentage of complaints that confront doctors have a psychological component.

After I learned I had cancer, it seemed that every other person I met believed in this power of the psyche. People constantly reminded me about "positive attitude" and the salutary effects of laughter. They gave me tapes called *Self-Healing* and books with titles like *From Victim to Victor, Mind as Healer, Mind as Slayer,* and *Love, Medicine, and Miracles.* They encouraged me to "visualize" white light traveling through my body, cleansing and repairing, and blue light carrying off the poisons. Cancer cells, they told me, were "disorganized" and "confused" and easily destroyed by white blood cells, the body's own defense against disease. I was to imagine these "good" cells as on the offensive, multiplying exponentially, rooting out cancer cells and decisively destroying them.

There were differences of opinion about how much anger was appropriate to these visualizations. Those who saw anger as cathartic encouraged fantasies of white cells as victorious soldiers in violent confrontation, killing enemy cancer cells with weapons: spearing them, shooting them, eviscerating them. Others, believing that anger, even in fantasy, might mire one in negative feelings, suggested gentler means of destruction: cancer cells were killed by chemotherapeutic agents and "swept away" by white cells that kept a vigilant watch, or were gobbled up Pac-Man style, leaving no residue with which they could rearm.

Although quite skeptical, I found it hard to dismiss this thinking entirely. My approach was to consider anything that might increase my odds of survival. I underwent surgery, and then chemotherapy. As soon as it was feasible, I started a physical exercise program. I watched my diet closely. I started psychotherapy. I joined a cancer support group. And when I was feeling especially low, I visualized myself as happy and carefree, lying beside a quiet pond in Vermont where I had spent many wonderful summers, the sun gently warming my skin, the wind ruffling my hair and caressing my body, with birds calling above me as they flew against wisps of cloud in the late-afternoon light. I could breathe in that air, that light, even in my bedroom a thousand miles away—and whether or not doing so affected my prognosis hardly mattered, because it did help me cope.

Similarly, for me, the appeal of the !Kung healing ritual had little to do with its mystical component. The ritual appealed to me because it provided an avenue of action for those who suffered from illness or misfortune, and perhaps even more important, it mobilized the community around them. It was also about touch, about taking sickness seriously, and about caring. A trance dance belonged to everyone: participants expended tremendous energy to ensure not only that the sick among them got better but that all were protected against future bouts of illness.

Of course, sometimes a cure didn't work. Then the !Kung acknowledged that God or the spirits had their own agenda. The healer may have worked hard—pleading, begging, bargaining, insulting, and battling—but failed nevertheless.

Is this so different from ourselves, with our advanced medical technology, which also sometimes fails? But who would say that the effort was not worth it? Or that believing in something—whether it be prayer or medicine—does not impart some measure of comfort, which itself may influence health?

And when a !Kung "cure" did work? Then the concept of healer as intermediary was affirmed, along with the belief that when trouble struck, as it invariably did, someone, somehow, was there to intercede.

The "spirit travel" or "soul travel" that !Kung healers describe is real. I do not mean to claim that the !Kung actually accomplish the mystical feats of which they speak. I only mean that the healer really does journey, symbolic though the journey may be, into the psyche of another.

When a healer discovers the "cause" of someone's illness, the explanation is said to come from the spirit world. The healer's soul, having left his or her physical body behind, travels—in the form of a wild animal, such as a lion, or just as itself—to this nether world, for there the source of human suffering can be found. Sometimes the soul need go no further than the dark shadows at the edge of the dance, where a vindictive spirit may be sitting. More often, the responsible party is at a distance, in the heavens, where the spirits normally reside, living near and attending to the Great God.

Through "soul travel," !Kung healers explore the psychological needs of others, reflecting intuitive knowledge and often profound insight. In trance, relieved of the necessity to process information within "normal reality," healers open their minds to the subtle conversations people have within themselves, those rarely, if ever, expressed openly. They "listen," they "see," they intuit. Heightened sensitivity enhances their perceptions and allows them to recognize unconscious motivations and needs.

It is therefore not surprising that the explanations !Kung healers advance for illness touch upon many tensions described by Freud. A man, near death, is said to have become sick because he tried to thwart his son's ambition to become a healer; the man felt threatened that his son was becoming more powerful than he. A woman's serious illness is linked to her recently deceased father, who is pulling her to join him in the grave. The healer convinces the father to let her live, thus helping to dispel the woman's guilt about surviving his death and about turning her attention to others. The healing gives her permission to go on.

Richard Katz, a psychologist studying !Kung trance, wrote in his book *Boiling Energy* of a healer who had been trying to help his sick wife, after having cured her, with variable success, for years. Asked what he saw while he "pulled" sickness from her in trance, he said, "I pulled her dead father's testicles out of her heart. Then I told her dead father not to pursue her anymore."

!Kung sacred knowledge—knowledge of the mysterious and esoteric—may be difficult to acquire, but the route is available to all. Anyone willing to undergo the rigorous, often painful training required, and possessed of a personality amenable, under certain conditions, to fluctuating states of consciousness, is eligible. About half the men and a third of women have successful apprenticeships. Not all who begin, however, become healers. Some are so cautious that they hardly advance. Others become so overwhelmed at the start that they discontinue their training.

Still others, mostly women, enter the trance state but do not gain control over it: when violent trembling or intense pain rises up, they drop to the ground, and they never learn to direct the energy into healing. Both men and women, however, do proceed through the rigorous training—usually years in duration—and become very powerful healers.

Watching Kasupe and Kantla in trance, I yearned for them to touch me, for their eyes to open to the darkness within me, for them to tell me what they saw. As I squeezed myself into the circle, however, the two men stopped curing and directed their efforts toward each other, helping to maintain their trance state and their control over it.

Disappointed, I turned to the music, trying to clap the intricate rhythms of the song. But even the simplest of patterns escaped me, and I stopped. No one commented. No one tried to teach me. No one even seemed to notice. Wanting to be part of their world, wanting to be cared about, I suddenly felt alone, the outsider I really was. What was I doing standing there, watching others live their lives?

I envied the integrity of their lives. Here were young women, many of whom I had known as children, clapping and singing ancient melodies at the top of their voices, hour after hour. They were dedicated to their tradition, carrying it forward to the next generation. So, too, were the young men who beat the drums, sometimes three drums at a time, with heroic energy, undiminished as the hours passed. Even the two old men, shakily embracing the power of the trance state as it coursed through their worn frames, set the context, making it right. I didn't romanticize the problems of their lives. But right then, the dance, for young and old alike, expressed group cohesiveness and the passion they shared for their culture: they knew they belonged.

Lost in thought as the music swelled around me, I felt a tap on my shoulder. It was Bo, telling me that Nisa had arrived. Perhaps it was the extra wood someone put on the fire, or perhaps just Nisa's appearance, but the events that followed dispelled some of the darkness, as well as some of my loneliness; in memory, the scene is imbued with warm hues from the lights of many fires.

Nisa looked stunning. Someone preparing for a royal ball could not have taken much more care in choosing her clothes, or have adorned herself with more of her most striking jewelry. She wore a colorful dress of pink and yellow; two beaded headbands of bold stripes and diamond shapes circled her head. Beads sewn in small clusters were strung in her hair, along with copper hoops. Multiple strands of many-colored beads hung loosely around her neck and were wrapped tightly around her wrists, knees, and ankles. She was radiant, both in her physical appearance and in her mood, which was energetic and excited.

Nisa and two other women only slightly younger than she, each comparably adorned, joined the group. As the three stood together, their faces glowed in the firelight, reflecting the red, fragrant oil they had applied for the occasion. Their energy and purpose were infectious; driving the music, they now took the lead. Clapping loudly, they echoed one another with responsive melodies and alternating counterpoints, mirrored by the equally insistent rhythms of the drums. As the pace of the dance accelerated, the two old men retired to the sidelines.

Supported by the singing of the circle of women, Nisa became more concentrated, her eyes fixed on the fire. Her voice endlessly repeated the refrain of the song. Beads of sweat formed on her face and her arms. The back of her palm rested on her forehead as her body started to tremble. She swayed slightly to one side, then the other, losing and regaining her balance.

As her *n/um* came to a boil, the vibration in her middle moved like a wave over her frame. Then came a sound, rising from deep within her, gaining strength, and building to a crescendo that broke in a cry, plaintive and powerful, piercing the night. She was in trance.

The circle of women closed tighter as Nisa tried to gain control of the chaos within, to direct her energies to the task of healing. Not yet ready, she wavered, holding her shaking arm over her chest. She sang the refrain over and over, pushing her trance deeper and deeper. She stepped closer to the fire, staring at it with unswerving attention. The singing and drumming intensified. Imploring and passionate, the music fueled her state, prodding her forward. Trembling the length of her body, she emitted another cry.

At last she was ready. Turning to the person closest to her, she rested her hands lightly beside his ears and around his chest, laying on hands and "pulling" out sickness with a fluttering touch known only to those who heal.

〴〴〴〴〴〴 Watching from a distance, I remembered what Nisa had said about her experiences with healing during our conversations years before. She had first learned about healing while a young girl, from her mother. Her mother had prepared a root for her to eat that tasted so terrible it made her throw up. But it also made her tremble, the first step toward learning how to "break out of my self and trance." Her mother guided her for a number of years, until Nisa felt comfortable handling the state. But she stopped training when she reached childbearing age. The experience was so physically demanding and *n/um* was considered so powerful a substance that custom didn't allow her to continue: doing so could endanger a fetus or a nursing child. When she finally returned to healing as a mature woman, she became an able trancer. She was one of a handful of women who actually laid on hands in cure.

At the time of my last visit, fourteen years before, Nisa had been capable of entering trance during either the traditional ceremonial dance, ancient in origin, or the newer drum dance. She had felt her powers most strongly, however, when the drum sounded. But she had still considered herself a novice because she hadn't yet spoken directly to the Great God, or visited where he lived, feats accomplished only by the most experienced healers.

This night, I stood watching her exquisite control of her trance state and the fluidity with which she laid on hands in cure. I wondered why it had not occurred to me earlier that she might be the one to "cure" me. Indeed, it seemed perfect: Nisa, who had taught me about life, would now engage me in a conversation about my staying alive.

Peering through the crowd, I saw there were now three in trance: Nisa and the two women who had sung beside her. But the crush of people was great and my vision was obscured. Excited by my new thought, I left for another fire that blazed nearby, where people sat in intense conversation, warming themselves from the cold night air.

〴〴〴〴〴〴 Gazing around the fire, my eyes came to rest on a woman whose face was somber and drawn. Her left thumb and wrist, wrapped tightly in a thick, dirty cloth, were cradled by her right hand. It was Nai, Nisa's niece, who had been part of my interview study years before. Beside her was her husband, Debe.

They both greeted me with warmth, but Nai's smile was taut, reflecting pain. Debe explained that she was sick: something had penetrated deep into her finger. The swelling had split the outer layers of skin. The pain and swelling, once confined to her hand, had traveled to her armpit. Worried, I asked why she hadn't gone to the clinic earlier in the day, when we had taken the truck to Kangwa for water.

Her answer reflected the tenuous relationship the !Kung have to services provided for them by the local government. "I saw the nurse when he last came," Nai said, referring to the monthly visit of medical personnel to Dobe. "He gave me medicine, but"—her voice dropped to a whisper—"but I didn't take it right. If I go back to him, he will be angry with me."

"Nai," I implored, "he is a very kind man. He won't be angry. He only wants you to get better. I'm worried that if you wait any longer, the sickness will kill you."

Under the bandage her thumb looked swollen to the width of four fingers, and her drawn, ashen face spoke of intense pain and sleepless nights. Making a quick calculation, I offered, "If you say yes, I will send Baitsenke with the truck to Kangwa again tomorrow, to take you to the clinic. You will get more medicine and it will make you better."

She looked uncertain. I told her I would write a note to the nurse and explain about the medicine. Her expression cleared, but she still didn't answer. I turned to Debe, "It's very important that she go. This is serious." He nodded in agreement. I said, "See what you can do. If she says yes, bring her to my camp early in the morning. Of course, you can go, too."

The drums beat on. The night air was cold against my back. I inched toward the fire, warming my hands. Then Nisa was there beside Nai, undoing the bandage, revealing Nai's grossly swollen, cracked, and discolored thumb. "Working" on Nai—her only blood relative at Dobe—Nisa held the infected arm gently: laying on hands, she repeatedly threw off the illness, violently spitting it out into the darkness, crying out a plaintive wail. She used her sweat, considered a powerful manifestation of *n/um,* rubbing it onto Nai's chest; she flicked her fingers hard against Nai's sides and pressed hard, transferring the healing medicine into Nai.

Then Nisa turned to Debe, to cure him. This meant she would probably go around the circle; this meant she would come to me. The singing and drumming crescendoed again, loud and furious, inspired by three in trance at once. Nisa broke from curing, temporarily, to drive her trance state deeper; she stamped dance steps into the hot sand beside the coals, staring into the fire, singing intently. She swayed and her footing became uneven. Suddenly she was falling toward the fire. Arms reached out from behind, lightly encircling her, propping her upright, protecting her from the flames. As a cry exploded from within her, passionate and heart-wrenching, she resumed curing, first one, then another, making her way around the circle. Then it was my turn.

"Ah—oh—ohya—oh—oo—yeh," went the alternating women's voices in the sound tapestry, supported by the drum. Leaning over me, Nisa echoed the melody, her tone deep, her attention unwavering. Her arms traveled down my chest, stopping when her pulsating hands reached the spot they had been searching for, just above my waist. With one hand in front, the other behind, she sang the refrain, loud and resonant. I closed my eyes, my senses alert to the sounds, the smells, the feel of her touch. Her "cure" culminated quickly with the healer's scream, "Kow—hi—de—li"—the sound folding down after the first syllable—and she moved on to the person next to me.

The heavens didn't open; nor was it a miracle, the stuff of dreams. Indeed, it seemed distressingly perfunctory: I was just another body to attend to as Nisa worked her way through the group. Yet I was moved. The tension of the previous week—a week in which I had left my family and come thousands of miles to this world that was both strange and familiar—dissolved in a torrent of feeling. Tears streamed down my face.

And it wasn't just the tension that found release. In the tears also flowed some of the pain, fear, and sadness that had defined much of my life for a year. These didn't disappear, but the tears felt cleansing, even healing. It felt good to acknowledge how bruised I was, how hard the year had been.

Nisa continued around the circle. I drifted in and out, sometimes joining the clapping, other times remaining lost in thought. No one seemed to notice me. Yet this time I didn't feel lonely. I felt grateful to be there, to be surrounded by the sounds of the dance, the fragrance of the wood fire, and the cadences of a language I loved. Most of all, I basked in the luxury of just sitting, observing as I wished. While the presence of the others supported me, they asked nothing of me, at least for the moment: I didn't have to smile, to respond to social obligations, even to engage in conversation. But they allowed me in, and that was what I wanted. I breathed in the clear night air and looked up at the stars, bright in the black firmament above us.

Nisa was now beside Kantla, her lover since her youth. Did others also know, as she knelt behind him, resting her body against his back, draping her arms around him as she laid on hands in cure, that the touch was familiar to them both? That it reflected a love of nearly fifty-five years? Kantla, his voice no longer clear, his body gaunt, his face somewhat sickly, spoke in low tones as Nisa cured him, commenting to anyone who would listen about where he was weak, where he was in pain. Nisa sang tenderly, embracing his thin frame, pulling out the bad, putting in the good. She remained with him a long time before returning to her niece Nai.

Chuko, another of the women in trance, joined Nisa at the fire. Younger than Nisa by about fifteen years, she lacked Nisa's centered grace. The angularity of her body lent sharpness to her movements as she went, somewhat frenetically, to one, then another, around the circle. Her hands were firm as she touched me, quivering on my chest, rubbing my sides. Ending with the characteristic cry of the healer, she continued on, making her way back to Nisa to help with Nai.

A pattern of unison clapping signaled the end of one song. Laughter, joking, and general talk, accompaniments to most dances, filled the air, only to be obscured again almost immediately by the opening melody of the next song. Nisa and Chuko, unaffected by the break, continued to work on Nai. Then Nisa started around again.

When she reached me, she leaned down on her knees, singing and laying on hands, rocking from side to side. When her face was close to mine, I said, "My aunt, see well what is inside. The doctors in my country found a terrible sickness. They tried to get rid of it, but they don't know if I am cured. They said it may still kill me."

There was no sign that she heard me. Perhaps I had not made myself clear. Or perhaps she couldn't decipher normal speech while she was in trance. Whatever the cause, she finished healing me and quickly moved on. Yet, from her touch, and from having spoken the words, tears again filled my eyes. Hidden from the others in the dim light, they flowed down the already charted path, unstifled and unnoticed.

Later in the dance, Nisa came around once again, as did the two other women. Each time they approached me, I closed my eyes to soak in the moment. Each time they left, I wanted more.

By two in the morning I felt depleted. With the dance still going strong, I asked Bo to show me the path back to my camp. Knowing that I would probably get lost, he took a flashlight and led the way. The sounds of singing, dancing, and healing receded into the background as we pushed into the dark quiet. It was good to be with Bo. He was considerate and supportive, gentler than Nisa.

He spoke of my kindness and generosity, of the cows and the branding iron I had given them. He told me they had traded many cows to get a horse, a horse that one day, when it was old enough, would be used for hunting. He even mentioned a heavy sweater I had sent him, which he was then wearing. He thanked me for caring about them and for helping them. He spoke clearly and slowly, and I felt deeply connected to him and to Nisa. The strangeness of my journey slipped away as I again began to feel part of this world.

Nisa Is Inside

Returning to Africa had been my dream. But within that dream, I had another dream: to take a group of people to the bush as we had done in the old days. I wanted to go hunting with the men, to go gathering with the women. I wanted to walk mile after mile in a world untouched by people, in a land quietly continuing its past, inhabited only by plants and animals, wind and sky. I wanted to read animal tracks in the parched sand and to search for scant vines signaling succulent underground roots. I wanted to camp with the !Kung in the nut groves where the air was clear, where sound was gentle to the ear, and where light from the stars reached the earth unimpeded.

I expected that such a trip would take place near the end of my stay. It made sense: by then my work with Nisa would be finished, and I would have gained a perspective on the people's lives. But that logic was derailed on my first day in Dobe, when the army officer kept trying to pin down my plans, asking many times, "This trip . . . when would you do it?" When I finally came up with an answer, it was not the one I had planned. "If it is all right with you," I heard my voice saying, "I'd like to go as soon as possible, perhaps within the next few days." Then I added, "Of course, I have to talk to the people about it first."

Soon after the army trucks drove away on that first morning, the conversation with the people began. And the idea of an immediate trip to the bush quickly gained momentum. A host of problems, both logistical and social, had to be worked out. When would we leave? (The next day.) Would I feed the people in the bush? (After much discussion: Yes.) Would I pay them? (No.) How much water should I transport? (A lot.) And especially, Who would go?

With only thirteen seats in the truck, I suggested that two people from each of the five San villages of Dobe join us, a suggestion no one, including me, loved but all accepted. Since these people would not, under normal circumstances, camp together, the social dynamics of our group would be an unknown. Nevertheless, this seemed the best solution.

Places remained for Nisa, the driver, and me. Bo was invited to be a fourteenth, but he chose to stay behind. He had cows to supervise, he explained. Then, asking "Don't you need someone to keep watch on your camp while you are gone?" he smoothly parlayed our absence into a job: he would assist Tuma, the camp helper, during the day, and at night, after Tuma went back to his village, Bo would sleep at my camp. He had done the same, he said, for other anthropologists who had been at Dobe the year before.

Each village agreed to send two people, a man to hunt and a woman to gather. Because of responsibilities at home—herding cows or goats, tending crops, preparing crafts for market, caring for children or older people—three couples split the trip, with one spouse staying home. Kumsa-the-Hunter brought his daughter Kxaru and her three-year-old son, Dem. When one man backed out, Kumsa brought the husband of his other daughter along. Nearly thirty years older than his wife and close in age to his father-in-law, Toma was also a hunter in his own right.

As we sat around camp thrashing out plans, Nai and Debe approached. Nai walked slowly and carefully, looking as wan in the daylight as she had in the firelight the night before. "I am so glad you've come," I said. "Does this mean . . .?" Debe nodded yes. "Then I'll send the truck to the clinic before we leave for the bush."

Confusion reigned while people rushed to claim whatever room remained in the truck after Nai and Debe, and others with medical problems, took their seats. Baitsenke and Tuma loaded empty water containers, I handed Nai a note for the nurse, and they left.

〰〰〰 "Many years ago, when you and I last spoke," I said to Nisa in a private conversation after the truck disappeared. "Many years ago," I repeated, making sure the tape recorder was working, "I told you that I wanted to write down our talk."

"Eh, hey. I am listening. Mother,"* she responded, her tone almost childlike.

---

* Mother: an expression that emphasizes the truth of what the speaker is saying, similar to "I mean it" or "I swear."

"But when I left here, I didn't know whether I would write something good or whether I would write something bad."

"You wrote something very good."

"Many years passed and I didn't . . ." I paused, looking for the right expression.

"You didn't come," she offered.

"I didn't . . . finish it," I continued. "Only later, years later, after I gave birth to Little Nisa, only then did I finish writing down our talks. And make them into a book."

Thus began—in the quiet of a mud hut used once a month by the visiting nurse, its plank door pulled closed, its elegantly thatched conical roof rising to a point high above the circular walls—my first interview with Nisa. Apart from the villages, apart from the whirlwind of activity that surrounded my camp, and shielded from the eyes of others, we sat facing each other, getting to know each other again. With the tape recorder propped between us and with cups of hot tea, hers sweetened to saturation, beside us, we talked as we had done long ago.

I asked, "Have you seen the book?"

"Eh, Richard showed it to me," she said, referring to Richard Lee.

"Well," I said, handing her a copy, "I have one here to show you too."

We both looked at its colorful cover. Then I said, "There's something I want to talk to you about. I met Royal in Maun, the man who knows English."

I described my conversation with Royal. He had asked me, "This book, are you the one who wrote it?"

I said yes, and, hoping he wouldn't know Nisa's identity, I asked him, "Do you know which woman it is written about?"

He answered, "Yes, I know her."

That made my heart sink, since I had hoped to preserve Nisa's anonymity. Then I asked, "Who is she?"

He pointed to the picture on the book jacket—a picture of Tasa, not Nisa—and said, "This one, this is the woman."

When the possibility of publishing Nisa's story first arose, it seemed clear that I should conceal her identity. After all, in a particular time and place, in a particular frame of mind, and in the privacy of a hut, Nisa had opened the intimacies of her life to me. There was no doubt that she had done so willingly, or that she had welcomed the recording of our conversations. It also was evident that she had understood, and had even felt pride in, my having chosen "her" words to take to women in my country. But did this mean she had had enough experience with the "modern" world to understand that these words might one day be read by thousands of people?

Furthermore, Nisa herself had expressed concerns about privacy long before publication had ever been considered. During our first interview years earlier she had instructed me: "Fix my voice on the machine so that my words come out clear. I am an old person who has experienced many things and I have much to talk about. I will tell my talk, of the things I have done and the things that my parents and others have done. But don't let the people I live with hear what I say."

Four years after those first interviews, when I returned to the field, it seemed conceivable that Nisa's life story might one day be published. By then the work had gained some recognition: a handful of scholars had been very encouraging; I had published a paper in an academic book; and I had been awarded a fellowship with a small stipend (by the Bunting Institute of Radcliffe College) for the laborious and time-consuming job of translating and editing the original fifteen taped interviews.

I was concerned that Nisa's words not come back to haunt her. So as not to let "the people I live with hear what I say," we changed her name and the names of all the people and places mentioned in the narrative. She was delighted with the name "Nisa," which I suggested because it scanned so well, but which she said was also one of her own names, "given at birth." She enthusiastically helped me choose other pseudonyms, laughing aloud as we invented names for her husbands.

At that time we also reviewed stories she had told years before, the "nice" ones and the "not-so-nice" ones. When given the option to exclude certain incidents or details, she told me, without hesitation: "All the talk that the two of us have done—all that this tape recorder, this old man, has heard—wants to enter the paper."

The talk had indeed entered the paper and had been published in book form. And our strategy of disguising people and places with pseudonyms had been effective—as long as the !Kung could not read English. But, within the last two decades, many !Kung children had attended school, and a few, like Royal, had become proficient enough in English that they had found paying jobs. I recognized that Nisa's confidences might one day be read by someone who knew her—and who would be able to identify her.

The thought that someone like Royal might read the book made me uncomfortable, for several reasons. Would Royal think I had represented his culture accurately? What would he think of Nisa's story? Had she revealed too much? Or not enough?

And how could I continue to protect Nisa's identity? With Royal, I had been lucky. So far he had not actually read the book and had just assumed that "Nisa" was the beautiful woman pictured on the cover. The next literate !Kung, however, might not be fooled. All that was really needed, aside from the ability to read English, was the desire to find out. Anyone who knew the area could easily figure out who "Nisa" was. Who else had had so many husbands, had a daughter whose husband killed her, had no living children, and had lived in villages so closely aligned with Bantu settlers? What other woman had the skill to elaborate a story as she had? And in case additional clues were needed, one only had to ask which woman had spent the most time with me. Or which one had received cows from me.

The truth, of course, was that I could not guarantee her anonymity. Hoping to discuss what this would mean to her, but wanting to be sure, first, that my story about Royal had been clear, I continued, "Because you . . . it's . . . she's on the page."

 Some things defeat you (a !Kung expression that seems apt for my stumbling), and with some things, no matter how well your brain knows them, your tongue refuses to cooperate (another useful !Kung-ism). So it was when, in recounting the story of Royal, I variably referred to "he" and "him" and "she" and "her" and "you." In the !Kung language, all these terms are expressed with the same seemingly simple syllable: "ah."

This simple sound had been my undoing years before, and now once again it was undoing me (not a !Kung expression). Just imagine how confusing communication would be if you couldn't tell, when talking with others, whether they were referring to you or to someone else. The !Kung do distinguish "you" from the neutral gender "he or she" or "him or her." But they do so, not by assigning these concepts different words, but by using another facet of language that is difficult for outsiders to master: tone.

For example, to express the concept "you" in !Kung, you say "ah" in a high voice, or a high tone; to express the concept "he or she" or "him or her," you say "ah" in your lower register, or with a low tone. Simple enough. Well, my brain understands its simplicity, and I have no difficulty distinguishing tone level when the !Kung themselves speak. But when it is my turn to talk, and I get started with phrases like "he asked her" or "you asked him" or "she asked her," a glaze usually comes over the eyes of the person I am talking to, along with a bemused smirk I can only interpret as meaning my attempts at communication are utterly hopeless.

When I was first learning the language, I could barely hear, much less use, tones to distinguish word meanings: I relied on emphasis and content to help me make sense of what people said. I gradually learned to hear tones in other people's speech, and eventually I began to use some of them correctly.

꧁꧂ My husband, Mel, was also new to the language back then. On one memorable day, our inability to discriminate among tones put us in danger.

We left our bush camp, which sat on top of a gentle rise near the border with Namibia, for a late afternoon walk. Reaching the bottom of the slope, we followed the track along the border. As we left the commotion of camp life behind, we entered the familiar warmth of our relationship.

We walked awhile, then turned back, retracing our path. At first it was only the children's voices we heard. Then, as we neared the bottom of a rise, we saw them near the top, a group of !Kung children. They seemed excited. Walking on, we finally realized that their excitement had something to do with us. "See the *gxi!*" they shouted. "See the *gxi!*"

We recognized the word for a wildebeest. Intrigued, we scanned the fields of grass, which glowed in the late afternoon light. "We don't see a *gxi,*" we called back. Somewhat puzzled, we resumed our conversation and our walk back to camp.

But the children persisted. Jumping up and down on the slope, they begged for our attention. "There's a *gxi!* See the *gxi!*" they cried, gesturing emphatically toward where we were now standing. We shook our heads, smiled, and held up our hands—a universal sign of incomprehension. Brushing past the thick grass that grew shoulder high in the depression at the bottom of the slope—a vivid contrast to the short scraggly grass on the hillside—we climbed the hill to camp.

I immediately looked for Tuma, the man who worked for us. Although Tuma spoke no English, he was usually able to translate complicated ideas in the !Kung language into words we understood. We could also count on him to speak slowly and carefully. "Tuma," I said as best I could, "when Mel and I were out walking, the children said they saw a *gxi. Gxi* means the animal with horns, right? Why would a wildebeest be near camp? And why were the children so excited? And why, if they saw a wildebeest, were they telling us instead of a hunter?"

Tuma's eyes twinkled. "Did the children say *gxi,*" he asked, using a high tone, "or *gxi?*" using a low tone.

I asked, already wary of the answer, "What's the difference?"

Using a combination of words and gestures, he explained. "Well, *gxi,*" he said, his voice low, "is a wildebeest."

"And *gxi?*" I asked, raising my pitch.

"That's a puff adder!"

At last I understood the children's frantic attempts to communicate: a puff adder is a highly poisonous snake.

〰〰〰 Now, twenty years later, talking with Nisa, I was struggling with the language again. Trying to get the tones right, I stuttered: "Because you . . . it's . . . she's on the page . . ."

Nisa, unruffled, responded as though she knew exactly what I was trying to say: "Because I'm there."

"No," I countered. Did she mean that she was there in the book (correct), or that she was there on the cover of the book (incorrect)? Frustrated, I said, "No, that isn't you [or did I say her?] on the cover."

"Her . . ." Nisa echoed—or was she referring to me?

Desperate to move on, I tried another tack: "Because people don't know . . ." I wanted to say "They don't know it's you," but the pronoun defeated me.

"They don't know, mother," she prompted.

"Eh," I tried again. "The cover of the book says Nisa. Ni-sa. I left out the click. Because, long ago, when we two last talked . . ."

"Mother," she broke in, "you, you listen to me again."

"Eh-hey," I said, afraid we were headed for another language snafu.

But we were not. Instead, she summarized our long-ago conversation about her pseudonym as she recalled it: we had agreed to call her Nisa, one of her names given at birth, because there were too many people with her other name.

Her interpretation surprised me, but that would have to wait. For now, discussing the problem of confidentiality seemed more pressing. And yet, the more we talked, the more the concern with keeping her identity a secret seemed mine, not hers. Indeed, she described, in an animated manner, a stranger who had visited with Richard Lee: "a tall white woman who came here with her son and young daughter. She had the book, the one you gave to Richard Lee's wife. Did you not give one to Richard Lee's wife? Well, she had the book, the one called *Nisa*."

I felt a need to defend myself. Did she think I had told Richard? Interrupting her story, I assured her that I had not revealed her identity to anyone, not to Richard, not to his wife, not to anyone else. "Richard just knew. I never told him. He just knows you so well. When he read your words, he knew who you were." Richard, who had worked in the Dobe area for more than two decades, had recognized her easily. "That's why," I said, "I could send money with him for you to buy cows."

Our conversation moved to the five cows she had bought with the money I sent. They had done very well, she said, multiplying every year. Then, one year, some got lost in the bush. People searched for them, but they were never found. "Oh," said the man who had been herding them. "This woman has no son. She also has no husband, because he is old. And those cows . . . her daughter [meaning me] helped her with them, but they died in the bush."

Nisa told the man, "Eh, I have no children and now these cows have died. Those were what my daughter gave me to keep me alive. She said that I was old and gave me the cows to live on. Now, those have died in the bush and I just sit."

But they had not all died in the bush, and she did not just sit. Enough cows remained that, a few months before I arrived, she and Bo had traded some for a horse. Now she had six cows: three females and three calves born that spring. The horse would eventually be used for hunting, she told me, but now it was still too young. In the next rainy season (about four months away), she would employ someone to hunt with it.

"Because," she said, quite delighted by the custom, "if someone rides it and kills an animal, all the meat belongs to the owner of the horse. I am the one who tells the person, 'Here, this piece is for you. The rest I'll eat—it is mine.'"

With a second gift of money I had sent with Richard two years after she bought the cows, Nisa had bought a branding iron. That was to stop people from stealing cows in the bush and selling them.

"Then, when Richard came another year," she continued, sounding a criticism that came up often throughout the interviews, "I said, 'Did Marjorie give you any shillings to give me, so that I could buy even one more cow to put with the others?' Richard answered, 'Marjorie didn't give me any money. This time, Marjorie didn't employ me to do anything.' I asked, 'What! Marjorie! How is Marjorie treating me? Why has my daughter dropped me? I can't gather, I can't do much of anything. The cows she gave me are my only sustenance.'"

I tried to turn the conversation to another topic, but she quickly turned it back again. "The only thing I don't have," she said, "is a donkey. When the horse goes hunting and something is killed, I will have to ask others to use their donkey. But they will refuse. That's why, as I see it, without a donkey, I can't really use the horse to hunt for me."

Now I knew what she wanted for her next payment. Her request seemed reasonable, as did her questioning of the rewards for our work. But before I could determine how best to help her this time, I needed to know more about how my previous gifts had affected her life. With a noncommittal "Uh-huh," indicating that I had heard, but implying that we would talk about it some other time, I asked, "What did others think? Did they ask why Marjorie gave you so much money . . ."

She interrupted me: "Some of the other women said . . ."

I tried to finish my question: "or . . ."

"I'll tell you, mother," she said, quieting me. "The others said, 'How come she worked with all of us, yet she only gave money for cows to you?' And I said, 'That's because you all had cows. I was the only one without.'"

Then her voice became gentler, more thoughtful. Still quoting what she had told the other women, she said, "My tongue . . . my tongue bought these cows. So don't kill me about it."

I agreed. "Yes, and although the other women also spoke to me with their tongues, you passed them all!"

They had themselves to blame, as she saw it. "Eh, we all talked. But, with their tongues, they didn't buy cows. They themselves didn't buy cows, but drank beer!"

She quoted an elder in one of the villages who also blamed the others: "This older woman, she bought cows. She didn't drink beer. All the rest of you also received money. But you ruined yourselves with that money. But not this older woman here. What she did was excellent!"

I explained that my payments to the other women years before had been too small to buy cows, and that I had sent additional money to her—and only to her—later on. "When I got home and listened to the interviews, yours surpassed the others. You put your heart into our work. Maybe they didn't know how to do it. Yours was the best!"

Nisa offered a different interpretation: "Perhaps they were hiding their talk from you, holding back. But me, I don't know how to hide the things I see. Those things are the talk I give you."

"Yes," I responded. "The people where I live have listened to your words. Women have said, 'How is it that when this woman—this !Kung San woman who lives so far away—speaks about the things she has seen, she sounds like one of us?'"

"Eh-hey." Nisa interjected enthusiastically. "A woman like that was here. A tall white woman and her husband, also tall, they were with Richard Lee when he came. They greeted me! And greeted me! And greeted me! They said, 'You are such a fine woman. You are a fine older woman. Your talk is beautiful!'"

The breach of confidentiality appalled me, but Nisa did not seem concerned. In fact she sounded proud to have been recognized.

I picked up the book and held it out toward her. "When you first saw this, what did you think?"

"I hope that it took my words very well." Then she added, almost in a whisper, "This book has given me life . . . given me life." And with more animation, "Nisa is inside."

"Do you like that?"

"This book holds Nisa inside. I especially like that."

Gifts and Payments

"Richard, I've dropped him," Nisa said suddenly, with great bitterness. "Richard dropped me, so I've dropped him." Her list of complaints was long. Richard gave everything to others. The money he had, he gave to others. The clothing he had, he gave to others. A trunk, he gave to others. Water containers, he gave to others. "That's why I say that he refused me. Ri-chard!" she said, exploding his name emphatically from her lips. "Richard, he is worthless!"

Then she voiced an accusation that would come up again: "I even told him, 'Don't go to Marjorie. Because if you go to Marjorie, she will give you things for me and you will give them to others.'"

She had asked Richard's wife to write to me. "I said, 'Go tell Marjorie to come back so I can see her with my eyes, my eyes that are almost dead. There are so many things that Marjorie will do for me—she will give me clothes, she will give me beads. Because today I am old. Marjorie will come and clothe me and give me a few shillings so that I can eat.' And she wrote it using my name, Nisa, and yours, Hwantla."

I couldn't help feeling somewhat amused by Nisa's description of me as the ultimate benefactor, although there was no humor in the underlying disparity it reflected: the substantial means available to researchers versus the meager ones available to the people they were studying. Nor did those with greater wealth see much humor in being constantly badgered by those wanting a larger share. During my years of fieldwork, when similar accusations were lodged against me, they were a source of great pain.

Accusations of stinginess were a quintessentially !Kung mode of expression and, with somewhat different emphasis, were just as likely to be leveled at an anthropologist as at a close relative. This type of conversation helped equalize material wealth and discourage social posturing. "Ooh, look at that," was a typical refrain when a person had something of value. But it was usually followed by "Why don't you give it to me? You haven't given me anything in a long time." Depending on the relationship between the two people, the article might be given on the spot.

Nisa's anger with Richard Lee came up more than once in our conversations. She listed others he had helped, others he had given gifts to, others he had paid with money. "The only thing he gave me was tobacco. I don't know why Richard, a grown man, my in-law, refuses me. Why? What wrong have I done him that he hates me?"

Her hurt was deep. And her needs, like those of the others around her, were real. Nevertheless, I confess to feeling some satisfaction when I heard Richard—the fieldworker among fieldworkers—blasted in the same tones that over the years had been reserved for others, including me.

KKKKK Nisa's tone changed to one of tenderness as she reminisced: "As I lived on, I said, 'When is Marjorie going to come? Oh, but I refuse other white people! I want Marjorie. I want her to come here so that I can see her again.' When others called out, 'Richard has come,' I ran to Richard, hoping that perhaps your truck was coming after. 'No, Marjorie's not here,' people told me. 'It's Richard and his wife.'"

Her words caught in her throat as violent coughing erupted, typical of all !Kung who smoked heavily. She fumbled for her pipe and lit it, inhaling deeply. The spasm had barely subsided when she commanded me, as sternly as her still raspy voice would permit, "When I cough, turn the tape recorder off. Don't let it record me coughing."

When she spoke again, her talk was a litany of accusations and complaints. Yes, my initial gift had been generous, she conceded. But when Richard returned years later, she was sure he had given others money I had sent for her. Had it not looked that way, with money in their hands, and none in hers? When, at the end of his stay, Richard finally gave her a gift he claimed was from me, her suspicions were confirmed. "No, Marjorie wouldn't give only that much," she insisted. "Marjorie is someone who is generous with money."

What she didn't know was that I had been eager to match my first gift, but that I had left it to Richard, who would be in the field, to determine the exact amount. And when Richard saw Nisa, already one of the wealthiest !Kung at Dobe, he feared that another very large gift would do her more harm than good. The sum he gave her "from Marjorie" therefore was modest, although it was still more money than most !Kung received in a lifetime. It had covered the cost of a branding iron and a few smaller items.

What and how to pay the !Kung for their labor had never been easy questions. During my first field trip, the people preferred material goods to money as payment for services. The local hourly, daily, or even weekly wage would never have covered the cost of the shoes, cloth, clothing, or beads they wanted—and even if they had had the money, those items were rarely available for purchase. Nevertheless, the issue of payment had caused considerable dissension among the anthropologists.

Some feared, rightly, that Western goods and money would disrupt the very fabric of !Kung culture, a culture many hundreds if not thousands of years old. These anthropologists took seriously the tenet that we were there to understand, not to change, the !Kung way of life. Except for tobacco, a "necessary evil" that allowed admission into the area, no other "handouts" were considered legitimate. (Of course, it was in the anthropologists' interest to avoid disrupting !Kung traditions: their academic reputations—and future livelihoods—depended, in part, on collecting data on "unsullied" traditional life.)

Others felt, also rightly, that the people should not be expected to shoulder our presence for free. Why should they? For the sake of (Western) science? Tobacco handouts and medical assistance were widely appreciated, and were adequate, by and large, for the general population. But when someone worked for an hour, a day, a week, or longer, payment was the only ethical choice. Otherwise, it was exploitation. These anthropologists accepted the risk of affecting, not only how the people lived, but also the delicate balance of the researchers' give-and-take relationship with them.

It was not just for the tobacco and gifts, however, or as ready (and generous) customers to buy their crafts, that the !Kung at Dobe welcomed the anthropologists. We were also a source of pride. Never before had the spotlight shone on their culture in this way. Never before had outsiders, considered wise in the ways of the "modern" world, taken time to understand !Kung ways. The dominant message from other groups with whom the !Kung San came in contact—mostly Bantu and whites—could be summed up in the epithet "bloody Bushmen," which fell as surely from the curled lips of whites drinking too much as water falls from a dripping faucet. The Bantu were not much different. Their view of the San was so low that they classified them in a category with animals and things, rather than with people like themselves.

The anthropologists never did establish consensus on payment. And this meant that different anthropologists worked it out for themselves in different ways. One couple about to return to the States, for example, dug a huge hole and burned, then buried, all the goods they no longer wanted—clothes, utensils, truck parts. What the !Kung must have thought as they watched items of great value (to them) being willfully destroyed, I can hardly imagine.

Were the two anthropologists hard-hearted? They didn't think so. They felt strongly that their legacy—to the people, and to later researchers—should not be the proliferation of Western goods. Distributing the goods would have caused tension and precipitated power struggles within and between the villages. The goods would also, eventually, have left their mark on the landscape, in the form of scattered debris. The anthropologists knew the !Kung had fared quite well before they arrived, and believed they would continue to do so after the last anthropologists left—as long as they did not become too dependent upon outsiders whose presence in the area was short-lived.

As significant as the distribution of these goods might have been at the time, the impact would have been small compared to the effects of the monumental forces of change that were reshaping the daily lives of the !Kung: the Bantu settlers who now shared most traditional !Kung waterholes; the Bantu headmen who maintained law and order; the fence between Namibia and Botswana, which partitioned !Kung traditional lands and affected game migrations; the local trading post, which bought Bantu cattle and which, when stocked, sold sugar, salt, flour, cloth, and other items; and the monthly, if not biweekly, traffic that now traversed the area.

At first, I too was a purist. And quite a romantic. Although I flinched when the goods were burned, I thought that !Kung hunting and gathering traditions should be given every chance to be preserved. They were, after all, among the most elegant—and among the most ancient—traditions known to anthropologists. They embodied power, freedom, simplicity, and pride. And though !Kung life was consistently hard, laughter often seemed easier than in our own complex lives. It rose and fell in the night, passing from village to village after darkness suspended until morning the unfinished work of the day.

To me, this world was a breath of fresh air in contrast to the musty traditions of my own life, many of which I was eager to leave behind: accumulation, greed, vanity, locked doors, closed living spaces, anonymity, crowds, pollution, noise, and vision that was hemmed in by tall buildings and developments. Yes, I was a romantic. And, yes, I was willing to accept the charge of being stingy if it meant I was not driving culture change at full throttle.

One researcher, an archaeologist, did not worry about this issue. He needed men to dig trenches and to sift earth. The !Kung wanted the jobs, so he hired the men at Dobe, where he lived. Nearly every morning his truck left carrying just about every able-bodied man from within a three-mile radius of the Dobe well, to return late in the day. About once a week he paid the men for their labor—in cash. Talk about impact! But he saw it differently. The people were begging to change, he explained. They wanted to enter the market economy, and he was proud to be their benefactor. "Back in graduate school, I was a nobody," he once told me. "When I return, I'll be a nobody. But here . . . here I'm a king."

Of course, the steady money pouring into Dobe made it untenable for certain kinds of research, and created havoc within the traditional, egalitarian community. But few of these complexities were clear to me when I first arrived. I was so happy to be there that it was easy for me to assume that, for the people, having anthropologists in their midst was an even exchange. But, very early on, I was taught a very valuable lesson.

When I left for the field, I knew I would have to learn the !Kung language. It was a badge of professionalism among anthropologists, and most who worked for long periods among the !Kung wore it. Yet, with clicks and tones, glottal stops and flaps, implosive and explosive sounds—and with words that prompted some Westerners, when hearing it on tape, to say, "It doesn't sound like language"—the challenge was formidable.

The anthropologists who introduced my husband and me to the field got us started, teaching us words and phrases—and a standard orthography with which to write the clicks. Soon, armed with the ability to say "When I do this, what is it called?" and "What is the name for that?" we placed our recalcitrant tongues in the hands of Kxau and Tashay, two !Kung brothers who, with much patience, agreed to teach us the language. Each day they came to our camp and, after we gave them something to eat, they talked with us. Mel and I used the few words we knew and pointed and acted things out. We tried to distinguish the sounds and then to write them down.

After a few days of this, the archaeologist asked me, quite casually, if we were going to pay the men for the lessons.

"Pay?" I asked incredulously. "Pay them?"

It's hard now to understand my frame of mind back then, but paying seemed utterly shocking. Why? Because the brothers were our friends. Because we laughed together and had a good time. Because we gave them presents and fed them. Because we put salve on their burns and gave them medicines for their ailments. And because they were part of the camp staff. They helped us, and one day we would help them. Wasn't that how relationships worked? They understood, I was sure. Only the archaeologist didn't.

When I finally found my voice, I gasped, "Are you saying they want money?"

"Ask them," he said, an amused gleam in his eye.

I certainly felt contemptuous of him: of how he studied the past, not the present; of how he meddled with the people's traditional economy; of how he wanted to be a king. Indignantly, I walked to the nearby village, finding Kxau and Tashay near their huts.

We exchanged afternoon greetings, the blood hot in my face. "Tom . . ." I began, speaking the archaeologist's name. Then I realized I had no idea how to ask my question. "Money . . . we two [I meant 'you two'] . . . like . . . money?"

These brothers had the anthropologists down cold, at least their speech. No matter how much we butchered the language, they always seemed to understand. When I became more fluent, I saw how they watched our faces and body movements for clues. A hand that pointed away took precedence over (wrong) words that said "come here," a nodding head over (mistaken) words of denial. So I was well met. I, too, would be understood. "Yes," they said, smiling broadly and speaking slowly, "we'd love to be paid."

Yes? Yes. Devastated and speechless (I had so few words at that time anyway), I retreated to my camp with my wounded pride. I wish I could say that I learned my lesson then and there, just two weeks into my stay, but I didn't. Of course, we paid them (retroactively, as well), but I never gave up my hope, unfulfilled to the end, of finding a medium for more spontaneous exchange.

$\mathbb{K}\mathbb{K}\mathbb{K}\mathbb{K}$ A month or so later the issue came up again. Wanting to put my shaky vocabulary to the test, I went to visit the nearby village. Tashay's wife, Nukha, was sitting near her hut, roasting and cracking mongongo nuts for her family. It was midday. The youngest of her four children was nursing. No one else was around. I greeted her and pointed to a spot on the ground, asking if I could join her. She nodded. I sat down and watched her work, marveling at her economy of movement. With unerring accuracy, she cracked the thick outer shells along a small fault line, then pulled out the still-warm kernel.

Soon she extended a hand filled with bare nuts, cleared of both the outer shells and the thin inner shells. I thanked her and ate, savoring the full roasted flavor and rich texture.

"Now what?" I wondered, as I sat mesmerized by her rhythm. How could I get a conversation going? There we were, two women together; what should I say? I felt awkward. I thought about leaving but persuaded myself to stay.

It amuses—as well as embarrasses—me now to recall what I did say. "Go for what you want," I had told myself. What I really wanted was friendship and shared intimacies. So what did I ask? I suggested we tell each other about what happened when we first "saw the moon," which meant first menstruation.

"Tell me about you," I asked eagerly.

Roasting, cracking, and shelling, her work continued. She answered flatly, "Nothing happened." (I would learn, months later, that this response meant that nothing unusual happened.)

I was taken aback. Perhaps she would open up after I took my turn? I told her how my mother had prepared me and how she had helped when my period first came. I filled in details as best I could, although with my sparse knowledge of the language the event remained hazy and generalized. She listened as she worked. "That's how we do it in my culture," I concluded. "Tell me about you."

Again she brushed me off. Again I offered Western customs in hope of starting a dialogue. Back and forth we went. She never did tell me anything. Finally, frustrated, I stood up to leave. Then, using more words than she had during any of our interchanges, Nukha asked, "What are you going to pay me for the interview?"

Again, as with Kxau and Tashay, I was crushed. I felt unseen and used. But as time passed, I began to understand. Would I have confided my intimate memories to someone I hardly knew, someone who barely spoke English and who asked personal questions about my life? Probably not. In retrospect, it seems quite reasonable that Nukha didn't confide in me. After all, I was the one who wanted something. Surrounded by family and friends, she did not need friendship from me. She needed to provide for her family. I learned, ultimately, that if I wanted the women to talk with me about intimate topics, I needed both better language skills and a better approach.

⧫⧫⧫⧫⧫ Learning the language was a matter of time. As for an approach, I learned to make contractual agreements when asking for someone's time or for a special favor. "I'd like to ask about your pregnancy," I began months later, when I had slightly more mastery of the language. "I will pay you two shillings or the equivalent in oil, beads, matches, or cloth." Sometimes the payments were higher. Much to my surprise, I eventually discovered that paying did not detract from relationships. Rather, it allowed them to flourish.

But that lesson took time to learn. A letter I wrote to friends in February 1970, six months after we started fieldwork, evokes the difficulties:

It's very difficult to write when your mind and soul are steeped in sadness. The Bushmen thing hasn't been working out too well. We both feel defeated. Nothing striking has happened. It's just that we're realizing that there is no way of reaching any kind of "human" compromise in our relations with them.

No matter how we strip ourselves of comforts other field workers here couldn't live without, no matter how we try to minimize the cultural differences and the language barriers, no matter what we do, we're always too rich and they, too poor. We're too powerful and they, too powerless.

The blacks in the area look down upon the Bushmen, even as the Bushmen look up to the blacks. Meanwhile, the blacks look up to us. The Bushmen are on the bottom and they know it. They also know we're the ones on the top-top. We've got a truck and clothing and food and everything they could ever want. And when we try to communicate on any kind of meaningful level, nothing happens. That is to say, nothing good and a lot of bad.

If someone comes over to you in the morning and greets you in an especially nice way, you can be sure he's going to ask for something or scold you for not having given him something, or anyone anything, for that matter. And if you remind him, "Didn't I give you X just last week?

And what about the tobacco you get every few days. And how come you haven't given me anything after all I've given you?" he tells you that he is poor and you are rich and that you are bad. Then he goes off to tell people what a bad white person you are.

We've tried every approach to get around this. First, we gave out nothing, for that was one of the other anthropologist's policies. That didn't work. The people told us we were stingy and didn't give anybody things. Then we tried giving things to everybody, equally, but found that they took this as a dole, that it meant nothing personal if everyone got it. Then we tried giving selectively; that's where we are now. If someone gives us a present, we return the gift a hundredfold. Even so, very few people give to us. We're not included in their give-and-take exchange.

It's easy to buy friendship. If you give someone things often enough, you can be sure he or she will tell you how much you are liked and how, when you go away for a few days, you are missed. There was one woman who was so kind to me and friendly and I gave her little presents all the time. Then I noticed that she never gave me anything, not even a token. So when I had things to give, I didn't give to her and asked why she never gave me anything. After that she wasn't so friendly and didn't tell me how sad her heart was that I was going away.

It's such a hard fall from my dream. I was going to learn about "Woman." I was going to learn how to face myself as one. I was going to become "cosmic." I was going to sit in the shade of the trees and gossip with the women and they would tell me about their childhoods and their marriages and I would drink in their radiance and I would become at one with myself . . .

Enough. It's too depressing to go on. Suffice it to say that the women here are not very different from anywhere else. They are petty and selfish and constantly demanding in all their dealings with us. If I sit in the shade of a tree where some women are talking, they immediately ask for matches, tobacco, water, or whatever else they think they might get. If I ask them questions, informally, about themselves, I am given "I don't know" type answers, and "That's the way it is, that's why." If I persist, they want to know if I'm going to give them something when I get through questioning them.

So, I've been working up an interview about marriage and related things. When I want an answer, I'll go up to a woman and say, "I'd like to ask you some questions. When we finish, I'll give you the following . . ."

᠁ Of course, while we were trying to figure out the !Kung, they were working pretty hard trying to figure us out as well. Once, when the requests (more like demands) seemed unending, my husband asked the younger of the two brothers, "Kxau, do you think anthropologists have as much money as there is sand?" "Perhaps," Kxau answered, amused, yet serious enough that we could see he thought it within the range of possibility. Another time, Kxau was watching my husband write furiously in a notebook. "When you return home, you will sell those papers for money, right?" he asked. Little did he know how close to the truth he was. Field notes, did, ultimately, translate into jobs.

᠁ When I first worked with Nisa, paying her wasn't difficult: I gave her the same combination of money and presents I gave the other women in my study. But once I recognized her extraordinary conversational gifts, I was glad to shower her with additional presents—as long as doing so didn't cause problems with the other women.

"Marjorie," Nisa would say, eager for the moisturizing cream, the perfume, the bottle, the scarf, or whatever else she had marked among my things, "that's mine when you finish with it."

If I could, I'd just hand it to her. "Now, don't let the others see, or they will be angry with me."

"Eh-hey, mother," she would whisper, slipping it into the folds of her clothes or her carrying sack. "No one but the two of us will know."

How that could be, I never understood. But unlike less conspiratorial approaches to giving presents, collusion worked: it rarely provoked demands from others for equal treatment.

᠁ But what if gifts were fairly distributed to all? I tried that, too. Once, on our way back to Dobe after several days at another village, and still hours from "home," we passed two gargantuan baobab trees, the largest living forms in the desert environment. A !Kung couple traveling with us asked us to stop so they could collect the fruit. On the ground or still hanging from the trees were long pods covered in green velvet. In shape and size the fruit resembled spaghetti squash. Inside, however, it was bone dry. Seeds like cherry pits were encased in a thick white pulp and held firm in a net of strings attached to the pod. The dried pulp tasted more sour than sweet; some Westerners claimed the taste was pure vitamin C, or perhaps cream of tartar. But although it teased one's salivary glands and stripped one's teeth clean, its flavor was full, like that of premium lemon candy. When not eaten directly from the pod, the pulp could be pounded clear of the seeds and the fine powder consumed with water, either as a drink or cooked as porridge. The seeds could also be swallowed whole, with the pulp, or roasted and pounded to release their rich, nutty flavor.

I took a pod for myself and watched as the couple gathered a half dozen or so. Then it occurred to me that I could share this treat with the people at Dobe. I gathered what I could, amassing enough to distribute at least one pod to each family, and loaded them into the truck. Dark was falling as we drove away, the headlights ricocheting off the deep ruts in the road. These gifts would be much better, I thought, than the usual tobacco, refined corn meal, or sugar. I looked forward to our return.

As soon as the truck stopped at Dobe, I grabbed the baobab pods and walked to the village. I stopped at the first hut, saying, as best I could, "I gathered what was too far away for you to gather for yourself. It is a small gift, to be sure, but I wanted to bring something back to you." I walked from one family group to the next, repeating some version of my speech. I felt virtuous, even triumphant. This proved, I thought, that there were other choices besides "being stingy" and a giving free-for-all.

Part way around the village, I became aware that something was very wrong. People were not smiling. Instead, they were angry and demanding. "I need more than three. I have many mouths in my family." "Give me another, I'm hungry." As I handed out more pods from the bag I carried, the chorus of complaints grew louder. My bubble burst. I stopped telling people how glad I was to see them again, gave out the last pods as fairly as I could, and escaped to my tent. Giving to everyone equally? No, that didn't make people happy. When everyone received the same thing, no one experienced it as a gift.

During my second field trip, paying Nisa was still relatively simple: for our six interviews, she received the customary monetary compensation, along with many not-so-customary additional gifts. Of course, by then I knew she was special. I had already translated our original fifteen interviews, and had edited some of her childhood stories and published a selection as a chapter in an edited volume. But the next step—writing a book about her—was still a distant dream.

It was a dream, however, that I took seriously enough to discuss with her during that second visit. I explained that it would take me many years of work to turn her story into a book. And when I finished, people might not buy it. "People may look at the book and leave it on the shelf."

"Yes," Nisa said, showing her understanding of the market economy of which the !Kung were becoming a part. "They say, 'very nice,' but their hearts don't go out to it." Then she added, "But if they do help the two of us and buy it and you help me, then I will buy a cow."

Six years after that second field trip, the book was published. One year after that, a paperback edition appeared. It would take almost a decade for the royalties I received from "people buying it" to balance the expenses of so many years of work. Nevertheless, Nisa's story had enriched my life, and it seemed to touch others who read it. There was no doubt that Nisa deserved her cows. But how to provide them in a beneficial way?

Then Richard Lee told me of his plans to return to Botswana. As one of the first anthropologists to study the !Kung of Botswana, Richard was sometimes called the "father" of !Kung ethnography. Along with other researchers, he mapped !Kung life, collecting data on what the people ate, where they lived, how they earned a living, whom they married, whom they chose as their leaders, what they fought over, and when they died. He collected plant specimens and had them matched with scientific names. He studied hunting and gathering and how the !Kung used the resources available to them. He calculated the work done by men and women and took a census of the entire population at nine waterholes—more than a thousand people by my second trip to the field—going from household to household, writing down the names of the living and the recently dead.

Could I ask Richard—who had been there from the start, so to speak, who had arrived when the !Kung were still hunting and gathering, who had extolled the small differences in wealth between the most and least advantaged, who had understood sharing as the great equalizer in this essentially egalitarian culture—could I ask Richard to buy cows? And for just one person?

Major changes had taken place in the twenty years since Richard had first visited Dobe. By 1975, the time of my second field trip, !Kung ownership of cattle, though still rare, was no longer unknown. Villages sported "contemporary" mud huts beside the traditional grass ones. Adolescent boys, bows and poisoned arrows in hand, walked the land tending communal herds of goats. Many people owned donkeys, bought with money earned by selling crafts. Domestic animals were being husbanded instead of slaughtered, precipitating crises within families as sons-in-law no longer sacrificed goats to feed in-laws who complained of "meat hunger." In the past, a man would hunt a large antelope to satisfy the demands, and the requirements of respect, of a close relative. But wild animals now stayed far away, beyond the ever widening grazing areas of cattle and goats. And the young men, who as boys had herded domestic animals, now lacked the tracking and shooting skills of their fathers.

I summoned my courage and asked. Richard said he was more than willing to take money to Nisa for cows. I was thrilled. If anyone could handle this assignment in a way that caused the least dissension, it was Richard. And, from his own accounts afterward, it had worked just fine. Now I got to hear Nisa's version.

"Richard took me from where I was living," Nisa told me. "He said, 'Come with me to Dobe. There, you'll take the money Marjorie gave you and buy your cows.'" Her husband and the Bantu-speaking husband of one of her relatives negotiated the deal. Five pregnant females! Some of the offspring lived; others got lost and died. But for years now, Nisa had had milk to drink.

Nisa stayed at Dobe, where her cows were, because "I am without strength. Mother, today I am without strength. I didn't see any person who would pour water for the cows because I am without my own child. Only my older brother's daughter Nai, the one who has the sick finger . . . her son is the one to whom I say, 'Take care of these cows. For me. For me. Put them in a corral. For me. Have the babies drink the milk. For me. Milk the cows and bring me the milk so that I can drink.' Later, he comes to me and says, 'Here's your milk, Aunt.' And I have it."

"Very good!" I responded. "The cows are helping you and your husband."

"Eh, mother. I'm not feeling pain. My mother, I'm not in pain." Pointing to me, she added, "You . . ." Then, emphatically, "You . . . !"

"Uhn-uhn," I broke in. "It was your tongue that did it."

"This book here has saved me. Because, even if people yell at me, it doesn't matter. It doesn't bother me. You really are taking good care of me. Mother!"

"And you," I replied, "you also took good care of me when first we talked."

Later I asked her another question about the cows, and she answered with the eloquence and enthusiasm that had marked her interviews years before.

"And what if you had never seen the money and had no cows—how would you be living?"

I'd just be living. If you are living where just people are living, people eat and eat and eat, whatever they have. Even a little thing that you have, you say, "What I have is very little and I won't give it to you. I'm going to eat this myself." You are the only one to eat it.

But after that, the other person says, "What's wrong with you, that with that food, you don't give me any and eat it yourself? If you eat it yourself, what do you suppose I will eat?" That's what happens when there are a lot of people living together.

And you say, "Didn't you sit with a small amount of food and eat it yourself? I didn't yell at you about it. What are you saying I should now do with mine?"

But Richard did bring the money and I'm living well. And I am thankful. Very thankful. Because a cow . . . it is like a real person! A real person that you live with. It cries and goes, "Bahhn . . . bahhn . . . bahhn . . ." And you run and tell it, "Nisa is getting up to take care of you." And the two of you talk. A cow is a wonderful thing. "Nisa, get up and help me," it says, and your heart is happy.

Into the Bush

It took half the morning to make the arrangements: collecting water, packing food and supplies (including tobacco), and settling who was to go. As agreed the day before, each of the five San villages of Dobe sent two people so that the potential gains from our bush living—meat, honey, and vegetable foods—would be distributed fairly.

At midday, the heavy wheels of the truck began to turn. Eleven people—ten adults and one child—were seated in the back, on the "game viewing" benches bolted high above the truck's chassis. Packed beneath them were our food, water, and equipment. Voices rang out as last-minute goodbyes, bits of advice, and humorous exchanges filled the air.

Baitsenke drove westward. The rumble of the motor reverberated as we passed !Kung and Herero villages, cattle and goat corrals, and fields long since harvested. One mile from Dobe stood the border fence separating Botswana and Namibia. There Baitsenke turned north along the road that ran parallel to the border. Foot trails became fewer, and clusters of tall grass—out of range of the grazing herds nearer the villages—collected the afternoon light.

Nisa sat beside me in the cab of the truck, our bodies pressed together in the cramped space, bouncing against each other as Baitsenke negotiated rough patches on the grassy track. My eyes feasted on the view beyond the open window: a landscape so familiar yet different from any other landscape of my life. It was a place of great beauty. A place of great stillness. I had visited it often in recent years, but only in memory—and now it surrounded me. Graceful acacia trees, sculpted termite mounds, massive dunes, earth tones that ranged from deep red to chalky white and earth textures that varied from soft sand to hard clay to rocky outcrops, each with its own signature and its unique vegetation, all pristine, unsullied by human presence. My journey had led me to a place I loved.

〟〟〟〟〟 To be sure, I hadn't loved it from the start. On my first trip to the field, the landscape had sometimes frightened me. Two days from medical help, the post office, or a telephone, emergency services were essentially nonexistent. Lions, leopards, cheetahs, hyenas, and wild dogs were known to live in the wilds beyond the village boundaries. And an array of lethal snakes made the desert their home: puff adders, green and black mambas, boomslangs, spitting cobras, vipers.

We did have contingency plans in case of an emergency. Plan A was to drive to Maun, the nearest place with a hospital and medical personnel. The drive took about fourteen hours in the best of circumstances; packing (petrol, water, food, truck parts, and bedding) and leaving camp made it even longer. In the rainy season, however, or if the truck broke down along the road, that fourteen-plus hours could stretch into days, even weeks; vehicle traffic to the area, let alone to our camp, was rare.

In case of a dire emergency, there was also plan B. We would drive to the border, one mile away, cut the fence, then speed along the graded road to Chum!kwe, the !Kung settlement thirty miles inside Namibia. There we would ask someone to radio the Namibian capital city, Windhoek, and request that a helicopter be sent for us. Of course, the success of this plan also assumed optimal conditions: that it would proceed without complications (What do we use to cut the wire fence?) and without delay (The radio is broken? It's Sunday and no one is there? The helicopter is already out on a call?). Again, hours upon hours might pass before we found help.

Knowing in advance how tenuous our connection to outside support would be, we had gladly accepted training from specialists in tropical medicine before we left for the field. We also carried abundant medical supplies, including antibiotics, anti-malarials, anti-diarrheals, and anti-snakebite serums, as well as creams, salves, pills, solutions, and bandages of all sizes and shapes—a treasure trove for almost all situations and a cure for practically anything that was curable. Once in the field, our how-to book of medicine, the *Merck Manual*, was never far from reach. Referred to religiously, it was perhaps our most precious possession.

But, filled with the exuberance of youth, we had enough naiveté, courage, and faith—and, as it turned out, good luck—that instead of worrying about what might possibly happen to us we were able to focus on what was actually happening. And, during our first year, what was happening absorbed all my attention.

▨▨▨▨▨ Now the task was to find out if I could become that absorbed again: if I could leave behind exquisite observation of my internal world for the challenges of a world outside. I had traveled a long way to break the emotional paralysis that had become, in some bizarre way, comfortable. With no doctors to see, no tests to take, no reassurances in technology to ease my frightened soul, deliberation and worry could serve no purpose here. I stopped my fingers from searching for things strange beneath my skin, and I brushed aside discomfort, pain, and concern, telling myself, "One month won't make much difference."

But, of course, one month did make a difference, not to my illness, but to my health. Traveling once again in that ancient desert, with Nisa by my side, I felt at peace. Dry, cool air blew in through the window, playing about my arms and neck, dissipating the heat that rose from the engine. And on we drove, following the contour of the land, its sand dunes and hard flatlands, its risings and fallings that stretched before us (and around us) beyond where the eye could see.

Near the crest of a dune in an area called Gaing Na Ho, Baitsenke slowed down, put the truck into four-wheel drive, and turned into the bush. People swayed from side to side as the truck mounted the embankment, much as they might in a sailboat negotiating waves upon the open seas. Gau, one of the men, walked ahead, guiding Baitsenke around holes and thorn bushes.

A quarter of a mile from the border, beneath a group of majestic mongongo nut trees, Gau signaled Baitsenke to stop. There, surrounded by the great expanse of wilderness, we set up camp.

The promise of meat and vegetable gatherings beckoned, so everyone worked quickly and efficiently. The ground was cleared of underbrush as sleeping and living arrangements were defined: Kxau and Bau, a middle-aged married couple, set their blankets together a short distance from the main fire, beside a small fire of their own; Dikau, Kxau's sister-in-law, placed her blankets adjacent to theirs, securing branches upright in the sand between them—the skeleton shelter delineating their separate living spaces. Except for Baitsenke, whose well-fortified tent displayed his respectful fear of the bush, we all cleared spots around the central fire, which was already alight: a dead tree, large enough to burn through the day and into the night, had been dragged roots first into the middle, its trunk breaking our circle like a hand on a clock.

My own blankets I placed beside Nisa's, nearest the truck and Baitsenke's tent for whatever protection they might offer. On the far side of Nisa were Kumsa, an aging widower of great strength and hunting ability, known as Kumsa-the-Hunter; his daughter Kxaru; her son Dem, about three years old and the only child in camp; and Toma, the husband of Kumsa's other daughter, who had stayed behind with her own son at Dobe. Kumsa was the benign patriarch of this group, inclining himself, and his village, toward older traditions as the way of life he knew best.

Kumsa had been married to Tasa, my daughter Sarah's namesake, and they had had three children. But while still in her mid-thirties, this thoughtful, handsome woman had died, probably from tuberculosis. Recently, years later, Kumsa had entered into another marriage, but his bride, thirty-five years his junior (and younger than either of his daughters), had spurned him a few months before my arrival.

On Kumsa's far side were three people from Kxoma's village: Kxoma's energetic wife Nisa, his niece Nukha, and her husband, Kantla. Kxoma himself, the namesake of my son Adam, had not accompanied us; he was still away on a hunting trip. The last in the circle was Gau, a tall, modest man who lived in a small compound at Dobe. Including Baitsenke and me, we totaled seven women, six men, and one child.

Tea, thickened with dried milk and sweetened beyond saturation, was made, passed around, and consumed. (A more substantial meal would be prepared after the daylight hours.) Then people were off, the women to gather *kama ko* berries, the men to try their luck in the hunt.

I would join the hunters. Walking at a brisk pace behind the men; watching them decipher animal tracks in the sand and plan strategies with a whispered word or phrase; sharing the excitement that electrified the air when an animal was near; feeling strong, fully alive, and fearless in this world as long as they were beside me—this was what I had come so far to experience again.

With my cameras, canteen, and notebook secure in a cloth tied, traditional style, across my right shoulder—arranged for me by one of the women—I fell in line behind the men, following Kumsa, who had agreed to be my guide. The men walked quickly and surely through the wild terrain, beyond the mongongo nut trees, beyond the ridge to the flats where the groves ended, through thickets of thin trees and meadows of low brush. Talking openly as we left, they lowered their voices only slightly as they discussed tracks too old to hold promise. The clicks in their speech were expressive and subtle, like the breaking of a twig.

On they walked, and on I followed, keeping their rhythm as best I could, losing it when my heavy boots dropped through the sand and fell into mouse tunnels below. The sun shone in the western sky, warming our faces and arms, even as the winter breeze felt cool and refreshing. The air was clean, the land unblemished. A rush of excitement swept through me as I breathed deeply of this world.

After a kudu—a large antelope—jumped from its hiding place, its footsteps pounding into the distance, too far away for the hunters to stalk it, the rush became a torrent. I heard a chorus of voices in my head. "Marjorie, you did it!" they called. "Here you are, back in the bush, walking with men with real bows and poisoned arrows, hunting real animals!"

I recognized the familiar voices of my friends, my family, and my husband—those who had hoped for my healing, for the lessening of my psychic pain. In my head I answered them. "Thanks," I told them. "Thanks for having stood beside me."

By sunset everyone had returned to camp. After setting aside their kama ko berries and other bush gatherings, the women arranged their bedding for the night. The men, who had had no success in the hunt, talked about animals, tracks, and possible strategies for the next day. Everyone shared cornmeal porridge seasoned with oil and salt (except Baitsenke, who cooked his own much more substantial meal), along with tea; everyone tasted roasted *gwea* and *sha* roots the women had collected. As the two fires burned brightly, I visited with one group and then the other. Then, wearing extra sweaters and socks, I folded my blankets on top of my sleeping bag and climbed in.

Talking more quietly now, the others also prepared for sleep. Seeking shelter from the cold, we few humans wrapped our bedding around us, legs shifting under blankets to capture warmth. Together, we fourteen people—small against the canopy of mongongo nut tree branches above us, even smaller against the primal landscape extending endlessly (so it seemed) beyond us, smaller still beneath the silence of distant stars—repeated a scene as old as human experience.

Hours later, I woke to a profound silence. Small sounds—someone coughing, coals shifting in the fire—retreated quickly, barely touching the immensity of the stillness surrounding us. "This is exactly where I want to be," I thought. Drinking in the beauty of the stars, the jagged strength of the towering mongongo nut trees, and the clarity of the cold night air, I returned to sleep.

I accompanied Kumsa and his son-in-law, Toma—both men over fifty—on our second day of hunting. The sun, bright in the winter sky, had been up for over an hour. Again we headed for the flats beyond the groves. Even minutes from camp, I could not have found my way back.

They moved quickly, taking long, steady strides. A snake retreated into its hole as we approached; had it not, the men would have killed it as a matter of course. We went on, and large tracks appeared. "Kudu," Kumsa whispered to me. His hand signed, "Two of them." With cameras, film, food, and my canteen, I scrambled along, trying to be quiet, grateful that I had started physical conditioning months before.

Half an hour went by. The men talked with their hands—talking, questioning, agreeing, disagreeing, forming strategies. Unable to read their hand signs, I watched the language of their bodies. Perhaps it was a sound. Or a call. Perhaps it was the fresh droppings they found, very fresh, they acknowledged, rubbing the droppings between their fingers and holding them near their faces.

Suddenly the men tensed. With every sense alert, they were still.

When they moved again, it was as though a dramatic twist had suddenly brought sharp focus to a previously meandering play. With hands still conversing, they advanced in slow motion, crouching low. Almost in unison, they reached for their quivers, withdrawing arrows freshly poisoned for the hunt. Lethal arrows at the ready, they pressed on, each foot touching the ground with care.

Knowing I was a handicap to them, I reluctantly dropped back; even the lightest of branches seemed to crack more sharply beneath my tread. I couldn't even take photographs: the camera shutter would have scared away any animal not savvy enough to be already running.

On they stalked, their bodies controlled and sure-footed, as in a dance. Suddenly a loud noise resounded, followed almost immediately by another. I was too far away to see anything more than a little movement and a flash of brown. Then the kudu were gone, their retreating hooves pounding the earth like a dimming heartbeat.

Only slightly discouraged, the two men decided to approach the animals separately. Toma went west. Kumsa, beckoning me to follow, went east.

Then it was just Kumsa and me. The kudu we were following was on the move, its tracks leading us through terrain thick with trees or with a scattered few, over rises where low thorn bushes reigned, through areas where vines crawled along the sandy floor, nourishing grapefruit-sized *dcha* fruits. Likened to prickly pears, these succulent fruits were so tart that their moisture was sought only as a last resort—by people as well as by animals.

No matter where the tracks led, we invariably stumbled (literally) into mouse burrows. Elaborate in scope, this underground mouse civilization was ill-prepared for the weight of creatures with booted feet. I would lose my stride, feet twisting, ankles sinking into the sand, off balance like a clown in oversized shoes. After extracting one foot or two, I would run to catch up; even though it was just two of us, Kumsa set a fast pace.

An hour and a half passed. Just as I began to wonder when—or if—we would ever turn back, Kumsa suddenly dropped down, motioning to me to do the same. Crouching low, he went on, his muscles once again taut, his every move considered. His hand waved me forward, his fingers signing, "Kudu . . . not far away." Trailing behind, I tried to move as he moved—precisely and quietly.

Minutes passed. More minutes passed. I had not seen or heard anything. I pressed on, feeling tired, thirsty, and hungry, and somewhat distracted from our purpose.

"Rrrrrrrr"—a loud rustling pulled me back to the moment. It came again, quite close, resonating like castanets. Silently, Kumsa set down his sack with his bow and quiver, stepped out of his Western pants and shoes (with more holes than covering), took off his socks (also filled with holes), and stood barefoot in his leather loincloth. Arrows poised, he advanced in the direction of the sound. This time his hands told me to stay behind.

He disappeared behind a tree. Then it was as though he had never been there. Try as I could to stretch my senses, he was thoroughly gone: there was no sound or sign of any creature but me. No distant foot-steps, no retreating hoofbeats. Just the wind gently moving the leaves.

Famished, I dug into my carrying sack for raisins, crackers, and water from my canteen. I rested awhile in the dappled shade, happy just to eat and drink. Then I looked for nuts under a mongongo nut tree, but there were very few to gather. I sat down again, feeling that Kumsa had been gone for a long time.

I looked at the bushes, at the mongongo nut trees, and into the scrub brush beyond. I saw a leaf moving. What was that sound? I got up, my senses keenly alert. I couldn't walk away—where would I go?—but I no longer felt relaxed enough to sit. After all, Kumsa had disappeared si-lently. What if some predator could approach me with equal stealth?

The sense of unconditional safety that I felt while Kumsa or the others were with me was gone. What if he didn't come back? What if a lion, leopard, wild dog, hyena, or cheetah—my imagination sparing none of the possibilities—found me first?

A lion had found me once. After twenty years the memory was still vivid.

𝕂𝕂𝕂𝕂𝕂 I had been in the field only a few months. Fieldwork had turned out to be more sedentary than I had expected. I moved around minimally much of the time: observing, writing, photographing, learn-ing the language, asking questions, organizing notes, and performing general camp chores. Or I rode in the truck: filling drums with water, collecting firewood, driving to other villages.

Add a diet more limited than I was used to, and I found myself gain-ing weight and losing conditioning. To burn calories, walking the one-mile track from camp to the border road seemed an ideal solution: the distance was reasonable, it wouldn't take much time, and I couldn't get lost.

I walked the route a number of times, usually alone. I would leave early to avoid the midday heat; in the hot, dry season midday tem-peratures in the shade typically topped 100 degrees Fahrenheit. In the villages, rhythmic pounding—"mortar talk," as it is called—could be heard, as women turned nuts and vegetables into paste for eating. The sounds dimmed as I passed the last village. I walked in the truck spoor, seeking the crushed grass or flattened soil that told of the frequent pass-ing of tires.

Traveling fast where the earth was hard and slow where it was heavy and soft, I walked on. The air was clear, the sun warm. When I reached the border, I stopped to rest, touching the five-foot-high barbed-wire fence that divided the politically opposing governments of Botswana and Namibia.

I rarely thought about danger on these walks: hunters typically went out on their own or with one or two others; gatherers did the same. Just a mile from camp, I felt I had little to worry about.

Then one morning, when the fenceposts of the border had just come into view, something caught my eye. It was big. It was brown. And it was moving. From a distance, I watched as it emerged from the bushes, its form becoming distinct on the open road. About halfway across the road it stopped and turned its head toward me. It didn't have horns. It walked low to the ground. It was a female lion!

"If you ever see a lion in the bush, walk away from it backward, and very slowly," was the advice I had heard in my travels. "Don't run from a lion, you'll only provoke it." I took two or three steps backward.

"Walk slowly . . ." But suddenly I found my back turned toward the animal and my feet heading for camp as fast as they could go.

That wasn't very fast. No matter how hard I tried to run, the soft sand held my feet like glue, slowing my progress to that of a child learning to walk.

Any second now the lion might be on me. I panicked. My breath heaving, I moved from the track to a spindly tree with an upright trunk. Climbing a tree might be my only chance. For some reason, I had the impression that I could somehow climb vertically while a lion couldn't.

Racing from tree to tree, looking back, stopping to catch my breath, I went on toward the village. By the time I heard "mortar talk" in the distance, the terror had subsided. Safe and in one piece, I finally arrived.

"There was a lion near the border!" I tried to communicate, afraid it might still be a threat to our camp. But people didn't believe me. "City girl. You wouldn't know a lion if you saw one," was the gist of their remarks.

Eventually, late in the day, the story was taken seriously, but only after three men who had been out hunting returned to the village and said they had seen my tracks. They could tell from the tracks that I had walked nearly to the border, stopped still, and then run away. Curious about what had frightened me, they had explored the area until they found animal tracks. They grinned as they described what they had discovered. Yes, the animal had been a lion, and a big female lion it was, too. Yes, it had started to cross the road. And yes, it had stood still, its body turned in my direction. "Then," they said, chuckling loudly, "when you began to run, the lion did, too—but in the opposite direction!"

After that I stopped my walks and never again ventured alone far from the village or camp. I also became wary, even in the company of others. In the beginning I had felt invincible, as though my heart pounded less vulnerably than the hearts of those who lived there; as though being foreign somehow shielded me from harm; as though the laws of nature that governed this land, laws that had prevailed before I arrived and surely would prevail after I left, didn't quite apply to me. This wasn't my world. I was only an observer.

It had seemed easy to watch events unfold before me, yet to stand apart, to translate experience into narrative, as if in a novel: "Our hero-ine arrived in Dobe today, two days after leaving Maun." Or to impose frames on the visual field, as if in a photograph or film: "A woman sits beside her hut, cracking nuts by the fire, the grass thatch alive with the yellows, oranges, and reds of the late afternoon sky."

But my body wasn't invincible, and the ending of whatever book or film was being created was not yet known. I was flesh and blood. I was vulnerable. And I, like other human beings, was tasty.

⟨⟨⟨⟨⟨⟨ Now, twenty years later, alone in the trees with lions on my mind, I again thought of climbing a tree. I walked purposefully to the nearest mongongo nut tree to rehearse my climb. Pushing aside thorny underbrush, I searched for a way to ascend. But the trunk was too broad for my outstretched arms and the bark too smooth for my feet. The trunk divided far above my head. Attending to sounds of the bush while eyeing the ground for snakes, I circled the tree slowly, seeking a place for my foot, a hold for my hand. Finding none, I moved on to the other mongongo nut trees nearby. But they all proved unscalable.

I was still working on the problem when Kumsa appeared—as qui-etly as he had disappeared an hour earlier. He had tracked the kudu quite far (yes, I suspected that!), he explained, and finally had been close enough to shoot. But his arrow had missed and the animal had run off. On his own he would have kept going, of course, but he had turned back for me, leaving the kudu to roam free, the deadly power of the arrow wasting in the grass.

We sat in the shade, eating crackers and raisins and drinking water. He talked of the animal, of his missed opportunity, and of his arrow still somewhere in the bush.

I shifted the conversation to the events of the last fourteen years, since my last visit. I asked about people at Dobe, about his own life, and about the death of his wife Tasa, the beautiful woman whose face graced the cover of the book *Nisa*. He first spoke of another beauty, the girl he had recently married. He told me she had left him after her first menstruation. Although she had been living with him for months, "When she went to her female relatives for the menstrual dance, she didn't come back." Because she was so young, they hadn't yet started having sexual relations.

〰〰〰 Tradition has it that a girl's first menstruation be celebrated by ritual, with singing and dancing and rejoicing. At least for the other women involved. While they dance and sing in high-spirited bawdy displays of femininity outside a hut, the young girl sits quietly inside, eating little and speaking less, her head covered.

A girl knows what to do long before she sees the first blood; others have traversed this path before her. She knows that her demeanor is expected to change. She knows that she is to sit down, cover her head, and stop speaking. Others, recognizing the signs, will string her hair with beads and ornaments and rub her skin with oil. Once "made beautiful," she will be taken into a hut prepared for the ceremony.

Men are not supposed to see the girl's face. "It could hurt them in the hunt," custom dictates. This is because first menstruation is thought to harness powerful spiritual forces, much like those harnessed in trance. One woman told me, "If a man sees a girl's face during the ceremony and the women find out, they'll take everything away from her that they had given her, even cut off her hair. Then they'll tell her the ceremony is over."

That is why the girl covers her head and the men sit at a distance. But not so far away that they cannot watch and comment vociferously on the proceedings, including the baring of women's buttocks while they dance, the only time this otherwise very private part of the female anatomy is publicly exhibited.

The girl remains in the hut for three or four days, eating little, leaving only for short trips to the bush (a !Kung euphemism with the same meaning as our own euphemism "going to the bathroom"). The dancing and singing continue sporadically during that time, ending with the cessation of the menstrual flow. The girl is bathed, rubbed with herbs and oil, and brought out of the hut. Subject to new food taboos, she resumes normal life, although her manner remains "reserved," reflecting her new status. At her second menstruation the ceremony is repeated, after which time she slowly—ever so slowly—starts her journey into the adult world.

Traditionally, half of !Kung girls marry before their first menstruation, which occurs at the average age of sixteen and a half—much later than the average of twelve and a half years for girls in the West. It is not clear why it occurs so early in our culture. Various explanations have been advanced: better nutrition, less exercise, artificial lighting. The pattern of early menstruation, however, seems relatively recent in origin, perhaps within the last 150 years. Before that, Western women—like women in most third world countries today—experienced first menstruation in their mid-teens. And even in our culture, many girls who exercise strenuously, such as professional athletes, begin menstruating much later and have irregular periods.

For Kumsa, the menstrual ceremony was a sad event, for it marked the end of his marriage. Once his bride left his compound, she never returned. After the two ceremonies, she stayed with her parents, refusing to live with him again.

Kumsa did not seem to know her reason. But it surely must have had something to do with age: he was about thirty-five years older than she. She was younger by ten years than his own youngest child. !Kung marriages are arranged, and while passion and mutual attraction are respected, parents make the best choices among those available. It is not typical for young girls to marry men as old as Kumsa, but it is also not unknown. Indeed, Kumsa's own daughter Kxaru, then in her mid-twenties, was married to Toma, a man her father's age, about twenty-five years her senior. And their marriage seemed to work.

Our conversation moved on. Kumsa had been considered a powerful healer when I was last there. I asked about his healing power. "I have very little left," he said quietly. "It wore out trying to heal Tasa." He described Tasa's sickness, how blood came from her chest. He never stopped trying to cure her, but her condition deteriorated. Some nights he didn't sleep for trying. Some days he did little but trance and heal, hoping to effect a cure. But in the end, "God refused to help me," and she died.

〟〟〟〟〟〟 We got up and walked on. Half an hour later, Kumsa pointed to some tracks in the sand. "Leopard," he said, without much concern. My nerves tingled for a moment. But with him—and his arrows—beside me, my shield of safety once again felt secure.

We soon reached the place where he had shot at the kudu. Kumsa searched among the dried grass and scattered bushes for his arrow, retracing his steps, his mind in instant replay, his hands signing an internal conversation about the aborted hunt. The scene, disappointing to him, seemed miraculous to me. I marveled at his intimate knowledge of the landscape, at the comprehensive internal map that had brought him back to this spot, as earlier it had returned him to me in the bush.

It took some time to find the arrow. I looked too, hoping I would be able to point to it hidden in the grass, and say, in a voice understated and deferential, "Is this what you were looking for?" I still cherished my nickname from years before, "Marjorie-Things-See," given after I had spotted an animal in the bush before a hunter did.

But the task seemed impossible. The bottom half of the arrow, made from a reed the color of grass, dried leaves, vines, even sand—practically the entire visible universe surrounding us—blended in more subtly than the proverbial needle in the haystack. The arrow point, although made of metal, would be buried deep inside whatever it had struck, much as it might have buried itself in an animal's thick hide.

Kumsa finally found the arrow, and we were off again, but no longer as hunters. Our path took us to thickets where succulent *sha* roots grew. I watched Kumsa delve in the pliant earth with a digging stick fashioned from a nearby plant, following the thread of life to the water root below. He first pushed aside the earth with his stick, then extracted loosened sand with his hands until the bulb appeared.

The bulb exposed, Kumsa continued to dig, following attached threads farther into the earth, tell-tale signs of secondary roots nearby. Extending his entire arm into the hole, he pulled the prize from the ground: an oblong root, the size of a sweet potato, with three smaller bulbs attached. My mouth watered as he gently tapped them clean, then broke off the larger bulb for me. It had been years since that clear, sweet taste had been mine. I savored its earthy aroma and the sudden burst of wetness as my teeth pulled open its outer skin.

I asked for a digging stick of my own, and together we dug for more roots. He taught me to identify the curve of the *sha* vine from among others, to leave a wide berth around the stem so as not to puncture the bulb, and how to follow the paths to the secondary bulbs. He showed me that some vines had no bulbs at all: holes in the sand indicated that honey badgers or other animals had already found them.

He worked quickly and economically, harvesting one area thoroughly before moving on to the next. In less than an hour he collected several pounds of roots. My efforts, in comparison, seemed dismal: the few roots I had unearthed had gashes in the white flesh, or in the vine, where my digging stick had penetrated, leaving grit that, no matter how carefully cleaned, would invariably reassert its presence between one's teeth when the root was eaten. Kumsa handed me his pile of roots and off we went, this time to check on some mongongo nut trees. The season had been poor, however, and few nuts could be found.

Occasionally he stopped at a tree to examine holes in its base or between its limbs. I thought he was seeking honey, but at one tree he knelt down and filled his hands with water. I polished off the little water left in the canteen and refilled it with the brown-tinged water from the tree.

On we walked, now toward camp, I carrying *sha* roots, other roots Kumsa had dug, some berries, some *dcha* fruits, and a graceful kudu horn I had picked up along the way (for one of my doctors, who had asked for a horn to make a lamp), in addition to my cameras, film, notebook, canteen, and food. It seemed appropriate, even intimate, when Kumsa handed the gatherings to me, the woman, the one who typically carries food. Traversing the wilderness, hunting part of the day, gathering the rest, we were comfortable. I, like the good !Kung wife carrying the load; we, like a married couple testing the vagaries of nature together, earning our livelihood.

We stopped once more to rest in the shade, finishing the food and water. He asked no questions, but answered mine carefully, repeating himself slowly when I didn't understand. This time I asked whether men ever hit their wives, and what he thought of it.

Yes, he said, a man has the right to hit his wife when she doesn't listen to him or if she is lazy. That is the custom. And yes, he had even hit Tasa.

Sadness crossed his face as he elaborated. "When we were first married, I hit her a few times. Then once, while she was still young, I took a strap and hit her so hard that it broke the skin on her thigh." His voice was quiet as he continued. "Afterward, I saw what I had done: I saw the hole I had made on her leg, the ugly spot. I knew I never wanted to do that again. And I never did. Although I was tempted, I never hit her again."

Young men were violent, he said. His voice gained force as he explained that young men's violence—especially after drinking—was the reason he had agreed to the marriage of his daughter Kxaru and Toma, who was almost an old man.

Years before, Tasa, while telling me about a fight with Kumsa, had said that a man's heart and a woman's heart were different: "A man's heart is important. A woman's heart is not, because she is without strength to fight back. If he throws her down, she can't do anything, because men are so strong. That's the way God made us." She went on, "A woman's heart in anger is just like that of a man, but she is without strength. Therefore, her anger is meaningless. Because I still haven't seen a woman with strength like a man, who can fight him off with equal power."

The sun, an hour from darkness, left long shadows on the land as we continued our walk back to camp. Trees, grass, and bushes rustled, whispering beyond human hearing of other worlds. The wind traversed the golden grass, mysterious and unknown. In the shadows seemed answers.

Back in camp, our lack of news spread quickly, as did that of others: none of the hunters had met with success. Two men, however, had seen a termite mound with a tunnel bored into it and fresh porcupine tracks around its opening. They planned to return to it the next day to search for the porcupine, hoping this would prove more successful at alleviating everyone's meat hunger than another day of traditional tracking.

The women, meanwhile, had had a stellar day. The kama ko berries continued to be plentiful, as attested by the large bags, once filled with food-relief meal, now bursting at the seams with small round berries the size of peas. Each bag would command a handsome price in the marketplace—perhaps even equal to a month's wages. Kama ko were highly valued by neighboring peoples for beer making.

The sun sank below the horizon and night descended quickly. Food was cooked. Tea was made. After six and a half hours of walking, my body was limp and my blistered feet ached. But, except that I craved fresh, lean game meat, it had been a wonderful day.

"The place feels so healing," I wrote in my journal that evening. "Even if it doesn't actually heal me, these are very happy days. The vast wildness around, opened for me by a Zhun/twa, is one of the joys of my life. The peace here, for me, is broad and deep."

In the firelit darkness, people conversed quietly. Sitting on my blankets within the circle of bodies, I watched three-year-old Dem, amazed by the smallness of his presence nestled in the protection of his mother's body. I longed to shelter my own children, especially the youngest, who I feared was most vulnerable to my absence. Even at this great distance, my children's presence didn't feel small. They seemed to occupy more space than any adult in my life, including myself. The demands from them, or from myself in relation to them, quieted only when they slept. No wonder I so often felt overwhelmed.

With great interest, I watched Little Dem. His eyes bright, his spirit seeming engaged, he spoke little. He didn't ask for things, nor did he expect anyone to amuse him. No one asked him questions or cajoled for answers. He ate when given food, nursed when he wished, and sat quietly the rest of the time, bathed by the voices of his mother, grandfather, and uncle, all nearby. (In his village at home, besides other adults, there also lived a cousin slightly younger than he.) The adults' conversation proceeded without interruption from him, his mother a full participant.

What a contrast to the culture I came from, where frequent verbal exchanges between children and adults were the rule, where continual teaching and prodding were signs of good parenting. Young, inquisitive minds needed infinite input, I had come to believe. How else would the children rise in the competitive world of their peers? How else would they to learn to trust their own capacities?

From this vantage point, then, Little Dem—sitting quietly without much verbal interchange initiated either by him or by the adults—was doomed to a life as an underachiever, a passive recipient of whatever came his way. Yet the competent, articulate, individualistic group of adults around the fire—as well as those back at the village—belied such facile generalizations, as did the above-average ability demonstrated by most !Kung children who attended school. Perhaps Little Dem sat so quietly because he was tired, or because he was the only child in a group of adults, or because darkness hugged closely outside the fire's glow. Whatever the reason, it was clear that I had much to learn. My longing for my family stayed with me into the night: for touch and for smell, but not for sound.

After visiting with those at the second fire, I shook my blankets to dislodge any snakes or bugs that might have sought refuge, crawled in fully dressed, and settled for sleep. I woke a few times during the night, drank in the sky, listened for leopards, and worried only slightly before falling asleep again, having decided to leave my fate in the hands of the people around me.

Lions in the Night

On our second morning in the bush, Baitsenke and some of the other men took the truck and went off to find water for our nearly depleted jerry cans. Their first stop would be a nearby water pan named Gautcha; if that was empty, they would drive on to the well at Dobe. The porcupine hunt would take place after they returned, since the man who had found the termite mound was in the truck.

I used the time to join the women, welcoming the break from hunting—especially unsuccessful hunting. I fell in line behind Nisa as she left camp with the others. We crossed a sandy meadow with tall grasses and low bushes and continued southward to the wooded areas where the coveted kama ko berries grew. Our path would not stray far from the border, for the truck was to pick me up on its return so I could go on the porcupine hunt.

The six women fanned out among the bushes, which were heavy with berries as if they had been fed by an exquisitely calibrated fertilizer. Stripping the tips of the branches where the fruit grew, the women worked with efficiency and skill; the dark orange pellets swelled in tin cups and buckets, or in cloths which were periodically emptied into larger carrying sacks.

I collected berries, too, although I was more interested in watching, photographing, and asking questions than in filling my sack. But what I picked I ate with gusto, both the kama ko and another sweet berry, *tori*, that grew in clusters. Throwing handfuls into my mouth, I broke the skins with my teeth, savoring the intense sweet flavor on my tongue. After working the pulp loose, I swallowed the tasty, fibrous strands, spat out most of the hard pits, and started again; the other women swallowed all the pits.

Suddenly the women were shouting: "Lion tracks!" "Hwantla," they called to me, "Hwantla, come and look!" There in the sand were tracks that looked something like a dog's, but magnified tenfold. "Two of them," a woman said. "They were here in the night." Then, following

99

the tracks a short distance, she gestured with her hands: "They passed that way."

The tracks were already hours old, I was told. The women moved on to nearby kama ko bushes, collecting as industriously as before. In the daylight, surrounded by others, my fear of carnivores remained distant. I followed the women's lead.

After about two hours, with the pace slow, the heat rising, and fatigue surrounding my eyes, I chose a spot ahead of the moving group—although it wasn't perfectly clear which direction they would move—and sat down. The dappled shade, really more sun than shade, provided modest relief from the steady sun. I pulled off my hat and let the thirsty desert air circulate around my sweaty scalp.

The women moved from bush to bush, steady and sure, concentrating on their work. Their conversation was animated, their mood gay. The exception was Kxaru, who was locked in a battle of wills with her son, Little Dem. From Kxaru's point of view, the order of the day was clear. As the only female representative of her village, she needed to collect as many berries as possible. But maximum efficiency meant free hands and an unburdened carrying sack. It also meant that Dem, old enough to keep up at this slow pace, needed to stand beside her and eat berries from the lower branches, or sit nearby and play.

But Dem didn't want to stand, he didn't want to play by himself, and, although he occasionally collected and ate some berries, it was just a matter of time before he began to complain bitterly. He wanted his mother, and he wanted to be carried, now! Kxaru would carry him until his weight became too great. Then she would set him down.

Under normal conditions, another relative would have given Kxaru a break, or other children would have distracted Dem. But in our bush camp there were no other children, and Kxaru had no relatives among the women who were gathering. Indeed, any of those five women might have lent more than a cursory hand to help Kxaru, but each was also working hard for her village, trying to harvest as much as she could. This didn't mean the atmosphere was competitive, or that no sharing or exchange took place: even I was a recipient of the many cups of berries that made their way from one to another, signs of friendship and goodwill. But serious work was being done.

Kxaru was not accomplishing as much as she would have wished. One moment Dem was hanging from her back; the next, around her waist. Then he was pulling at her skirts, winding himself around her legs, whining all the while. "Mommy, pick me up. *Mooom-my, pick me up!*"

Kxaru, adept at stalling, would answer his initial cries with a soothing "Mmm." When this no longer worked, she would put berries in his hand, saying how sweet they were. She would direct him to a particularly full patch, or set him down with a cup and a stick for a drum. Each maneuver worked for a while, enabling her to collect a bit more before the inevitable took place. Eventually, she would meet Dem's demands and tears sharply: "What is the matter with you? Do you think I can carry you forever, you crazy child?" But as she spoke she would pick him up and return him to the sling. He would be instantly happy and blissfully quiet; she, resigned—at least for a while—to his weight. The scene was so familiar. Was it only the night before that Dem had seemed so different from my own children?

By now, most of the women had long since passed the spot where I sat. Their voices were faint in the distance. I picked up my bags (and my berries) and moved closer to them, settling down once again in their midst, this time in the shade between two bushes. Although I expected to continue watching and listening, I found my senses dulled.

I hated to admit it, but the morning's activities had begun to feel commonplace, almost boring. Compared to gathering expeditions of the past, this kama ko enterprise lacked excitement. I yearned for the days when women gathered a wide variety of plants; when a large number of the 105 kinds of edible nuts, roots, fruits, vegetables, and legumes would come back in a woman's carrying pouch; when the women scoured the landscape in its open places and wooded ones, in its groves and its flats.

But efficiency was the mode of the day, and there was no doubt that capitalizing on this harvest was time-efficient. I lay down, surrounded by tall bushes laden with berries, the undisputed matriarchs of the area: no nut trees grew in this terrain. The wind rustled the leaves gently. A bird sang a song of rapidly falling notes, perhaps five or six, then repeated them, or varied them, or stopped after the first three. Other birds chattered, not working so hard.

I lay still, the sounds of nature and of conversation providing a soothing basso continuo to my inward journey. I breathed deeply of the clear air. Above, wisps of clouds touched the vibrant blue dome, suggesting forms familiar, then unknown. The child in me that had been able to turn scary cloud monsters into benign friends by changing my perspective joined me, reminding me that I could affect the universe, at least my part of it. I sank into the ground, trying to remember what life had been like before sickness, before children, before husband, and before I used words like "time-efficient."

"I feel so peaceful," I wrote when I finally sat up. "It's almost as if every breath I take is healing me—if not my body, then my soul." Yet the comfort itself raised questions for which I had few answers. Why had I really come here? Was it to do Anthropology? Or Photography? Was it for Nisa? Why did I feel so much love for this physical world and feel that the traditional ways of the people were so much a part of me? What was I to learn this time?

❮❮❮❮❮❮ I looked over at Nisa, at age sixty-eight going as strong and steadily as the younger women, and felt affection for her, the first since the first day of my visit. Since that day she had seemed insufferable, with endless demands and fervent reproaches, as though she didn't realize that she and I had a unique dialogue of our own.

Not that my perceiving Nisa as insufferable was new to our relationship. Twenty years before, as now, she had sat around my camp talking incessantly, commenting, asking for things, questioning me. To be sure, others with the same agenda had sat beside her. But Nisa's presence had seemed harder to ignore. Her voice had demanded attention even when her words hadn't been expressing demands.

Back then, after days of hearing an endless litany of my faults, I finally took charge. To be more exact, I took charge of her voice. Instead of trying to close my ears to her colorful and constant verbiage, I actually asked for it. But I asked for things I wanted to hear. I asked about herbal medicines that affected reproduction and about sexual play in children. I asked about adult sexuality and about early relationships within the family. I also asked, and heard in riveting detail, about Nisa's own life.

Then it was as though The White Woman Had Finally Seen the Light. Filled with pride in her newfound role, Nisa excelled. She spoke far more openly and clearly of her own life, and of the lives of others, than anyone else had—or would.

Now that I had returned, how could she understand the strength of my commitment to her, or appreciate the years I had spent translating and honing the nuances of her tape-recorded words into English prose? Perhaps she felt she was just one voice among the many competing for my favor. Of course, she couldn't deny the cows and the branding iron she had bought with money from me. But that was the past. New ground might need to be won.

With my tongue still struggling to make the sounds commanded it by my brain, I had told her, as best as I could, that she was a major reason for my return. If she was willing, I had said, I would love to work with her again. That might have reassured her, as had my insistence that she come along on the bush trip.

Even so, those first few days at Dobe had been difficult, and Nisa and I had had a hard time connecting. Confusion surrounded my arrival and the setting up of my camp. Our leaving for the bush two days after I arrived stirred things up even more. In addition, I had allotted time—and gifts—to shoring up old alliances and establishing new ones.

Here in the bush it was different. We could live beside each other without the artifice of my visiting her compound or she mine. She wasn't "waiting" for me, and I wasn't "visiting" her, self-consciously taking photographs, self-consciously asking questions. Here, as we woke together, ate together, and, now, gathered berries together, a new trust had formed. I, for my part, relied on her more with each passing day. And she, for hers, allowed a gentler conversation to rise between us.

A deep droning, resonating like a bow drawn faintly across the thickest string of a bass fiddle, signaled the truck's approach. When Baitsenke finally stopped to pick me up, I had been waiting at the border for a long time.

This would be my second porcupine hunt. Years before, I recalled, the men had spent hours digging and moving the compact earth of a termite mound, smoking out entrances and blocking exits—and sitting around and waiting. There had been a few minutes of high drama as the porcupine dashed from its underground home toward the presumed safety of the bush. In the fast-paced chase, it had been unable to elude the barrage of sharp spears and poisoned arrows the men hurled at it. It had quickly become that day's dinner.

On this hunt, all five !Kung men in camp had joined. We walked swiftly across the land, the sun beating down and uncomfortably hot. There was little discussion of fresh tracks, and even less inclination to follow them. The men talked freely, the noisy procession startling animals that might otherwise have been camouflaged—or tracked—in the surrounding bush.

I looked at my watch: half an hour had gone by. When I looked again, another half hour had passed. The next time I looked, it had only been five minutes. How had I managed three hours of nonstop walking the day before?

Termite mounds were often visually striking in the bush, but their true splendor was best seen near villages, where there was little or no grass to obscure their presence. Rising above the ground, these gray cityscapes (from a termite's point of view, virtual skyscrapers) spoke of complex adaptation and biological resilience. In the burning desert sun, tunnels winding within provided natural air conditioning, cooling the termites' nests and allowing their survival. Springhares, porcupines, and other burrowing animals—as well as snakes and even bats—were quick to become guests, making nests of their own in the cool, protected earth.

The men said this burrow had first been dug by a springhare but was now occupied by a porcupine. At the entrance to one of the four main tunnels the porcupine's tracks could be seen, beside a circle of wetness in the sand where the animal, in hasty retreat, had evacuated its bladder.

The next three hours proved a study in patience, in perseverance, and in the intensity of the desire for meat. With flashlight or matches in hand, the men repeatedly explored the tunnels. Toma, Kumsa's son-in-law, went in first, inching his way into the snug, dark hole. With only his feet visible, I worried about his breathing—how much oxygen could be in there?—and about his age. When he finally resurfaced, his skin and hair were powdered the color of ash. The news was not heartening: he had no sense of where the porcupine might be.

It took courage to enter that space, with walls so close, seeking a frightened, cornered animal that might strike at any time. But this was the men's way of earning a living—if they were lucky. Kumsa went next. He worked the tunnel hard, pulling out earth, pushing himself farther in. I admired his courage, his stamina, his determination, and his ability to be effective in a frightening situation, a challenge that I myself had only recently begun to explore.

The men took turns in the most promising tunnel and then in the others. Kumsa jumped out soon after he entered one of the tunnels near the top of the mound, closely followed by a flurry of surprised bats. Finally, the porcupine was located, deep in one of the lowest tunnels.

Next the men dug down from the top, hoping to strike the roof of the tunnel in which the animal was hiding. Other hunters must have been there before: in the midst of the mound was a round hole about eight feet deep. But the shaft had been abandoned before it had reached a tunnel.

After further efforts, the hard earth finally won—along with the porcupine. When yet another hole led nowhere, the men gave up. After they had worked for three hours, we turned back toward camp.

Another unsuccessful hunt! I wondered what had gone wrong. Five men working for three days represented a great outpouring of energy. Yet the animal protein netted was zero. A study of !Kung hunting had shown that the !Kung were successful, on average, once in every four days they hunted. The animal might be small: a snake, a tortoise, a hare. Or it might be slightly larger: a steenbok, a duiker. Or larger still: a springhare, a porcupine, a warthog. Or even a full-sized antelope.

But this time, nothing had come in at all. Were there fewer animals in the bush these days? Were the men less hungry? Were they out of practice? Or had it just been bad luck? Whatever the answers, younger men would surely not be lining up for lessons in the art of the classic hunt. And this was all the more disheartening because there were no young men in the village who were already skilled hunters.

Meanwhile, the women were doing well. Each day ended with bags of berries and pounds of roots.

On one hunt, twenty years before, the quarry had been a giraffe—and the methods had not been exactly traditional. We were driving south along the border road, headed for a Bushman camp half a day's ride away. The landscape was parched, the ground was dry, the air shimmered with heat. The motor droned on, straining through sandy stretches, quieter on hard rocky ones. The posts of the border fence glided past.

Suddenly there was an urgent thumping on the top of the cab. We slowed, then stopped. "Giraffe . . . giraffe . . ." the men in the back of the truck whispered. They pointed toward the scrub bush to our left. A few hundred yards from the road, the animal stood looking at us. The men thumped again, and the truck moved forward slowly.

Had the giraffe headed deeper into the bush, it would have been safe.

But, in its panic, it moved where it could run fastest: the road in front of us. Great excitement filled the back of the truck as the men readied their bows and arrows. The truck gave chase to the giraffe, its long spindly legs and huge haunches carrying its heavy body forward as fast as it could go.

"Stop! This isn't fair!" I cried. "Besides, it's illegal to kill a giraffe!" But meat hunger was very strong, and everyone was impassioned. So, eventually, was I. "This is not trophy hunting," I reminded myself. "This is food."

Not far ahead was the camp we were to visit. A deep rumbling had long preceded our arrival, and people were out in force. What they saw was a giraffe running past their camp, followed closely by a truck filled with eager hunters.

It didn't take long for the poisoned arrows, lodged in the animal's rump, to have an effect. The giraffe soon slowed to a walk, then turned from the road into the bush, the only safety it had known. The engine was shut down to a shocked silence, and every eye watched the dying animal. It was as if the world itself held still for the last moments of that huge life. The giraffe's great neck began to sway as it resisted collapse. When it fell, the end was swift. It lay there, immobile, no longer dangerous to the hunters standing nearby with spears. Then it was dead.

I exulted almost as the !Kung did. This meat, cut into strips and dried, would last weeks or even months. Nothing would be left uneaten or unused. Bones would be roasted and cracked for marrow; the skin, too thick for tanning, would be dried and saved to be eaten later; even the hooves would be cracked for their savory parts.

This chase and a number of others were part of my early education. Many months later, when I saw the most beautiful of bush animals— the large kudu, with delicate white body stripes, a regal head, large eyes, and massive spiral horns—I started to salivate.

Returning to camp at nightfall after the porcupine hunt, I was exhausted. I had walked nearly four hours that day, following about ten hours the previous two days. My feet hurt. My body ached. And my sensibilities were overloaded. I was thrilled to be in that world—but the thrill was tempered. Perhaps a juicy, flavorful chunk of fresh game meat would have helped.

Perhaps. But I was also uneasy—and I was not the only one.

Throughout the day, lions had dominated most conversations: the tracks found by the women had made us all uncomfortable, evidence that the predators had passed so close to our vulnerable selves, deep in sleep, in the night. In the fast-paced conversations that swirled around my ears, the distinctive sound *n'!hei,* lion, seemed to be on everyone's lips.

Uneasiness was also evident in the fires blazing in camp. Whipped by a steady wind, they were bigger and brighter than those of the previous nights. Logs, heavy limbs, and dead trees were piled nearby, ready reinforcements. And a third fire had been lit, the biggest by far.

Yet in other ways things seemed normal. Dinner was cooked, roots were roasted and passed around, tea was drunk, and blankets were set out for sleeping. By eight o'clock it had been dark for nearly two hours. At the end of the third day of strenuous activity, my body was ready for sleep.

While others talked, I covered myself with blankets and closed my eyes, the wind testing the folds of my sleeping bag. Then my eyes popped open. I looked around, assessing my sleeping spot in relation to the rest of the group. Had I really thought the truck and tent would offer protection? Here, at the outer edge of the group, at the end of a line of women, it seemed to me I was the most vulnerable of all.

In fact, I thought, the truck and tent were perfect screens, obscuring the shape of danger advancing in the darkness. I sensed stealthy steps in the bush beyond. Our scents were a beacon, a stream of primal knowledge carried in the air, leading the predator to its violent livelihood; beckoning it, as the tantalizing aroma of cooking meat would beckon us.

Kxoma's father had been killed by a lion when Kxoma was a young boy. He had been pulled from his hut in the middle of the night and dragged away. Kxoma's wife told all she knew, her voice weaving its distinct pattern within the tapestry of other voices also telling lion stories.

I myself had heard a lion story only two days before, when the truck had stopped at a Herero village. "Why haven't you visited me before this?" the village matriarch scolded me. She had treated anthropologists well over the years, to the benefit of all. "And what did you bring me?"

"Here, take a look," I said, pulling a package with cloth and beads from my bag.

"Mmm . . .," she said, pleased with the gifts, which she quickly put away. Then her face filled with pain. "Did you hear about my son? He was killed by a lion."

Her first-born son had killed about thirty lions in his life, and even an elephant that had been ruining the village well. He and three other men had gone off with their dogs to hunt a lion. They had one rifle between them. The dogs tracked the lion, but instead of fighting the dogs, the lion turned on the men.

Her son, who had the gun, shot but missed. The lion lunged and began to maul him. He managed to shoot again, but again missed. The lion stepped back, snarling and growling. "I am already dead," the son cried. "One of you get this gun and kill the lion that has killed me." Another man grabbed the gun and fired. But he too missed, and a bite to the neck killed him instantly. The other men hid. The lion stalked around for a while, then left. The wounded son and the dead man were put on donkeys and taken to the nearest village. The young man died that night.*

We sat, an island of human presence, our borders defined by the light of the fires. Beyond were the wild places I knew—with roots and berries, with gentle animals and ferocious ones, with termite mounds and hidden tunnels—and the wild places beyond my experience.

Restless in my bedding, I felt as far from the core of the group as if at the farthest tip of a peninsula. I was sure that, if a lion did come, it would take me first. Does a lion go for the leg, gripping it tight in its jaw, hauling the rest of the body, struggling and screaming, into the night? Or does it go straight for the neck—as it had with Kxoma's father—breaking it within seconds with a snap of its head, then pulling the limp, cooling flesh through the grass to its bushmates, eager for fresh meat?

Would my journal be all that survived me?

What was that? The wind? Or something moving quietly like the wind? I got up and moved my bedding to a spot between the two circles of people. Here, with both men and women nearby, I felt more insu-

* Thanks to Henry Harpending for the details of this story.

lated. If I was dragged off, at least others would know about it; they might even be able to help.

Then a thought occurred to me, repellent and yet irresistible: I could sleep in the truck. If lions were stalking in the night, the cab was safer than the ground. I could take myself away from danger while the others remained in it.

That action might actually have been reasonable, even sensible, given my outsider status. I could easily have rationalized it: the others had knowledge of the bush that I didn't; they were more able to handle this kind of fear than I was; they had experience with lions. And if they thought it was too dangerous to sleep here, they just had to say the word: we could drive back to Dobe immediately.

But the thought was also renegade. It flew in the face of one of anthropology's most sacred tenets, participant observation. To fully appreciate what one observes, one must participate in it, one must "do as the natives do." It also flew in the face of my personal determination to explore the !Kung world to its fullest—not for anthropology, but for myself. So how could I remove myself when things got tough? No, I told myself firmly, I couldn't, and I wouldn't.

Of course Baitsenke could, and he did. He had no stake in doing anything the way the !Kung did. Indeed, he had little interest in learning about, and even less concern about showing his ignorance of, the !Kung people and their way of life. Soon after dinner, Baitsenke had checked the supports to his tent, secured the ropes, and zipped himself inside, his blue nylon tent standing out from the land like a space-age cocoon.

Baitsenke had heard about the lion tracks from me and from the !Kung: most of the people spoke Setswana, his first language. And he had heard many stories about lions over the years. Encounters with dangerous animals in the bush, especially encounters fatal to humans, were often reported in the newspapers or on the radio, and additional details always spread by word of mouth. Most of the stories were believed, and they invariably held some truth, truth that fed the hearers' wariness of the bush.

Baitsenke himself—a for-hire driver who shuttled tourists around—was a prime source. "I heard that lions ripped through a tent in the campgrounds at Moremi National Game Park and dragged a tourist out," he told me once, emphasizing the "tourist" (as opposed to "citizen"). And: "A lion once attacked someone sitting in the cab of his truck. The lion crashed right through the front windshield and got him."

But, for now, Baitsenke could rest comfortably within his nylon walls. The rest of us, out in the open, were the likely targets, not he.

I didn't have walls, but for a while I felt I had right on my side, and that gave me comfort. I lay in my blankets, listening to the wind. "I can always go into the truck later," I thought, as the treetops swayed above me.

I had tested the idea earlier, fearing the others would laugh at me. "Maybe I should sleep in the truck," I had said, so lightly that no one took it seriously enough to laugh. It was a seemingly offhand remark, spoken to no one in particular yet loud enough for others to hear: that is the way the !Kung themselves do it.

For example, someone annoyed at an in-law is not supposed to complain directly. The "respect" relationship among such relatives precludes a confrontation. However, grass walls do little to obstruct sound, and talking aloud to oneself in the privacy of one's hut is unlikely to be considered impolite. Especially if it's done right. "Others are so stingy," a woman may say, carefully avoiding names. "I work hard and share as best I can, but I get nothing in exchange."

Even if the person intended to hear this does not, the message will travel. And the woman, having made her grievance known, is likely to receive support. Even in minor disputes, others usually line up on each side, with all views having their champions and detractors. A truce ultimately will be worked out—often without the original participants ever becoming directly involved. And it is all accomplished within the bounds of acceptable behavior.

So, even though I spoke to no one, everyone heard. And I too, received support, one of the most gratifying experiences of living with the !Kung. (So central a concept is this that a term exists, *wi,* specifically to describe it.) "Maybe you should sleep in the truck," some of the women had responded, doing *wi* to me.

But Kxoma's wife disagreed. She heard my fear loud and clear and was not about to support it. "No," she said, grabbing my mat and blankets and, with a gesture both firm and determined, setting them down where I had slept before. "We women should sleep together."

Now, hours later, the talk went on—unusual for that time of night. Fear moved from group to group like wind in the treetops. "This is their world," I thought as I nestled deeper into my sleeping bag. "They know best how to handle this." Surely, I told myself, they had a plan. Perhaps they would keep vigil all night, taking turns staying awake, stoking the fires. They were not talking of retreat, so neither would I. My imagination quieted. Their words filled our clearing, strong like protective armor, soothing like a lullaby. I slept.

Hours later I woke to the sound of one voice: only Toma was still sitting, still talking. The others lay on the ground, covered by blankets and by soft firelight. The wind raised a cloth here, blew the edges of a blanket there; and people turned toward the heat of the fires. A man rose and added wood to one of them, his spear conspicuously in hand. Skittery shadows expanded their play, poking beyond the dappled trunks that framed our world.

Eventually even Toma lay down, still talking in low tones. His story—almost a recitation—was about lions. Gau, a younger hunter lying nearby, grunted "Mmm" or "Eh" every few phrases, either from respect or from genuine interest. Then the spaces between Gau's responses lengthened until only his steady breathing was heard. Toma continued, either not noticing or not caring that he was now talking to himself. Then his voice also halted. A word, then another, and he too slept, leaving his story unfinished.

Moments later he was awake again, startled by rustling leaves. "Was that the wind?" he mumbled. "Mmm," Gau answered without rising. Their breathing resumed deep and slow, a gentle duet.

But I was wide awake. I looked at the stars, distant and neutral, incapable of intervening even with a wish, and then returned to my search of the moving shadows and the inscrutable darkness beyond. My heart started to race. Where were the three blazing fires? Where were those who were to keep watch?

I sat up, singular above the sleeping forms. Alone. The wind stopped in a low bush, rustling the leaves, then raced on. What was out there, beyond the wind?

Smoke from the fire blew in my direction, then excited flames burst forth. Jagged shadows poked at the trees. My eyes would not close. My mind would not quiet. Should I keep vigil? The camp was quiet except for the medley of breath and the tentative sounds from the fires, once again burning low. This time no one rose to replenish them. Beneath a lacy cover of gray ash, their glow was fading.

The shadows were soft. The wind blew. The stars were uncaring. I shook the wind from my ears, trying to listen. If danger was coming, I wanted to hear its approach. Dying instantly, being plucked from sleep to death without awakening, seemed a travesty of all I had been through. At the very least I wanted to be able to exult, "It wasn't cancer. It was a lion!"

A coughing sound, a shuffling of cloth. Then Nisa was awake, shaking violently, raking the sand for her pipe like the addict she was; smoking was considered an antidote to congestion. The wind blew out her matches mercilessly. Finally, leaning over, she isolated a small, glowing coal from the fire. Carefully manipulating it into the pipe, she inhaled deeply, holding the smoke, savoring its effect. Eventually her coughing subsided.

I was pleased to have company. Especially hers. "Eh," I began as she pushed a stick into the end of the pipe, keeping it lit, keeping its flavor strong. I paused to be sure I had her attention. "Why . . ." I started again, signaling that there was something on my mind. Then I asked rhetorically, a form that in !Kung is both familiar and polite, "Why is it that sleep refuses me tonight?"

"Eh," Nisa responded immediately. "Mother . . ." She pulled in smoke, held it deep, then spat in the sand and covered the wet spot with a precise, practiced motion.

I spoke again, the preliminaries over: "I don't know why my eyelids refuse to stay closed. Sleep and I are just not agreeing."

"Eh," she said, showing that she was listening. I waited, but she didn't say anything more. She set down the pipe and lowered her body toward the ground, then buried the pipe's tip in the sand.

It seemed she would soon return to sleep. Then I would be alone again, negotiating this endless night. I summoned my courage, attempting to sound unconcerned: "Maybe I should sleep in the truck . . ."

"Eh," she answered in the same tone of voice, respectful but not fully engaged, her body rehearsing sleep. "Maybe you should." I sat there unable to move, unable to admit how much I wanted the safety of the truck, how frightened I was. Then I started again: "Sleep . . ."

Before I could finish what would have been my next mournful whine, she interrupted. "So, go and sleep in the truck!" she said emphatically.

"Okay," I answered, as though responding to a command. "That's just what I'll do."

◆◆◆◆◆ I picked up my bedding and carried it to the truck. There was little length (my legs alternately dangled diagonally from the seat to the floor and were pushed against my chest), and there was even less width (the steering wheel was large and intrusive). But no sooner had I arranged my blankets, lain down and, ever so quietly, closed the door, than a sublime feeling of safety came over me. Only one week earlier, safety had seemed a concept beyond me. Death had almost seemed welcome compared to the panic that gripped my life. Yet here, now, I felt safe.

But what would the !Kung think of me? I opened the windows of the cab—very slightly—and with the air rushed in a multitude of voices: voices only I could hear. They crowded into the little space, pushing, laughing, joking. "You should have seen her scamper into that truck," one voice exclaimed. "She headed for that door like an ostrich rushing to the road to escape a truck!"

In my imagination, guffaws pierced the air. When frightened by an approaching truck, an ostrich will run away. But in which direction does it usually run? It usually runs along the cleared road. But what comes up right behind as it runs for its life? The truck. Is there enough intelligence in the tiny head that sways from side to side like a weathervane in rough wind—its huge eyes seeming to occupy more space than its brain—to swerve off the road and into the bush? No—because the ostrich can't run as fast in the bush.

"I must have looked ridiculous," I thought. The voices pushed on. "She was so scared that she slept in the truck!" People would tell and retell the tale for years, reenacting it with exaggerated effect. I remembered the way they had mimicked an archaeologist after he left. "Whata ya doin?" they would yell, eyebrows raised, lips pursed, voices high, bodies straining to their greatest height. "Whata ya doin?" they would repeat, imitating his frequent outbursts (which usually took place after someone had dug too deep without first sifting the higher layers of earth).

But other voices came to my rescue. I had done the right thing, they said. What would my family, my children, feel if something happened to me? They were sacrificing a great deal by my being gone this month. But to be gone forever? When I could have moved to safety? They would never forgive me for having taken an unnecessary chance.

The hard surfaces enclosing me gave me comfort, a steel and glass womb. I lay listening to the wind. Then another thought tormented me. Everyone else was sleeping. Even Nisa had gone back to sleep without a problem. The danger had been only my imagination.

But when I looked out the window, people were not asleep after all. They were piling wood on all three fires. They were sitting, talking as if at midday. Their voices were loud, edgy. Activity was everywhere—as if the sun had neglected to rise today yet people were going about their usual daily tasks. This gave me a new worry. Had my moving into the truck precipitated this? Had I, ignorant in the ways of the bush, some-how given credence to their fear?

Slowly people returned to their blankets and to sleep. Then came a sound I will never forget. The voice of a woman. To call it eerie or pri-mal, a cry, a wail, doesn't begin to touch its power. It was a rhythmic moan, a cascade of pain. It was repetitive. It was trembling. It was breathy. It came from the unguarded depths.

Minutes went by. The sound continued, filling the night. No other human sound joined or stopped or soothed it; no other sound dared, so great was its urgency. Was it the sound of a bad dream? The sound of terror? Should I do something? Should I suggest that the woman—and the others—sleep in the back of the truck? Should we pack and leave?

When the sound finally subsided, it stayed in my ears. I eventually slept, grateful for my berth.

༺༺༺༺༺ I woke just before dawn, when the thick dark gave way to tentative grays. The fires were out. Everyone was asleep. The danger seemed past. Quietly, I moved my blankets from the truck to my sleep-ing place on the ground.

Light slowly poured into the sky, and people stirred: a blanket pulled tight, an arm outstretched, a body upright, making peace with the morning. "I slept in the truck," I ventured to no one in particular, yet loud enough to dispel any thought that returning to my blankets had been a ploy to hide the obvious.

"Eh," said Nisa, now awake and lighting her pipe. "You did."

I braced myself for the jokes. But there were none. Instead, the others seemed as relieved as I that the night was finally over. I turned to Kxau, an old friend. Surely he would tell the truth. "The lions never came," I said cautiously, then added, "But was I ever scared!"

"Me too," he said, showing great respect for the ordeal we had been through. "Everyone was!"

Emboldened, I responded with humor, giving him an opening to respond in kind. "I was shaking so hard I almost died from fright. I pleaded, but my eyes wouldn't close. I finally slept in the truck."

"That was very wise," Kxau said without a hint of derision. "We were all shaking. Didn't you hear Bau, my wife? She was trembling to death, crying out."

"Yes, I heard, but wasn't sure what was wrong. Was it a bad dream?"

"Uhn-uhn, it wasn't a dream. She cried out in fear. Of lions!"

Village Reflections

We could have prolonged our bush trip, but no one was willing to spend another night like the last one. As for me, after three days of walking and watching, of hunting and gathering, my need for the experience had been met, at least for the time being. I was also physically exhausted. My body ached—my back, my legs, my feet. My left hip was black and blue—from strenuous walking, dropping into mouse holes, brushing against thorns, and traversing the hard and soft sand.

Kumsa-the-Hunter and Toma left to go hunting. The other men had given up on hunting; they asked to be driven south along the border, toward Dobe, to a grove of mongongo nut trees. They hoped these trees would have been more productive than the ones near our camp: the amount, timing, and location of rainfall determined the harvest, which always varied. We would pick the men up later, on our way back to Dobe.

The women had collected enough kama ko berries for themselves (finally!), but wanted to collect for the men in camp who "hadn't brought their wives." There was no meat, and few mongongo nuts, but at least the men would have kama ko to take back to their villages. I followed the women through the tall grass, as I had the day before, although my step was more considered now and my spirit more worn. I photographed, ate kama ko and tori, and collected berries—despite my gross inefficiency at picking them—to give as presents.

Time passed slowly. After about an hour and a half, I sat down, surrounded by old lion tracks; the lions had never made their way back to us. The air was peaceful. Birds, flies, and crickets lent depth to the cheerful interchanges of women working, like a chamber orchestra behind a group of soloists. But my inner world was anything but harmonious. Anxiety—my all too faithful companion—had risen again, defiant and inescapable. My aching body refused to quiet; it called up my deepest fears; it reminded me about living on the edge. And why wasn't that pain in my elbow getting better?

I was tired, and my defenses were down. Sitting in the sand, surrounded by the pace of a different millennium, my personal concerns reasserted themselves. My pain felt heavy again. The thought of returning to Dobe—to village life; to cattle, goats, and scrawny dogs; to agriculture and overgrazing; to the droning of trucks and the fearful might of armed soldiers; and to inequity and material aspirations—was hard. The bush was freedom: visually pure, with vast amounts of space for the body, mind, and spirit. The bush was as far as I ever traveled, or wanted to, even in my imagination. Nowhere else did I find a comparable haven for my spirit when hurt, when seeking solace, when needing solitude. And although lions, leopards, chimerical porcupines, blisters, and physical exhaustion came with the territory, they didn't lessen its appeal to a lover in love.

Returning to village life was the downswing of the pendulum. It was a move toward—not away from—the life I so fervently wanted to leave behind. My trip was not yet half over, but it seemed the best had passed. Perfect freedom, pure air, supportive voices crying out in the wilderness, life pared down to the essentials—how was I to return to my "old" life after this? How was I ever to return to my family?

〰〰〰 My family: as complex as a thought can get. What was my connection to them now? How could I be so content on my own, nine thousand miles away? Was this an artifact of the stress of cancer? Or was this the real me? The devoted mother seemed so distant and unreal. Was it all phony? Had it all been a big mistake?

I thought of my first child and remembered telling friends that having her, at age thirty-two, had added a quality of happiness to my life that I had never known before. I thought of the magic of her heartbeat heard through a stethoscope held against my belly; of my fervent dedication to giving birth without any medication, like a !Kung woman; of my first morning in labor, when a Canada goose with head high walked proudly ahead of a gaggle of babies at a quiet pond in the country—a magical omen of fecundity; and of the surprise, when she was born, that this baby had come from my insides.

I thought of my second child and remembered bursting into tears—in relief and excitement—when told that amniocentesis had indicated a healthy child. And, although I had planned to wait until the birth, when the technician asked, "Do you want to know the sex?" my heart pounded as I whispered, "Yes." Then more tears as I learned that my child was a boy. I thought of my son's speedy birth, of his gentle singing voice, and of his talking long before he knew words.

One girl. One boy. I could have stopped. Yet, five years later, I yearned again for life to grow within me. What else was so intense, so fulfilling, so passionate? At age forty-one, I too held my head high—the mother of another girl—proud of the brood I had borne. She was fifteen months old and still nursing when I received the diagnosis of cancer. Weaning her in one night, the night before my mastectomy, nearly broke my heart. What conversation could we ever invent that would match our practiced duet? And how could I give up the vision of myself, a Bushman woman, nursing her last child until the child herself chose to stop, perhaps at age five?

No—the children were not the problem. They filled spaces I had not known were empty. They pushed against all limits, transforming what had been—unbeknownst to me—an angular life into a rounded one, like an inflatable cube, infused with air, that eventually turns into a sphere. They sparked compassion and tenderness, giving out and taking in, protectiveness and nurturance, and laughter along with tears. No—there was nothing phony there.

Yet I did not want to go back. And the appeal of living solo the rest of my life frightened me. With heartbeats and singing and duets, with cubes and spheres, had also come responsibility, minute-to-minute demands, whining, fighting, and the constant tallying up and dividing of resources. The din had become so great that I no longer heard my own voice. Or had it just stopped speaking? Here, at last, I had heard it again, even if only as a whisper. And it sounded so good that I hated to think of ever losing it again—or of how much I might be willing to give up to keep it.

The women had long since moved off; only distant voices suggested their whereabouts. I would have followed them the rest of the day, but Kxaru, the mother of Little Dem, was returning to camp, worn out from struggling with her son while trying to collect berries. I went back to camp with her. There we found Toma, who had ended his hunt early, talking to Baitsenke.

The heat was oppressive, and I lay down in the shade of the truck, desperate for sleep. When I woke, Toma and Kxaru helped me fill in a census I had begun earlier, telling me who lived in which villages. I also asked them about plants I had been collecting for my study of vitamin E in the natural human diet. We talked of the plants' edible parts and how they were prepared for eating.

Hours later the women returned, their carrying cloths filled to capacity—an impressive haul for six and a half hours of gathering. The sun was lower in the sky when Kumsa-the-Hunter appeared, tired, dusty, and once again without meat. We packed up, loaded the truck with hundreds of pounds of berries, nuts, and roots, and drove off—leaving behind a camp filled with signs of our comings and goings, a treasure trove of clues for anyone who could decipher them: crushed grass trails, partially burned logs, a dampened fire, cleared ground, organic remains. Even the most average of !Kung would be able to reconstruct most of our activities: for them it was, literally, all written in the sand.

The sun followed us along the border road. Its rays, long and orange, highlighted the tips of tall grasses and gave depth to the bark of trees. Everyone seemed content. The women sang their pleasure in "the truck song," which I remembered well from earlier years. "We live in the nut groves, ooh ooh ah ya oh ah," they shouted, refrain upon refrain. I hummed along—it was a melody associated for me, too, with good times. I leaned out the window. The rushing air pulled at my hair. I drank deeply of the beauty of the end of the day.

The men, waiting for us by the side of the road, were greatly relieved when we arrived. It seemed they had had much excitement—too much. Instead of finding mongongo nuts, they had found lions; or rather, the lions had found them. Kxau—who had trembled in fear of lions the night before even as his wife had moaned out her terror—told his story.

After Baitsenke dropped them off that morning, the men had wandered in different directions—as men typically did when hunting but women seldom did when gathering. By mid-morning Kxau was alone. He heard it first, a throat sound that took his breath away. Then a huge male lion appeared in the grass, walking toward him. He flung his arms about and shouted. The lion stood still. Kxau again yelled out, with curses and insults, trying to look and sound bigger than he was. The lion didn't move. Then, after they stood face to face for a long time, it slowly backed off, retreating into the bush.

Kxau didn't have much time to enjoy his success. Soon there were two lions, sounding their fierce roars, circling just beyond the periphery of his space. Hours went by in this stalemate, Kxau never knowing whether or not the lions would lunge, whether or not he would live. The sound of the approaching truck frightened the lions away, finally releasing Kxau from his imprisonment.

He shook as he told his story. We shook too, standing in the open, listening. Then Kxau and the other men, who had not had such encounters, threw their bags into the truck and we were off.

I recalled my very first impression of Kxau, from my second day in Dobe twenty years before. That was the day he found his father's shoes in the bush, covered with blood. Kxau's concern was evident. He had reason to worry: a huge buffalo, which had been wounded a few days earlier, had just been killed nearby.

The African buffalo is much bigger and more muscular than the American buffalo or bison. It is black and has large, wide horns that curve upward to sharp points. These horns—resembling an absurd rendition of a 1960s hairdo, the "flip"—drape over a powerful body. The animal looks like the work of an eccentric artist, deliberately mismatching parts of various living forms, but the horns are a well-designed weapon protecting a noble beast.

The buffalo story began when a Herero cattle farmer borrowed a rifle and went hunting. Near a seasonal pool of water a few miles from a group of villages, he shot a buffalo. But he didn't kill it; the wounded animal ran off. The man went after it that day, and the next day, but it seemed, he said, "as though it had disappeared."

The lore of the bush, along with legend from the Big White Hunter tradition, has it that a wounded buffalo is one of the most dangerous of animals. Its size, its speed, and the breadth and sharpness of its massive horns are reasons enough. But the buffalo is also legendary for the shrewd and seemingly calculating way it seeks revenge. If wounded, it crouches low in tall grass, or hides in a thicket, waiting for its attacker—or any acceptable substitute—to return. Silent and unseen, the animal lies still, husbanding its remaining strength, until its pursuer comes into range. Then it is usually deadly.

So hot is its rage that wounded buffaloes have been known to attack villages or randomly kill people they happen upon. The !Kung fear the buffalo's ferocity, and rarely hunt it. They do not eat its heart, because the animal "has too much anger."

The Herero farmer tried several times to locate the buffalo. Once he actually sighted and fired at it. But, as before, the shot was not lethal and the animal ran away.

This news worried everyone. The !Kung San asked two of the anthropologists who had guns to help kill the buffalo. The plan: they would go to the water hole where the buffalo had probably stopped during the night, and the hunting party—the anthropologists and eight !Kung men—would track it from there.

Of course I wanted to go with them. Only my second day at Dobe, and the mysteries of the !Kung San world were already opening to me!

In the mid-morning heat of that August day, a preview of the approaching hot, dry season, we piled into the truck and drove to the well—a broad expanse of flat rock surrounded by low brush and thorn trees, its central depression filled with water. A stray cow drank at one end, but it was still too early for herders to have brought their herds for water.

As we walked the edges of this desolate moonscape searching for traces of the wounded buffalo, everyone seemed jittery. The men stopped at one set of tracks. Had they been made by the buffalo, or by a very large cow? After heated discussion, the men concluded that the buffalo had not been to this water hole in the night after all.

The Herero farmer joined us then, and suggested that he show us where he had shot the buffalo the day before. We drove north along the border road, then stopped to let the hunters out. The truck, carrying anthropologists, followed close behind them. The wounded animal's tracks were found, but they were a day old. They told where the buffalo had lain down, gotten up, and later lain down again. After half a mile, the hands of one man started talking: "Fresh spoor!" It was no more than an hour old, his hands told us. The buffalo was probably lying down in the thicket just ahead.

The men walked toward the thicket, bodies tense, senses alert, no longer talking. The drone of the truck and the cracking of bushes and thin trees plowed down in its path obliterated smaller sounds. On they walked. Then, for a split second, the wide black horns of the buffalo could be seen in the tall grass! The truck stopped, restoring sound to the scene, and the men scattered. The hunters climbed nearby trees; excited whispers came from the lower branches where they sat.

One of the anthropologists climbed from the truck into a tree for a clear shot. It rang out and the buffalo bolted. Again he took aim and fired. This time the animal limped away, concealing itself in the thick bush.

Some men on the ground, others in the trees, me standing atop the truck trying desperately to see and understand what was happening—and the decisive moment arrived. It seemed to proceed in slow motion, with every gesture amplified. The Herero man, now carrying the anthropologist's rifle, walked tentatively toward the thicket. He circled one way, then returned with three !Kung hunters, their arrows poised, and circled the other way. They disappeared into the thicket. There was an unsettling quiet. A shot cracked through the air, followed by more quiet, then an explosion of excited voices. The drama was over. The beast was dead.

As the men butchered the animal, they traced the shots that had struck it, discussing the damage each had caused, determining, as best they could, which had been the lethal one—critical in determining who would distribute the meat. They worked efficiently, stripping the hide, removing the legs, cutting the flesh into long strips. All parts of the animal except its horns, which were useless to them, would be distributed.

A terrible stench emanated from the stomach as it was opened, the site of the first bullet. Festering for days, the wound had filled with bubbling rottenness—the animal's defense against infection and disease. Repelled by the scene and with my head spinning, I lay down in the shade at a distance.

Suddenly there came an urgent shout from near the truck, its distress piercing the atmosphere of celebration. It was Kxau, and in his hands he held his father's blood-covered shoes. Lying nearby, as if thrown away, were the old man's pouch and beads. The sand told of his struggle with the buffalo.

We got into the truck, leaving the Herero farmer alone to continue the butchering, and rushed back to Dobe. If we didn't find Kxau's father there, we would return to his tracks. As we approached the village, people ran toward us, their voices excited. Yes, they told us, the old man had been attacked by the buffalo. But he had made it back to Dobe. An anthropologist had washed and treated his wounds. Considering what he had gone through, he was doing fine.

As we drove to Kxau's village, I thought of my visit with the old man the night before and how dignified and proud he had seemed. About seventy years old and one of the most respected men at Dobe, he was a "traditional" man who, with his two wives, spent about nine months of the year earning a living from the bush. Unlike his sons, he kept a respectful distance from the anthropologists, and he never asked for favors.

We found him bruised and hurt, lying down, his legs wrapped in bandages. But the generous smile indicated he was alive and well, as did his telling of his story, which was as lucid as could be. He had left camp early that morning to gather fruit in a nearby field. He did see a large animal lying in the grass, but, with vision somewhat impaired by age, he thought it only a Herero cow. He walked on. Then the animal rose and charged him, throwing him far into the air.

He landed some fifteen feet away. Immediately the buffalo was at him again, butting him, trying to gore him with its horns. Somehow he slipped between the animal's legs, and as it backed up, he backed up. Anticipating its movements, he managed to keep clear of the horns. Eventually, the animal walked off into the bushes and lay down. The old man quietly crept away, open sores on his legs where the buffalo's hind legs had scraped him, his arm swollen, and his head bruised from having been thrown by its powerful horns.

When details of the incident reached the Herero farmer, he gave up his claim of ownership to the meat. We trucked the meat back to Dobe, where most of it was distributed to the !Kung San.

〜〜〜〜〜 Nisa and I talked little on the drive from the bush camp back to Dobe. But as we swayed and bounced against each other in the cab of the truck, she mentioned that my breast was pushing against her. Perhaps it was uncomfortable for her; more likely, she thought it was uncomfortable for me.

"That's not really a breast," I said, adjusting my body, our days together in the bush having made me feel more trusting. Yet I was pretty sure she already knew. Megan Biesele had carried that message, along with the one that I would soon arrive, to Nisa months earlier.

"Did Megan tell you I had been sick?" I asked.

"Eh, Megan told me," she said simply, without emotion.

"Well," I said, "my doctors found a terrible sickness in my right breast, so terrible that they took my breast away." I wondered what sense she could possibly make of that. Breast cancer is not known to occur among the !Kung, and they have no concept of it. Indeed, there is no translation in their language for the whole panoply of illnesses we categorize as cancer.

"Today, I am like a man on that side," I continued, wanting her to know. "What has been pushing against you is something else, something I put in so people won't see."

"Eh, I, too, had sickness in my breast," she said, pointing to her left breast.

How could she understand? Removal of a breast for sickness must have sounded barbaric, even primitive. It was probably as difficult for her to accept my explanation of my illness as it had been for me to accept hers concerning the death of her son: "little spiritual arrows sent by God."

"Oh, that's not good," I said. "But mine would not have gotten better. It would have killed me." Then I added, "And it still may."

"Chuko and I will lay on hands and see what is there."

The words were simple, but they were ones I had been longing to hear. She would help me. The pain and fear of the previous year once again flooded in, moistening my eyes and softening my words. "This past year was awful." I confided. "My heart felt so much pain."

Without encouraging me to go on, she said, "I will try to help."

Back at Dobe, a !Kung messenger brought me a letter from Megan, who was now working in Namibia. She had been on the Namibian side of the border just minutes after I passed by. Her messenger handed me the note an hour after Megan had written it—not very speedy for a distance of only one mile. I rushed to the border, hoping to see her, but we had missed each other again. "I waited until 6 PM, then left," said a paper freshly pinned to the fence. "I plan to come back this way again soon. Hope to see you then."

The people from the truck had long since dispersed to their villages, carrying food and stories. How I would have loved to hear the stories as they told them! Baitsenke and I were back in our camp. Tuma and Bo sat around while supper was cooked and water was heated for baths—which we would take in a shallow basin under the cover of night, the hot water momentarily warding off the cold air. After supper, Bo returned to Nisa, Tuma went back to his father's village, where he slept while employed, and Baitsenke, as usual, went early into his tent.

The winter wind pierced the blanket I had wrapped tightly around my legs. The crescent moon, which had just "struck" (a !Kung expression also used when an arrow hits its mark, successfully striking an animal), had long since set. Once again I sat by the fire. Once again I was alone. Perhaps too alone, I thought, especially after days of living in a group. Jackals whined in the dark, but were not to be feared, or so I had been told. And somewhere in the night there were lions. But even if the lions were close, I was not worried. There were cows and goats, donkeys and horses for them to feed on; not me, in my tent.

Two weeks to go. With the initial adjustment behind me, the heart of my journey still lay ahead. Two weeks: to interview Nisa, to reconnect with old friends, to make new ones, to find out about people's lives, to discover in what ways I could be useful, to photograph—to test out the rest of my dreams for the trip.

Kumsa-the-Hunter, one of the most industrious people I had ever met, would serve as my model. Kumsa loved the bush, and loved earning his living from it. He was the only one at Dobe who refused to herd cows for the neighboring Bantu people. To be sure, he would take government food handouts when they were available: corn meal and mixed porridge "drought relief" that continued even after the drought ended. But he wouldn't give up his independence—even though others who had done so had been reasonably successful. And his daughters and sons-in-law followed his lead: his was the only village at Dobe that was not economically tied to Bantu cattle.

It wasn't so much his independence as his tenacity that inspired me. Though older than the other men on our trip, Kumsa never quit early. On the porcupine hunt, he worked the mound for hours before giving up. When he hunted, it was for the entire day, and it was every day—even that last one when all but he and Toma had given up. And whereas Toma returned to camp around noon, Kumsa kept at it until nearly dark. Kumsa wanted meat. He wanted to strike an animal. He would try, even in the face of repeated discouragement. His body was hardened to the rigors of being pushed to the limit. His determination and skill had made him one of the most successful hunters in the region, earning him his nickname: Kumsa-the-Hunter.

And my nickname? It had once been Marjorie-Things-See, because I had been able to spot animals easily, sometimes even before the !Kung. And now? Marjorie-Make-Every-Day-Count? Or Marjorie-the-Adventurer? Or the-Anthropologist? Or the-Photographer? Or the-Self-Healer? Perhaps the next two weeks would hold some answers.

〰〰〰 The roosters crowed while it was still dark, as though hoping to hasten the coming of dawn. I lay in my blankets, secure in my tent, pleased that I need not get up right away. After days of group living, privacy was luxurious.

While I was eating breakfast, the soldiers returned. "How was your bush trip?" "What exactly did you do?" "What are your plans now?" "Are you planning any more traveling?" "How long will you stay here?" Although they were friendly, their purpose was clear: I was to be watched closely. Equally clear was that little that I did escaped their radar. I tried to be open and agreeable, hoping to be allowed to stay the next two weeks. When they finally left, I breathed easier. Now I could get on with my day.

With papers and cameras, I headed off toward the villages. My plan was to visit a different !Kung village each day. This way I could catch up with people I had known in earlier years, meet those I did not know, and see for myself what present conditions were like. Kxau, who had faced the lions the day before, would be my guide. He had come that morning to ask a favor: Would I send the truck to pick up grass that he and his wife, Bau, had cut not too far from the village? The grass would be used as thatch. "Not too far" meant a walk of close to two hours each way; that was how far the villagers had to go to find grass undisturbed by cows and goats. "Yes," I had told him. "When you are ready, show Baitsenke where the grass is and he will take it to your village."

I followed Kxau along worn paths in the sand, with crisscrossing paths intersecting at angles as if in a maze, one in which I had little sense of where I had come from or how I would find my way back. After half a mile or so the path opened onto a clearing, with few trees and a large expanse of sand held level by a clutter of low thorn bushes. Three villages were within hearing, if not sight, of one another.

How those villages had changed! Twenty years before, villages at Dobe had had no fences, no mud walls, no neatly thatched roofs. The village grounds then, as now, had been bare sand to prevent snakes and other creatures from finding hospitable hiding places. But back then, behind the simply constructed grass huts, natural vegetation had hummed with life, so vigorous that it had to be cut back periodically to keep it from encroaching on the village. The huts had described a circle, each with its opening facing inward, the social life of the group flowing around the edges and across the center. Possessions were few and were shared, either by choice or by coercion. From a distance, a village might be hard to detect, blending quietly as it did into the surrounding bush.

What stood before me now did not blend into the bush. Shoulder-high posts formed a fence, guarding the possessions within. Cut thorn bushes, placed at the foot of the posts, prevented even chickens from entering (or exiting) except at the prescribed entrance. Trees useful for shade remained, but other vegetation had been banished far beyond the fence, the battle long since decisively won. Inside the fence stood four or five huts, sturdily constructed with mud walls and thatched roofs—the result of weeks, if not months, of intense labor. The circle formation had given way to a sort of meandering line, with all doors facing the opening of the compound.

We shouted greetings back and forth through the dry air to people in two villages as we passed by, then stopped at Kxau's village. Inside the fence, four neatly built mud huts stood beside two traditionally framed huts belonging, respectively, to Kxau's elderly dependent sister and her husband, and his somewhat eccentric younger brother and his wife. The airy frames of the traditional huts, loosely draped with cloth rather than covered with grass, provided more light and breeze than did the mud huts. Now symbols of economic impoverishment, they were nevertheless a welcome sight to me: they represented a past that, despite its problems, had had integrity and dignity.

I joined Kxau's wife, Bau, at the fire. She and her three youngest children were eating cooked corn kernels that had simmered for hours in a three-legged iron pot. As their guest, I too ate the tough, lima bean–sized kernels. I gave presents of tea, dried milk, and sugar, along with articles of clothing I had brought from home. I took a census and asked to be shown around.

Kxau proudly led me to the far end of the compound, where a faded red forty-four-gallon water drum, marked and dented, lay on its side. Reaching inside, he pulled out a handful of large corn kernels, the kind we had just been eating. He told me, with visible pleasure, that this harvest was from his own garden. The rains had been good that year, and those who had planted had done well. Later I saw a comparable stockpile of melons, as big as watermelons but not as sweet, in another enterprising family's compound.

〈〈〈〈〈〈 Looking at this "modern" village and this successful family, I thought of Kxau and Bau as I had first known them, twenty years before. I had met Kxau very early in my first trip to the field. In fact Tashay, his older brother, had been the first Bushman I ever met. The anthropologist who met my husband and me in Maun—the last stop in our plane journey and the first stop of our truck journey—had brought Tashay with him from Dobe.

Earning a living almost exclusively from hunting wild animals and gathering wild plants, the family had divided their time between the bush and their village at Dobe. They were the group pointed to when anthropologists asked about "traditional" !Kung San, those who lived apart from their Bantu-speaking neighbors. Kxau and his extended family—his father, his mother and her co-wife, his older brother, his older sister, and their respective families—were the ones who welcomed the outsiders, and were the core group of the early studies.

Yet even their village would soon lose its independence. For years it had been protected, in part, by its poor well—a rocky outcrop that provided little water during the dry months for people, let alone for goats and cattle. But hard labor had deepened wells in neighboring areas, and Dobe probably would have been no exception. What saved it, at least for a while longer, was its location. One mile from Namibia, it was too close to the border to interest the Herero—the !Kung's most numerous neighbors and the ones most likely to settle on !Kung traditional land.

It was not that the Herero did not like Namibia. Rather, they considered it the homeland of their hearts and their culture. But neither country's government would allow the Herero to move back across the border, with their livestock and possessions, and settle in Namibia. Nor would it have been politically possible: in Namibia, the area immediately west of the border was legally considered !Kung San country. The Namibian police on patrol shot any cattle found on that side of the border, and scouts routinely checked for footprints and other signs of activity along the road. Thus Herero who settled too near the border risked losing their cattle.

But after the border was fenced in 1964, it became more difficult to hold back the tide of Bantu settlement in the traditional !Kung lands in Botswana. By the time I arrived in 1989, cattle—and their Bantu-speaking owners—were deeply entrenched at Dobe.

〰〰〰 That night I sat alone by the fire with my journal. Bells of animals rang in the darkness. Cows bellowed in the distance. The voices of women singing in Kumsa-the-Hunter's village came to my ears across the night air. Baitsenke had commissioned a trance dance, paying a sizable portion of his monthly earnings for four women to sing and for Kumsa to lay on hands. It seemed Baitsenke, too, must be afraid.

The voices stopped, then started again, without much energy. Someone passed my camp in the darkness, strumming a Tswana melody on a local guitar—perhaps an "owner of the shade," as young men were called. Earlier in the day there had been reports of four lions a few miles to the north. Surely there were too many domestic animals nearby for them to come after me.

Two weeks to go. I missed my family, ached for them. There was much I wanted to accomplish before the end of my stay, yet I found myself counting the days. What was I doing here? Research? Yes. But why? Nisa didn't seem to care about me. No one else did either.

To break my lonely, self-pitying mood, I followed the sound of the singing to Kumsa's village. The dance didn't amount to much. Without passion, the participants did what Baitsenke had hired them to do: the four women sang, and Kumsa went into trance. A few other women showed up and joined halfheartedly. Kumsa laid on hands, making the rounds of the women, Baitsenke, and at a separate fire, a few men who sat talking. By the time I got there, Baitsenke seemed ready to leave. This was his first experience of a Bushman healing ceremony; whatever he had expected from it, he seemed satisfied. Yet the dance limped on, as if no one was sure how much healing Baitsenke's money had bought. "Mm, yes," Baitsenke said when I asked if he had had enough. The night was cold, the firewood almost gone. Minutes after I told the women what Baitsenke had said, the circle broke up.

Back at my tent, I lit the kerosene lamp outside the flaps. My flashlights were broken, and so was Baitsenke's. Perhaps if the lamp burned all night, the mice would not bother me. The night before, a mouse had got in and run round and round the small tent. I tried to get it out, but in the dark I never knew where it was. I'd open the flap for a moment and move wildly about the tent, hoping it would leave. Eventually I dozed off. But through the night it kept waking me up, once even nibbling my hair.

In the morning I walked to one of the villages, giving presents, catching up on who lived there, what they ate, how they managed. Then I visited Nisa and Bo at their camp, a tidy, well-kept place set

apart from neighboring camps. Tall wooden posts encircled their compound, which included two mud huts—the roofs thatched with dried
bush grass—and a fire and cooking area. Two roosters ran at top speed
among the posts, absorbed in a fierce struggle that stopped then started
again and again. A scrawny dog settled down near where we sat,
slowly inched toward us on its belly, hoping for a shred of food, then
backed off with a whine as Nisa shooed it away. As Nisa and Bo's
guest, I was offered tea, with apologies that there was no milk; Nisa's
niece Nai had not yet brought it. We talked about their living situation,
and for the most part they seemed satisfied. Their only direct blood relative was Nai, who lived a twenty-minute walk away. Other villages
were closer if they needed help.

The first hut, for sleeping, was pretty standard: blankets laid out on
the floor, a kerosene lamp, a few other items. The second hut, for storage, bowled me over, holding an array of goods unimaginable years before: trunks with locks, blankets hanging on a line strung from one
side of the wall to the other, containers of all kinds, tools, a pile of
mongongo nuts from our bush trip, beaded headbands (worn at trance
dances), bags partially filled with government food, including a twenty-
five-pound bag of a soy-milk-and-grain product (a complete protein)
and a similar bag of dried corn kernels (which took hours of cooking to
reconstitute).

Later Nisa and I sat down together for an interview, which,
though somewhat depressing, went very well. We talked about old age
and her future.

Her childlessness was her dominant regret. Our discussion of her future seemed to reemphasize the depth of her losses.

When I am old to death and just sit, I won't have anyone to fill up water
for me to drink. I will just lie there. Even firewood. I won't have a fire to
lie beside. That's what I see when I look at myself . . . I will be unable to
find food. Then cold and hunger and thirst, they will kill me. When even
my last strength is gone, I will be without my face. Finished. I will lie
there with hunger and thirst. And without fire. Those are the things that
will kill me. Because I am without any young person.

Even my cows. I sit and cry to find someone to milk my cows so I
can drink. That someone would have been my son, my son who

came from my insides, who nursed on my own milk . . . God is terrible
. . . If my son were still alive, I wouldn't feel pain. But today I just sit and
think and think and think.

She felt that one or two people, distant relatives, might help, but she
did not feel secure.

Other people will see us and say that we two are old to death, that we
are not their relatives . . . They won't bring firewood and start a fire: they
won't carry water and give it to us. It is only the child you give birth to,
who suckles your milk, that child is the one who helps you.

Me, I have no family. When Bo and I get old, we two will just sit together and die. But if God helps, when one of us is old, the other will still
have some strength and will help.

Even in her dark moods, the cows gave her comfort. She sometimes
talked about them as if they were her children.

When I am old and Bo is old, we will just sit together, and that's what it
will be. Because there is nothing that will come to help us. Only the cows
are with us, and they cry "bahhn." They are our children, those cows.

I am thankful. Because if you have cows, it's like living with a person,
a real person. It cries and says, "bahhn . . . bahhn," and when you hear it
talk you stand up and lead it away. The two of you talk. Yes, a cow is a
good thing. You lead it away and your heart feels fine. Eh, mother!

I asked again, as I had a few days before, what her life would have
been like without the cows. She would have stayed in her old village,
she said, asking others for food and gathering what she could.

But my heart wouldn't be happy. I would look at others who had cows
and say they had survival. And me, I'd gather food and feel pain. Do you
not gather and then it is gone? Doesn't your body hurt? Aren't you tired?
And, as I am today, not seeing well, how would I find food to eat?

Though the day's topics were grim, it was wonderful talking with
her, and she was as seductive as ever. Each time a new topic came up, I
wanted to interview her not ten but fifty more times, to get all the details on tape, to be sure I understood the nuances. Then I'd worry about
how many hours of tape I'd have to translate when I got home. The first
book had taken ten years to complete.

〘〘〘〘〘 The Botswana Defense Force made their daily visit in the afternoon. As always I tried to please them, offering tea which they seldom accepted, making polite conversation, asking about their lives, but gently, gently. So polite and with no expectation of answers, with no edge. They could so easily have kicked me out. They were very suspicious. The sun was near the horizon when they finally left, quiet filling the camp as the rumble of their engines muted into the distance.

Then came a different sound, a far-off thickening, moving toward us. Knowing something I didn't, people poured from their villages onto the path, talking in excited voices. In the red afterglow of the sunset, women danced and sang their undulating melodies. Children ran about, affected by the mounting energy. Then, out of the bushes, came the men—Herero, Tswana, and Bushman—some riding high on horseback or on donkeys, others walking, a parade returning from a successful lion hunt, their rifles gleaming, their bows and quivers high, their gait steady. As they passed by, exuding prowess and strength, a high-pitched yodeling rang out from the well-wishers, traditional congratulations in a responsive refrain, repeating, then changing, again and again.

The news was that a lion had killed a donkey the day before. Those who had joined the hunt that morning had known the dangers. The previous year, two of their own—including the eldest son of the Herero matriarch I had recently visited—had been killed in just such a hunt. He hadn't been the first. Nor would he be the last. But today the men had been successful: one female lion had been killed and one male had run off.

〘〘〘〘〘 A small note, marked "Marjorie" on the outside, was placed in my hand.

> I'm on the Namibian side of the border. I'll wait for you for a while. If you don't come, I'll try again tomorrow, when I pass this way. About 3 PM. Hope to see you then. How's it going? Megan.

I moved quickly. Baitsenke was resting and didn't want to go, so I got behind the wheel, the first time since Maun. What a feeling. To move out from camp with a truckload of people talking, shouting, arguing; slowing the truck under low-hanging thorn branches; cool breezes in the cab swirling the mounting engine heat; shifting into four-wheel drive, with gears grinding, to get us through deep sand; the tall grass catching the end-of-day light.

This time, the people who climbed onto the truck had come to see and exchange news with those working for Megan. As always, someone broke into "the truck song," and the singing carried far beyond the dust settling in our tracks.

I made a sharp turn onto the border road. There was the fence separating Botswana from Namibia, parallel roads on either side. The landscape was identical on the two sides of the man-made dividing line, undaunted in its continuing pulse of life.

To my disappointment, Megan had already left. I hadn't seen her in years. We had first met eighteen years before, in Botswana, when she arrived to begin her fieldwork during my last months in the field, when I was tired, bitter, and ready to leave. She was tender and thoughtful and sensitive, and I admired her greatly. Her work on stories carried through generations was passionate, and her commitment to the people—to learning their language and to helping them protect their land and culture—was inspiring. What better person to talk to, to share experience with, maybe even to get support from—someone to remind me, in this strange land, who I was.

But I had missed her. Her messenger must have had priorities other than getting the note to me quickly. I would try again the next day.

As we were about to leave, a truck with cloth flapping over the rear frame, marked UN in huge letters, drove up on the Namibian side. A group of Finnish soldiers, so young, got out and greeted us. They were there, they said, to see that the elections went smoothly.

〰〰〰 I wrote a long letter to Mel that night, hoping Megan would be able to mail it for me. I felt so out of touch with my family. I had managed to send a radio message to Maun to let them know I was all right, but the safari coordinator at the other end of the radio link had heard nothing from them.

Here are excerpts from my letter to Mel:

It's Saturday night at 9:50 PM, and the place is really hopping—donkey bells blare in stereo and the fire snaps and crackles to its own internal beat; mice tap out rhythms as they clean the dirty dishes. That's about it for excitement. Oh, yes, a bull roars somewhere in the darkness. The moon struck a few nights back, but is still small, so it doesn't give off much light. The stars, the Milky Way, Scorpio (in the middle of the sky, not rising), and the Southern Cross help define the billions of stars piercing through the darkness above.

It's hard to know where to begin. Time has been so condensed. I've been away from home for two weeks and two days, and it's as if I have another life altogether. Coming back here feels like resuming an old life—fully intact, like being a complete part of a separate world, yet not believing it possible. Will the real Marjorie Shostak please stand up!

I've been working well, feeling more or less on top of things, and in a reasonably good mood. It's been a terrific relief being away from the children, even though I have intense yearnings for them nearly every day.

My relationship with the Bushmen has been good—the demands seem so minor, the badgering so understated, the complaints fairly trivial. I think being only one is a great bonus—people don't give me too hard a time, don't ask too much or expect constant service. I think part of the change is in them: they are not as hungry, or feeling as deprived, as they were when we were first here. That is not to say they aren't still the underdogs in the economy, but at least they are beginning to be in on a little of the "action." And part of the change is in me: I know what to expect, feel more generous, less overwhelmed, and have continuing relationships with people from the past.

Nisa is vigorous and in good form. I'm just about able to put together a detailed picture of her present life. She's in good health and responding well to me. We've done five interviews, all on the present, and I hope to review the past fairly soon.

Emotionally, I'm engaged in life here. I have numerous downs, but they pass. I'm alone most nights and have been writing daily in my journal (the one you bought me). Although I'm confused about where I go from here, I'm essentially happy. I've enjoyed being on my own immensely. (When else in our twenty-two years have I had the concentration to write you a missive like this one?)

The anxiety about my health hums in the background—my elbow has not gotten better. But I've been successful in stemming the panic—there are no resources except myself here. Also, this environment feels so healthful. The air feels clear and healing; being outdoors all day feels wonderful.

Whether or not I survive the breast cancer, this experience has been great. Whatever happens with the work I do here, I will treasure this month for the rest of my life.

The people ask after you—you, too, have roots here. I think of you and the children often and wonder how you are doing. I miss the quiet moments with Susanna in bed, before she sleeps, or off alone with her during the day; Adam in bed at night, whispering his thoughts, private and deep; Sarah—well, holding her, listening to her working things out in her head. And you, my support and ally. What I don't miss is space closing around me—tending to their needs, resolving their fights, catering to their friends and activities. At this distance, the life I left seems overwhelming. Yet here the basis of camp life is family. Nisa has none and is suffering.

I don't mean to end on a sour note—because my heart is full for you and the three. I just want you to know that me-to-me has been extremely successful. I hope to learn how to incorporate it into my life as a mother as well.

It's 11:30 now—let me end with you: I wear your safari jacket and your shoes every day—wonderful gifts, foundations of my life here. I am here because you allowed me to dream. I couldn't ask for a better soul mate in all the world. I worry for your sanity through all this. I love you.

Nisa Remembers

"Can you tell me about things you have seen since I left?" I asked Nisa. "I don't mean about everyone else. I mean about how you lived during all the years. We have not talked about how things were with you."

I looked at her puzzled face. "Do you understand?" Before she could answer, I apologized: "Uhn, uhn . . . What's wrong with me? Today my tongue is heavy. Did you understand what I was saying?"

Nisa indicated that she had understood and that she would teach me. Slowly, enunciating each word, she started giving me my lines: "We separated years ago."

Obediently, I repeated, "We separated years ago."

"And I didn't come."

"And I didn't come."

She finished my part: "I have only today come back. And you, my aunt, as you have been living, have you been doing well? Your heart, has it been cool [as opposed to hot, angry]? Have you been well and working at the things you always do?"

"Yes!" I said, delighted. "Yes, that's what I meant."

"Well, that's how you say it."

She answered the question by telling me that she had often been sick. She would be sick, then feel better and begin to work. Then she would feel bad again and lie down. Sometimes she was sick for a long time. When it passed, she would return to her work. "Today, I'm an older woman. As I am here, I have gotten old. When I do some things, my eyes don't see well. When I do other things, my legs hurt."

She often thought about me: "Marjorie left long ago. Will she, another day, come back and help me again, with life-giving support? My eyes no longer see well. Marjorie and I separated a long time ago. Perhaps the government has stopped her and that's why she hasn't returned."

When village life bothered her, when it "ruined my face," she and Bo would go to the bush. "Kill a springhare or a porcupine so that I can taste it inside my mouth," she would tell him. "Today, the inside of my mouth is dead! Meat hunger is killing me!" But Bo would say, "With my one good eye, how am I supposed to shoot anything?" And she would agree, "Eh, that's all right. It doesn't matter."

One time they traveled with dogs, and Bo killed a springhare. Nisa put it in her carrying sack. They came to a place where a leopard had killed a horse and examined the tracks to see how it had made the kill. They stayed in the groves that night, skinned the springhare, and ate. The next morning they gathered mongongo nuts and left for another part of the nut groves. At the end of the day, it began to rain. They left while it was dark and walked back in the night. They walked for many hours before they reached home.

In the morning, Kumsa, her younger brother, announced that he was going to move away, to a Herero village. Nisa told him, "You can go live with Hereros, but not me. They make you work hard and give you nothing. Only white people pay you for your work. They give you money to buy food. I won't move into a Herero village. I'll just sit right where I am." So Kumsa moved and she stayed.

Nisa started to cough. "When I cough," she reminded me, with a stern look at the tape recorder, "kill that thing. Don't let it pick up my coughing. I refuse for it to hear it. I want it to talk only my talk." I turned it off until she was ready to continue.

"After that, Bo and I lived alone at Mahopa, lived and lived and lived."

"Were you living well?"

"We were living, eating ivory palm nuts," she answered, leading into a more detailed description of Richard Lee's arrival than she had given in our earlier interview.

We were living on the nuts because we were hungry. Hunger was grabbing us, so we ate them. We knocked down the nuts, pounded them, and ate them.

Then Richard came to Dobe, asking for me. "I'm looking for Nisa. My heart wants her so much it's crying." People told him, "What are you crying about? Nisa is living at Mahopa. Tomorrow morning, first thing, we'll go to her. So don't cry." They slept that night.

Richard had his children with him. In the morning, they came for me. I was in the bush, pounding the ivory palm nuts. Bo was in the village.

He told Tasa, "Go get your aunt. Richard is looking for your aunt so he can take her and we will leave." Tasa came and got me. I collected the ivory palm nuts and ran back to the village. When we got there, Richard said, "Mama . . . my grandmother . . . Mama mama. Marjorie told me to find you and take you. I have your money with me. Here it is. I'll give it to you so you can buy cows." I was so thankful! I said, "My niece, my niece is helping me."

Richard said, "The Herero may refuse to sell to you. Let Timina [a young Herero man] do it." But I refused. "Timina won't do it. A Herero won't hold my money. You give it to me and I will hold it. I, myself, will buy the cows." Richard said, "Well then, take your things and put them in the truck."

Richard had suggested they buy the cows at Dobe. Relocating there, Nisa explained, was Bo's idea. She had told Bo, reluctantly: "All right, if that's what you say, we'll move there." So they packed and put their things in Richard's truck and went to Dobe. Then Makongo, a Tswana man married to a !Kung woman, helped them buy the cows.

Nisa and Bo watched over the cows, all of which were pregnant. At first, after the calves were born, Bo milked the cows and Nisa poured the milk into containers. But after "sickness entered him," Bo stopped milking them.

𒀭𒀭𒀭 "What happened to your two nieces?" I asked, wondering why she and Bo were living in a compound by themselves, away from their relatives. "You were raising them when first we talked."

"Yes, when first we talked, I was taking care of Little Tasa and Little Nukha. They were just children and we raised them," she said, the "we" generously including me, "you and I, on food that you fed them. But after they grew, their mother refused to let me have them any more. She just took them from me."

She continued, "My brother wouldn't let me be with them. The oldest was as though I had raised her. But he dropped me. He said that I did not give birth to them. That I was an outsider. I had taken such good care of them. It was as though I had birthed them." Her voice was sad, "I feel terrible about it. Terrible. Because I have no child. My husband, he is the only one. We look at each other and that is all."

Bo also had no children. "He never married a woman and had a child. When he came to me, we didn't have a child together. I had given birth to others, but they had all died. God was stingy with me. And when Bo came to me, God refused and we never gave birth."

"Do you have any of your own people where you live?"

"Me, I have no people. If my younger brother wanted to be good to me, he'd help me. But instead, he's taken the children from me. Nai, my older brother's daughter, is the only one who helps me."

"Why don't you live in Nai's village?"

"When you give your niece to a man in marriage, you don't live in their village. Won't the two of them fight and insult each other? And when your ears hear them, won't your heart disagree?"

She said she was content to live alone with Bo because their compound was near two small villages in which she had some distant relatives and a few friends. She didn't visit her younger brother, because he yelled at her.

He says that I haven't given him a cow. I refuse! I won't do that. I won't give him a cow. He is blind. If I gave him a cow, he'd drink it up in beer. And these cows, they keep my stomach full.

I told him, "When Marjorie gave me cows, she told me I should milk the cows and drink. She didn't want me to have to gather bush foods. Because, she said, I was old. That's why Marjorie gave me the cows. She didn't tell me to give cows to you. No, you will just have to sit and take care of yourself. My tongue here, that's my cows. I won't give any to you."

After that, he dropped me.

Then, almost as a summary, she exclaimed, "Ooo . . . oh . . . his eyes are broken." She blew out a puff of air and said, "begone," as though spitting out badness. "He is killing himself. I said I would visit him and we would sit together. But he said, 'I'm taking the children.' So he took the children and went off."

He was also angry because she hadn't moved to Kangwa, where he lived, after she bought the cows. "Why are you still living at Dobe?" he asked. But she told him, "I'm going to sit where I have been sitting. Here. I will bring up my cows, and only after they are plentiful will I move to Kangwa."

"After that, he yelled at me and fought with me and yelled at me. And then he took his children from me."

When she moved to Dobe, she reminded me, Richard Lee had carried her and her possessions in his truck. Moving to Kangwa without a truck would be hard. "A donkey is the only thing I don't have. If I had one, that would be good. I'd just pack my things and go live at Kangwa. But I have no donkey. That's why I live here."

Then she said she had always wanted to live at Kangwa. If she moved there, she'd leave the cows at Dobe and drink milk other people gave her. Then, when her cows gave birth, her nephew would bring some to her at Kangwa and keep others at Dobe. She might even take the cows to a bush camp.

But, she complained, "My husband refuses! He says he wants to stay here and watch over the cows. I say we should move. But he says he won't leave the cows." Even if she had the donkey, she admitted, Bo wouldn't move. "He refuses and that defeats me, even though my heart would like to go."

"Why do you want to live in Kangwa?"

"It's too hard for me to get water from the well at Dobe. Someone else has to help and pour water from the bucket into my containers. When I am alone, I live with thirst. At Kangwa, there is a tap and I can pour it for myself." And if she lived there her younger brother might be friendly again.

"If you lived at Kangwa . . ." I started to ask.

"I wouldn't feel pain," she answered at once. But she would never know that, because her husband wanted to stay and watch over the cows. In any case, she wasn't seeing very well and couldn't get around to gather food. So even if she had a donkey, "I'd still just sit. I'd give it to my niece's children to get food for me."

"But," she added pointedly, "I have no donkey."

Again I put the issue of the donkey on hold. "Your younger brother's children . . . do they visit you?"

"They visit me. They like me!" she said forcefully. "It's their father who doesn't want them to be with me. Ooh, mother, that's what he says! But those children, they like me, they really do. But their father takes them from me."

As the interview neared its end, I asked, "As you and your husband live here, are you doing well?"

"Yes, I'm living well. Even if I am alone, I'm doing fine."

"If you had no cows," I asked, "Do you think you and your brother would not be enemies?"

"No. Even If I had no cows, he would still hate me. He just hates me, hates me and my husband. That Kumsa, he is too full of words. The only one who doesn't yell at me is my older brother. But today, sickness is killing him and he is doing badly. My husband agreed to let him live with us so that we can watch over him."

"Before you moved to Dobe," I asked in another conversation, "what was your life like?"

"The years that followed your leaving, I ate foods that I gathered. I was feeling fine, and my husband was still healthy. If we got sick, we took care of ourselves. Foods from the bush were what we gathered and what sustained us. He, a man, would bring back meat and we would eat."

"But," she added, "Kumsa started yelling at me and we began to fight. He just hated me!"

"Weren't you two getting along when last I was here?"

"Just barely. I alone liked him, but he didn't like me. He was filled with bad words, yelling at me. I told him, 'I have raised your children. I helped birth them and helped bring them up. So why are you taking them from me?'"

She had wanted her nieces to live with her. They would help her get food, firewood, and water. But Kumsa refused, telling her that he, not she, had given birth to them,* and that they had come from inside his wife's body, not hers. "Why should I give you the children?" he demanded before he moved away to the Herero village.

It hadn't always been like that. Nearly twenty years before, Kumsa and his wife had essentially given Nisa one of their daughters to raise. The girl, Little Nukha, called Nisa "Mother," as I had witnessed when Nisa and I had first talked. At that time, Nisa had described the arrangement this way:

> Not too long ago, my younger brother, Kumsa, and his wife gave me one of their children, little Nukha, to take care of for a while. They lent her to me so I would help bring her up. His wife was pregnant with their third child and wanted to wean her. But Nukha didn't want to stop and cried all the time. Finally, my brother said, "My older sister, why don't you take care of her for us for a while." That's what I did. I took her and kept her with me. I'm still taking care of her today. I am the one bringing her up; I am the one beside whom she is growing and whom she calls

* Both men and women speak of "conceiving" and "giving birth" to children (*//ge*).

Mother. She says her real mother is just another person, and refuses to sleep in her hut. She stays there during the day, sometimes, but at night she lies down next to me.

Taking care of her has made me very happy; it's as though I had given birth to her myself. I love children. So, when my brother had his second child, I took her and kept her with me.

That arrangement had held for more than two decades. "I carried her, fed her, and brought her up. I also arranged her marriage and gave her to her husband." Little Nukha—now a mother of three—still called Nisa "Mother" and was called "my daughter" in return. Nisa took obvious pleasure in the fact, also mentioned years before, that Nukha always called her biological mother "Tasa's mother," after one of her sisters, and reserved the more intimate appellation "Mother" for Nisa.

Nisa and Bo had also taken care of Nukha's sisters over the years. But Nukha was the only one they had raised exclusively. Nisa said, again with obvious satisfaction, "Nukha moved from our village to her husband's without ever returning to her parents." It was Nisa, not Nukha's biological mother, who assisted at Nukha's first birth, and it was Nisa who took the new baby to its father.

Nisa would have loved to have her niece living with her still—and Nukha would have found the arrangement highly agreeable. But Nukha's husband refused. He tended cows for the Herero and said he didn't want to leave his work. But Nisa thought his real reason was jealousy. Once when Nukha was visiting Nisa, her husband had come to get her, and after that he had refused to let her return. "He said Nukha liked me too much. He was afraid that if she came again, she would refuse to go home."

〽〽〽〽 "I still don't understand about your brother," I said. "When you were children, your hearts liked each other."

"When we were children, we hated each other!" Nisa corrected me, with such vehemence that she was almost yelling. "Do you understand? When we were young, we *hated* each other. That man was bad! We would hit each other. I would bite him and he would hit me and I would bite him. Kumsa! He is still mean."

She paused, then added, "But my big brother is wonderful. He has always been good to me."

She said Kumsa had abandoned their older brother, Dau. "One day

Kumsa told me, 'I'm leaving Dau and moving away.'" Dau remained in a deserted village in which just one other person, another old man, lived. Nisa had had no way of transporting Dau to Dobe. But news of my impending arrival had filled her with excitement. The day after we returned from the bush, Baitsenke had taken the truck to pick up Dau and move him to Dobe.

For this Nisa was thankful and expansive in her praise of me. Her husband was as well. "Even though Nisa too is sick," Bo told me, "she wants her older brother here."

Dau himself, weak and in great need of care, also praised me, calling me his daughter. "My daughter has brought me to my younger sister. I am so thankful. Nisa will cook so that I can eat, and I will lie near her fire and be warm."

I still didn't understand the rift between Nisa and her younger brother. What had their fight really been about? Had it been jealousy? Had Nisa's good fortune so overwhelmed Kumsa that he had wanted to hurt her as acutely as he could—by limiting her access to his children? And what had been his excuse for abandoning their older brother, leaving him in a deserted village?

These questions remained half-answered to the end, although I returned to the topic often. But the final outcome was perfectly clear: total estrangement. It was only after Nisa spoke of other problems in her younger brother's life that I gained another perspective. Perhaps he was too depleted, psychologically, to be able to deal with Nisa more effectively.

The problem was Kumsa's marriage, a union that even years before Nisa had found wanting. Now she told me that while their third child was still young, Kumsa's wife, Chuko, had left him for a "Goba," a term used for Bantu-speaking people who live in more distant areas of the country. The lovers fled, leaving Kumsa and his young daughter behind. Kumsa turned to Nisa for help.

The sun was low in the sky when Kumsa and the little girl arrived at Nisa's village. He said simply, "Chuko . . . the Goba has taken Chuko."

"Which Goba?" Nisa and Bo asked.

"The one with the short fingers. Goba Fingers, that's the one."

Nisa said, "Oh, Kumsa! You can hardly see. How are you going to raise Little Tasa? Now that you're here, stay with us." So they lived together a long time. But it bothered Bo that Chuko had deserted Kumsa, and one day he said, "This isn't good. Nisa, let's go to the authorities." So they traveled to the village where the police were stationed and said, "We're looking for Chuko."

Chuko was living in the bush. When she returned, Bo told the police, "That's the woman. That's Chuko. Goba Fingers took her away. Me, I am like Chuko's father. I want to bring her to justice and then take her home."

The police told Chuko, "Do you see? Your father Bo brought you to us. Today you are going to jail." And they sent her to jail for a very long time. The Goba only received a fine. He paid cows to Kumsa and left the area, and was not seen again.

Many seasons passed before Chuko was released. But trouble followed immediately after.

The very night Chuko came home, she started drinking beer. There was this Herero man—do you know the one they call Kashay? Well, that man grabbed Chuko, threw her down, held her and had sex with her. My niece, her husband, and another man who witnessed this ran to Kumsa, "Uncle," they cried, "Kashay is having sex with your wife!"

Kumsa jumped up and ran to Kashay. He grabbed him and threw him down. All the while, Kashay was screaming, "I'm screwing Chuko! Let me at her!" Kumsa wanted to kill Kashay. His hands were at Kashay's throat, but people pulled him away. After that, Kumsa took Kashay to the police. When they came, the police took them all to jail.

"Why were they all put in jail?" I asked, confused. "Was it bad for the others to have told?"

"Be quiet!" Nisa instructed me sternly, irritated at being interrupted. "Just listen."

They all went to the jail. The police asked Kashay, "Did you take this woman by force?" "Yes," Kashay admitted. "I took her by force and had sex with her."

The police asked Chuko, "This man, did he force himself upon you?" "Yes," she said, "he grabbed me by force and had sex with me."

The police asked my niece's husband, "Did this man take this woman by force and have sex with her?" "Yes," he said, "we were all together when he grabbed her and screwed her."

The police asked my niece, and the third witness. "Yes," they said, "he took her by force and had sex with her."

So that was that. The police said the witnesses should be given money, and Kashay was put in jail. Chuko came back and was given to her husband. But she didn't treat him well. Him, whose eyes are broken. Because, after Kashay got out of jail, she went to him. He had been in jail for years, but as soon as he got out, *wham!* That Chuko is really bad! Today she still sees him.

Nisa paused. "Yes," she said slowly, "these are the things I have seen while you were away."

〰〰〰〰 "What you have just told me—a man taking a woman by force—is this seen often?" I asked, aware that anthropologists had depicted traditional !Kung life as virtually rape-free.

"It's terrible! A terrible thing!" she said emphatically. "A man taking a woman by force is awful. A man asking you or you asking him, and two of you agree—that is very good. But a man who doesn't ask you but just grabs you, that's horrible! Terrible! Because you yourself don't want it."

"Has a man ever taken you by force?"

"Me? Me? No, I haven't been taken by force," she said, then changed her answer: "Once, when I was a young girl and my breasts were standing out like this, I saw that."

"Who did it?" I asked.

A man who lived in the bush. That man, he has died since then, and you don't mention the name of someone who has died. That man, he took me by force. Afterward, I came back and told.

This was before there were any police here. I told my husband, the one I had children with who died, "That man—that man Tuka—he took me by force."

It happened in the bush. I had gone out to collect firewood. I was carrying it when he stopped me and forced himself on me. I called out and hit him. I screamed. I kept hitting him but he didn't listen and threw me down. He grabbed my arms and held me down like this, and held my legs down like this. He caused me great pain.

That's why I told my husband Tashay, the one with whom I later had children. My husband went and hit him. Then the two of them started to fight, and fought and fought. I saw what was happening and said, "Eh-hey. That's how it is? When you tell, this is what happens . . . men kill each other?" And I thought "Eh. If that's how it is, telling is bad. Bad!"

After that, if a man propositioned me, I would just refuse. Just refuse. But I'd never tell. I'd just sit around. Even so, other than that day, no one else has taken me by force.

"Long ago," I asked, "while people were living in the bush, did men force themselves on women?"

People who lived in the bush . . . they would take women by force. Today, it still exists. Men still do that. But long ago, if a woman refused a man and she was gathering, he might go to her and take her by force. If she agreed, she would just lie down with him. And wouldn't tell. But if she didn't agree and he forced her, when she arrived at the village, she still wouldn't tell. Because she would be afraid that people might start to kill one another. She'd be afraid of poisoned arrows. If she told, people would start shooting.

Only a man without sense would force a woman, Nisa declared. A man like that would grab your body in one place and another and hurt you over and over. She told of a woman who was almost killed by two Gobas who raped her. "Oh, my niece," she exclaimed. "We women have really seen things!"

Nisa's thoughts moved to a scene from her young adulthood, a story she had told years before. Two men, both her lovers, fought over her in angry rage, each holding one arm, pulling her in opposite directions. One was Kantla, the man who was still her lover. The other was his younger brother Dem, "birthed from the very same place." Kantla told Dem, "She is my woman." Dem replied, "No, she's mine."

Amused, Nisa said, "Marjorie, long ago I really saw things!" then described the event. "I didn't have a husband then. My husband, Tashay, had just died. My breasts were huge, and stood way out here. Was I not still nursing a child?"

As told in *Nisa*, it was Nisa's mother who rescued her, shouting, "Can't you see you'll break her arms? You're going to kill her!" But in the new version her mother's language was much more colorful: "Are you going to tear Nisa's genitals apart and carry off the pieces?" Nisa laughed as she recounted her mother's words: "Is that sex of Nisa's so *hot?* If you pull it apart, what will you have?"

Nisa's mother whisked her off to the village even as she continued her invective against the men, cursing them boldly and ordering them to leave. Eventually both men left. But Nisa feared that the older brother, Kantla, would come back and kill the younger one. "That one," she said of Kantla, "was very bad. That man . . . he was *bad.*"

"That's why," she continued, "today, now that I'm old, I can finally say, 'Whhhewwww! I can rest.'"

I laughed out loud. Nisa said affectionately, "Eh, Marjorie."

⟨⟨⟨⟨⟨ With much laughter, Nisa told of another fight between her lovers. She had been lying down in a hut with an aunt, Old Nisa, her namesake. One man came to her, then another. The two men started to fight, each pulling her toward him. The aunt intervened, "Is she the only one with a sweet vagina?" she yelled. "Are other women's vaginas so bland? What's so different about hers?"

The men kept pulling her, yelling at each other, "You're not going to have her!" Finally, Nisa freed herself. But the next day the men chastised her aunt:

> "Old Nisa, you're not letting us have your namesake. You aren't a man, but a woman. So why are you keeping her from us?"
>
> "No!" my aunt told them. "There are many women around. Do you think Nisa is the only one with a vagina? Look at all those women with vaginas sitting there for you to screw. Screw those vaginas that belong to others. Screw those. But don't come for Nisa's."
>
> And she scolded me. "Nisa with the sweet vagina," she said, "I'm going to cut it out. I won't just leave it. Come here and let me cut it. Then I'll put it in the fire and bury it!"
>
> My namesake really yelled at me. "Close your legs," she cried. "Sit with your legs closed! Close your legs and hold back your genitals." Because she didn't want the men to have me. "You really are bad . . ." my aunt said. "Now, cover your genitals. Don't leave them open. Are you crazy for letting these men have you?"
>
> But I said, "Aunt, they are the ones bothering me for sex. It's not me who's doing it. Didn't you see them grab me by force? They grabbed me right next to you. Didn't you see that? Yet you still say I did something wrong?"

Another day, she recalled, her lover Kantla returned.

He sat down beside us. My aunt told him, "Today, you're not going to have one taste of Nisa's sex. How come you're back here already?"

She told me, "Nisa . . . Nisa . . . Nisa . . . don't let Kantla sleep with you." Then, turning to Kantla, she said, "Anyway, if you lie down with her, there won't be anything there for you."

Kantla was unhappy. He thought, "Is she going to stop me from being with my woman?" Finally, he told her, "Uhn, uhn. I don't want to be without your namesake. I won't just drop her. Now, let be. Other men she refuses, but me she doesn't."

My aunt said, "No! No! No! Is her sex that sweet?"

Kantla said quietly, "Old Nisa . . . Old Nisa . . . I really love your namesake. I love her, so let me be with her. Don't take her from me."

"That story was about my aunt . . . and about my body," Nisa added. Then her tone changed, no longer sounding amused. Other women also had lovers, she said, but after having sex, their lovers would leave. "But me, I sat there and was hurt." Her lovers hurt her arms, her genitals, and her back, "pulling and pulling and pulling." "Branches—branches were all over my back, and all over my body. Did they not hit me?" Sometimes the branches had thorns. "Bam, bam, just like a donkey, just like one hits and hurts a donkey. These . . . are they not things that hurt my back and my legs? Those men—they almost beat me to death."

"But now," she went on, "I have been old for a long time and I can finally rest. Because Kantla . . . he doesn't hit me. But when I was a young girl, he once hit me with a hunting bow. I had refused him, so he hit me."

Nisa mentioned a time in her youth when Kantla, already married to Bey, wanted her as a second wife. She repeated in broad outline a story that had appeared in detail in *Nisa*:

He came for me and took me back to his hut. Bey and I lived there to-gether. But after a while I refused him and ran away. They followed me and took me back with them. We lived together for a while. Then, an-other day, I ran away again. The two of them followed my tracks. When they tried to hold me, I refused and ran off. I went off, and later I mar-ried someone else. Kantla had set me with him, but we separated.

𝕂𝕂𝕂𝕂𝕂𝕂 Her thoughts were in the past; it seemed a good time to bring up my questions about her early life.

"Long ago, you talked to me about your parents, about things they did when you were small," I began, remembering both extreme bitterness and extreme fondness she had expressed toward them. "When you remember them now, do you think they brought you up well?"

"My father and mother . . . those who gave birth to me . . . and who raised me . . ." She paused to gather her thoughts. "They worked hard for me and did well in bringing me up. When I was small, they nursed me and fed me food. Nursed me and fed me. Nursed me and fed me. They killed small birds for me to eat. And fed me. They set traps and caught cori bustards and guinea fowl. And fed me. My father killed porcupines. And fed me. He killed large animals of the bush. And fed me."

This "home" scene seemed to be set earlier in time than the one that opened *Nisa*, which began: "I remember when my mother was pregnant with Kumsa." To clarify this, I asked, "This was before your younger brother was born?"

"Yes," Nisa answered, "I was very small, without a sibling."

They took care of me and raised me and I grew. Then, when I was fairly big, one day my father was hunting in the bush and my mother and I were gathering, collecting food. We picked berries and other foods, then left and returned to the village.

My father had killed a porcupine. When he came back, I said, "That's Daddy!" Because I heard something rustling in the bush in the night. He came back at night and I heard him. Mother said, "Maybe that's your father returning. Go look." I went and saw my father carrying the porcupine. I was so excited. "Yea, yea, meat! Daddy's here!" I called out. "Mommy, look! Daddy's got a porcupine! Mommy, look what Daddy's got! Yea, Daddy! Mommy, come look! Come look at Daddy carrying a porcupine!"

He put it down, and in the morning he cooked it and we ate.

We lived and lived and lived. After more time passed, mother was pregnant with Kumsa. It was just our family living together. My father's younger brother killed an eland. We had been out gathering, getting food, when I saw my father's younger brother. He was alone coming from the kill and told us, "Let's go and eat over there." We went back to the village and he told my father, his older brother, "I tracked that eland a long time and finally killed it, killed it to give to you. I've come to say that we should move there."

So they packed all their things and moved. We lived there, eating the meat.

That's when mother gave birth to Kumsa. She said, "Uhn, uhn . . . this child I am going to kill. I'll kill this child so you will be able to nurse. Now, run and get my digging stick and bring it to me."

I said, "Mommy . . . you're going to kill this thing? This? Is this what you are going to kill when I get the digging stick?"

She said, "Eh, get the digging stick and bring it to me so I can kill this little thing. Then you can nurse. You can nurse, so go run and get the digging stick."

I jumped up and started to run. I ran and got the digging stick. Mother's younger sister, who was in the village, asked, "Didn't you and your mother go out collecting mongongo nuts? Where is your mother?"

I said, "Mommy's still out there, and she has a little thing with her, a little thing that is lying beside her. She told me to run and get the digging stick to give to her, and she is going to kill that little thing."

My aunt—mother's younger sister—started to run. "Get up! Get up!" she yelled. "Is Chuko crazy? Is she crazy saying she will kill the child? Mother! She must be crazy saying that. Her husband—when he returns, he will shoot and kill us. Hurry! Get up!"

Mommy's younger sister started to run, and took the digging stick from me. When we arrived, she cut the baby's umbilical cord— Kumsa's—and carried him. "You're crazy," she told her sister. "Why did you say you were going to kill this child, a little boy? Why? Do you kill a boy child? If you did, then his father would kill . . . would shoot you with arrows."

Mother said, "Uhn, uhn. Nisa is little and I wanted her to nurse. Don't you see how she is, so small? That's why I said I would kill the baby . . . so that Nisa could nurse."

But her younger sister refused. "Uhn, uhn. It is a little boy. Now leave things as they are. Take him with you and feed him." So they took him back to the village.

I asked Nisa, "If a child is a girl, do they kill it?"

She answered, "People don't kill it. My mother just wanted me to be able to nurse."

〳〳〳〳〳〳 My mind was racing. Nisa had told me of these events before. The first time I heard the story, I didn't believe it. The idea that her mother had involved her in the decision to kill her brother had so disturbed me that I had essentially dismissed Nisa—and her story. I assumed that, as one of her earliest memories, this account had been more fantasy than fact. Moreover, I reasoned that whatever "facts" were involved must have reflected cleverness on her mother's part. What better way to neutralize Nisa's anger and jealousy than to claim that Nisa was the one who had let the baby live? Or perhaps the problem had been my misunderstanding. Back then, mastering the language had still seemed an insurmountable goal (although other stories told at the same interviews had raised no such problems).

Shaken by this story, I left it, and Nisa, behind. I searched out other women and interviewed them. My language skills improved and I started to tape conversations. Months passed, almost a second year. Mel and I made plans to leave. But I had regrets. I had spoken with seven women, but there hadn't been magic with any of them.

I thought again about Nisa, about how clear her language had been, and about how brilliantly—and seriously—she had responded to my questions. I remembered how forthright she had been on matters of sexuality. I recalled how colorful her words had been. If a girl grows up without learning to enjoy sex, she had told me, her mind doesn't develop normally and she goes around eating grass, like a crazy Herero woman who lived in the area. Grown women were vulnerable, too, she claimed: "If a woman doesn't have sex, her thoughts get ruined and she is always angry."

I also remembered that we had had a good time together. In an early conversation about extramarital affairs in the villages, I mentioned that I had heard they were quite common. Nisa thought I said I had seen this with my own eyes. She leaned over, quite animated, and touched me. With a conspiratorial laugh, as if eager for details, she said, "You mean you *saw?*"

After working with the other women, I realized how good the interviews with Nisa had been. Finally I set aside my reservations and asked her for more. During the subsequent fifteen interviews I collected most of the material that appears in *Nisa*. When the story of infanticide came up again—and years later when I returned, again—I accepted it as Nisa's truth.

However, that truth did change in interesting ways in each telling. In the first recorded account, when her mother asks her to get the digging stick, Nisa says, "What are you going to dig?" Her mother answers, "I'm going to dig a hole so I can bury the baby. Then you, Nisa, you can nurse again." Nisa refuses. "My baby brother," she cries. "Mommy, he's my baby brother. Pick him up and carry him back to the village." Her tears and entreaties (and the threat that she might tell her father?) change her mother's mind. "No. If my daughter is crying like this, I'll keep the baby and carry him back with me." The decision is made even before Nisa's aunt, alerted by Nisa's crying, comes running.

In the second recorded account, Nisa greets the baby's birth enthusiastically. "Yea! Yea! My little brother! Some day we will play." Nevertheless, when her mother instructs her to get the digging stick so she can bury the baby so Nisa can nurse, Nisa complies. But she cries all the way back to the village. When her aunt sees her, Nisa says, "Mother is going to take the digging stick and bury the baby. That's very bad. She wouldn't even let me greet him." The aunt runs to the scene and yells at Nisa's mother, mentioning the father's anger and the baby's size and sex. She cuts the umbilical cord and carries the baby back.

The differences in these accounts are significant. In the first recorded telling—as well as in the initial version told to me but not my tape recorder nearly a year earlier—Nisa sees herself as having singlehandedly saved her brother's life. In the second recorded telling, her protest is still strong, although the aunt is the more effective actor. In this latest account, however, Nisa sounds no protest at all. Did this reflect a change in attitude? Had her recent falling out with her younger brother revised her story of his birth?

I asked, "When your mother said, 'Go, get the digging stick, I'm going to kill the baby,' was your heart happy?"

"Yes!" Nisa exclaimed. "And when they took him and carried him back, my heart was miserable. Because I really wanted to nurse."

〰〰〰〰 In traditional times, infanticide was practiced very rarely— in cases of physical disability, of twins, or of dangerously close birth spacing. (The sex of the child did not seem to matter.) The welfare of the family, including the older children, was paramount. The decision was made by the mother right after the birth. Nursing was a critical factor. The !Kung did not have milk from domestic animals or agricultural products to substitute for mother's milk. Bush foods, introduced into children's diets at around six months of age, were important, but nursing provided the essential nutritional balance—and antibodies to infectious agents in the environment—throughout a child's first three years.

Even under optimal circumstances, little more than half of !Kung children lived beyond age fifteen. A child born too soon after the birth of a sibling could seriously jeopardize the health of the older child, and might mean the eventual death of both. Too close a birth spacing also would affect the mother's health: the burden of two young children, both needing to be carried and given maximum attention, would drain her energy. She would be compromised in her most important economic role, as provider of food.

Weaning took place, typically, sometime during the child's third year, soon after a woman realized that she was pregnant again. (Menstrual periods were relatively infrequent events in !Kung women's lives. Frequent nursing inhibited menstruation, and ovulation, for years.) The milk in the woman's breasts was thought to belong to the fetus. Harm would befall the child or the fetus—or both—if the child continued to nurse. For most !Kung children, weaning was swift and difficult.

〰〰〰 Had Nisa been weaned too early? Had Kumsa been born too soon? Had Nisa's mother truly considered killing him? Or did the story have some meaning of its own, apart from the actual circumstances?

I asked, "You said you were small when Kumsa was born. Why? Had people not brought you up well?"

"I had grown very well and stood this tall"—she showed with her hand a child of about three or four—"but mother still wanted me to nurse more. That's why she said she would kill Kumsa."

"Do you think that if your aunt hadn't been in the village your mother would have killed Kumsa?"

"If I hadn't seen my mother's sister, if she hadn't been in the village . . . she would have killed him and we two would have been together. But I did see her sister, she was in the village. That's when she took the digging stick from me. And went to her and carried the baby. And we all returned to the village."

〰〰〰 I asked no more questions about the threatened infanticide. When Nisa spoke again, her thoughts had moved on to her life after Kumsa's birth.

When they took him back to the village, I refused mother. I only liked my older brother. He would carry me, even if we were traveling from one place to another. I'd run for a while, then he would pick me up and carry me on his shoulders. I would run again and he'd pick me up again. If he saw something he wanted to track, he would set me down. He'd sneeeak up on it very slowly, perhaps a duiker, and strike it. I'd run and tell my father, "Big brother struck a duiker. Daddy, big brother has already struck a duiker." Then he'd carry me again and we'd travel on until we stopped to live.

That's how I grew up.

Deep Trances

It was a typical night at my camp. Tuma, my helper, was cooking his meal. A few people had come to visit and were sitting in the near darkness, their forms lit by the flickering light of a tired fire, discussing the day, their low voices blending into one. They would stay for a while, drink the tea with milk and sugar I offered, and taste Tuma's food, which he passed around to his guests before eating any himself. I would give Tuma some of whatever I was eating, as usual, but my usual vegetarian fare was less of a hit with him than with those with greater hunger. Tuma's meals, from my supplies, always included meat.

From the surrounding darkness came the sound of voices, and two men appeared. "Hello, Hwantla," one said softly, and even after fourteen years I knew the voice well. I greeted Kxoma, a friend from years before and a man I much admired. "My husband!" I exclaimed joyously. "I have been looking for you since I arrived."

"My wife," he answered warmly. "I am sorry I was away. I was hunting. Only today I came home. And I brought something for you."

"Koo koo, my husband," I said as a !Kung woman might. "Koo koo, my husband hasn't forgotten his wife." And he handed me a huge piece of meat, the fillet from a kudu he had killed. "Oh, you truly are one who knows how to think about a wife. Look what you have brought. No longer will I have meat hunger."

\KKKKKK This man was wonderful. In addition to a stellar personality, a talent for leadership, and a sharp mind, he had an uncanny ability to work with outsiders and a clear understanding of how to move with the times. Early on, he had seen the advantages of sowing seed and planting crops, even though in some years low rainfall made agriculture a failing venture. He also spoke the languages of the Tswana, the Herero, and the Afrikaners, people who had influence on his daily life. When anthropologists showed up, Kxoma began working for them, and he had worked for Mel and me during our two field trips. He was willing to help smooth out problems caused by our ignorance. And he was congenial and smart.

Once Kxoma and I got to know each other, our relationship was defined as a "joking" relationship, in which easy, informal, and often suggestive banter was the rule. It was determined that in the complex Bushman naming system my name was considered equivalent to his wife's name, and that his name was equivalent to Mel's Bushman name. So he called me "my wife" and I called him "my husband." Joking was as far as this went, with nothing more to the banter than the cleverness of the wit and the subtlety of the innuendo. This good-natured fun was shared by his real wife, who always greeted me as "my co-wife," as I did her. The joking allowed in these relationships was sometimes so humorous that once a pair got going, onlookers would laugh uproariously at the repartee.

Kxoma had grown up in the bush, and he was one of the best hunters in the area. Once, when he was in his forties, he startled a kudu in the bush. He ran right after the fleeing animal, behind it, alongside it, finally managed to spear the kudu, and brought it down.

I first took notice of Kxoma during the second week of my first field trip. We had traveled to one of the southernmost Bushman camps with an anthropologist who was finishing two years of research. After a day of following her around, trying to learn what I could, I heard the strains of a trance dance in the night. I had seen these dances on film and been told about them by others who had attended them, but I had not yet attended one myself.

Impatient with the discussion Mel and the other anthropologist were having, I walked toward the music. I shut off my flashlight far from the group and stumbled toward them in the dark. The dance was going strong when I got there, although the central fire was dim, giving off minimal light. What should I do, where should I sit? Not with the women, in the inner circle around the fire, singing and clapping the undulating songs that helped push healers into an altered state of mind called trance. Nor did I want to get in the way of the outer circle of men, whose leg rattles pounded out syncopated rhythms to the songs, their bare feet raising small clouds of dust as they danced by. Finally I sat in the grass beyond them, an observer to the dance.

The sounds were wild—women's voices weaving over one another in a seamless tapestry of sound, hands clapping complex sets of rhythms, alternating one with another, the group balancing the syncopations without any obvious leader. Competing rhythms were pounded out by the men's feet, and by the dance rattles on their legs.

Sitting apart in the darkness, I felt in awe of the ritual enacted before me, of the power this small group of people harnessed, and of a belief system that bound the community together, easing the hurts and pains of group living, touching upon the fears of sickness and death—participating together for the good of all.

The only person I knew at the dance was Kxoma. I watched him dance around the circle, waving a gemsbok tail, his taut, muscular legs wound in rattles. He went around many times, each time his concentration narrowing, his eyes becoming more focused inward. His singing became less melodic, more repetitive, more self-hypnotizing. Sweat gleamed on his face. Suddenly, close to where I was sitting, he fell to the ground. He didn't crumple, he didn't catch himself partway down. He fell like a tree trunk, straight over, every joint locked in a stiff descent.

What had happened? Kxoma lay face down in the sand where he had fallen. No sound. No movement. And no one seemed to notice. The singing didn't stop. The men didn't stop dancing, but stepped around his body where he lay so still.

I knew a great deal about trance dances, I thought. Of course the dancers went into trance. But wasn't this something else? Kxoma wasn't a young man, perhaps forty years old. He smoked all the time, and like all Bushmen, had a hacking cough. Since his fall he hadn't moved or even moaned. What if he had had a heart attack? His dancing had been extremely strenuous. Dancing one minute, dead the next? Why wasn't anyone helping him?

I turned to another observer and pointed toward Kxoma, my eight-day-old language skills not ready for the job. He said something I couldn't understand. Finally, Mel and the anthropologist approached. I accosted them. "Thank goodness you're here! Look at Kxoma. I think he's had a heart attack."

"No," the anthropologist answered, "he's in trance. Kxoma goes into very deep trances."

Soon two other men, also in trance, took on the task of bringing Kxoma back toward the living. They rubbed his body, trying to retrieve his soul from the spirit world. They laid on hands and rubbed him with their healing sweat. As though ascending from depths of pure blackness, Kxoma came back toward consciousness, pulled up, step by step, by the healers. Soon his chest started to heave and a sound rumbled inside him, like a wild animal working to get free. The sound rose and resonated, finally exploding as a scream: "Kow! Kow! Kow-a-dili! Kow-a dili!" Out to the heavens it went as he tried to focus the turmoil inside him. When he had wrested it into his control, he went around the circle, his healing powers then at their strongest. He stood up, swaying, his legs shaking at each step. Kxoma the healer laid on hands, pulling out sickness from some, preserving good health for others. Kxoma, waving the gemsbok tail as he danced, was considered one of the most powerful healers of all.

〰〰〰〰 When Mel decided to become a novice healer, he asked Kxoma for help. Kxoma willingly agreed to Mel's apprenticeship and took him along to dances at Dobe and in neighboring villages. Kxoma would lead and Mel would follow, pounding his bare feet as Kxoma did, leaning his upper body slightly forward while his legs moved with the rhythms. Around and around they went, sometimes with Kxoma behind, holding Mel's sides, until the music and the smoke from the fire pushed Kxoma into trance. Then Kxoma would leave Mel to dance on his own while he laid on hands, healing those who participated and those who watched. When he returned to Mel, he would tap Mel's waist on both sides to help the healing medicine enter. Sometimes he took Mel's full weight on his own back and dragged him around, Mel's six-foot-two-inch frame draped across Kxoma, not much over five feet tall. These scenes were repeated for several nights.

Once Kxoma gave Mel a drink with purported hallucinogenic properties to hasten the letting go, to help quiet the inner voices of reason. Mel reported that the drink, the repetitive dance steps, the hours of exertion, the pounding that moved up his spine into his head, the sounds of undulating singing, the power of Kxoma in trance, and the aroma and visual pull of the fire indeed took him into a mental realm that was strange and new.

One night there was a dance at a village about three miles away. Mel was eager to go; I was less so. The dances usually went on into the night, sometimes into early morning. Although I was no longer just an observer—by then I sat with the women, clapped out rhythms as best I could, and repeated the simplest melodic phrases—I tired after a few hours. My day's work was difficult: that of an outsider trying to make sense of the people's ways. When I was at a dance, my night's work became more of the same: I was an outsider participating, but not quite fully, in a complex drama that ebbed and flowed throughout the night, and in a subtlety of sound and rhythm that always seemed elusive. After spending many nights at trance dances, I had learned to leave early. I would listen to the receding voices and welcome the quiet in my camp.

This night I suggested that Mel go on ahead. He and Kxoma would be dancing for hours, and since at that time we had two trucks, I could meet them later, perhaps in a couple of hours. After they left I sat by the light of the pressure lamp, enjoying the solitude.

Maybe it was two hours later that I arrived—it wasn't longer. But as soon as my truck stopped near the village, Mel was beside me, very, very agitated. "Where were you? Are you all right? I was so worried. Did anything happen? Thank goodness you came. What took you so long?"

The words tumbled from his mouth, each one nearly blocking the next. His distress was so great that he hardly heard me answer, "I'm fine. What's wrong? I told you I'd come in a few hours."

He paced around in the dark. "Come here, I want to show you something." He led me through the sand and then stopped. In the beam of my flashlight I saw his truck, stuck on a tree stump, the front wheels lifted into the air.

Then he told me what had happened. "I was dancing with Kxoma and it was intense. I entered that place where things appear different and my thoughts went back to my childhood. And Kxoma was like my father. And suddenly I remembered you. Where were you? Why weren't you here? I got scared. I was sure something awful had happened to you. The thought consumed me: 'I have to save her.' So, in a half-frenzy, I ran from the dance, jumped into the truck, and floored the gas pedal. I didn't know where I was going."

He laughed. "I guess I didn't get very far." Looking at the truck, he added, "But I was terrified."

I thought of other apprentices and young healers who experience the heating of their healing energy. They say it's hot, hot to boiling. Then it is as though it is on fire and their insides are exploding. Not yet able to control the energy, they often provide high drama. Wild-eyed, they may take off into the bush. Or they may focus on the fire, throwing coals around, walking into the fire, or putting their hands or heads into the flames. Or they may throw sticks and yell insults at the spirits of the dead, who are thought to sit in the shadows watching the dance.

In this state the untrained healers are capable of doing themselves great harm. Others help them cool down. They lead them back from the bush, pull them out of the fire, redirect their energy back to the dance. Experienced healers rub their bodies and dance with them around the circle, teaching them to restrain the energy so it becomes bearable.

"I guess that's how they feel when they run off into the bush screaming," Mel said, laughing. "So what did I, the White Man, do? I ran off screaming too, but I took the truck so I could go faster." He put his arms around me. "I was really afraid for you. I'm so glad you're all right."

Later he rejoined the trance dance and I joined the women singing. This time I stayed close by. Mel followed Kxoma around the circle, the shock of each step rising to his head as a deep banging, as though shuffling the gray matter around. His tired body eventually slowed down, and his balance wavered. Kxoma wrapped Mel's arms over his shoulders, balancing Mel's weight on his back, dragging him round and round again. Finally, when it seemed Mel could take no more, Kxoma lowered him to the ground, his head facing the fire at a safe distance. Unmoving, he lay there. Grains of sand clung to the sweat on his face, catching the flickering firelight.

The women intensified their singing and clapping and urged me to do the same. "To support your man," they said. Singing as confidently as I could, I stared at Mel stretched out on the sand. His eyes opened, looking glazed, and closed again. Then he began to move, inching slowly toward the fire. What was he doing? Would he get burned? Were they waiting for me to help him? Should I wait for them? I turned my head from one woman to another, trying to let them know I was very concerned. They kept clapping and singing, their eyes riveted ahead. Just as the top of his head touched the edge of the fire, women's hands reached out to push the coals away and put cool sand under his head. He stopped inching forward and lay in a half-sleep for a long time.

Much later, when he "woke" from the trance, he told me he had known what was happening but had felt absolutely no fear. He had entered a distant place, where the sounds and smells around him no longer meant anything. As he floated in this pleasant space, the fire drew him in, leading him where he wanted to be. He vaguely understood what fire was, but it didn't matter.

Kxoma was very proud of Mel's success. Years later he told other visitors that Bushman medicine still resided inside Mel. He always asked when Mel would return so they could go on to the next level.

〰〰〰 Now, with the fresh fillet in hand, I asked Kxoma and his hunting partner to stay for dinner. Tuma, too. The meat made my mouth water. Lean, from the wild, killed by a man I was fond of, and given as a gift, it was the best meat I could get, and I could get it no other way.

It was not the rancid beef sometimes offered for sale from a slaughter site or from what was left when a cow was killed by predators. At the selling area, a leg or other piece of beef would hang from a tree, swarming with flies, the fat turned yellow with age, the smell ever so pungent. Tension would rise in the villages, with people pooling whatever money they had, or with wives yelling at husbands to provide them with meat. The meat, bought and cooked and shared, would be gone before anyone's meat hunger had been satisfied. That satisfaction only came from the wild, when a large animal was killed and people ate and ate and ate.

This night, I pulled out onions and potatoes and cut the meat into chunks to sauté. Top gourmet, by my standards. I set it out on plates, serving "my husband" first. I still liked it best cut into strips and roasted in the coals, as in the "old days," but the others seemed to appreciate my efforts and ate heartily.

Before the two hunters left, I asked Kxoma if I could visit his village to see how he had fared over the years. Would tomorrow be a good time? "Of course, my wife," he said. "Sleep well." And they were gone.

〰〰〰 Kxoma's village was actually an amalgam of separate compounds or camps. The people living there were connected through kinship and marriage, and all considered themselves part of "Kxoma's group."

It was clear, even from a distance, that people here had succeeded in the "modern" mode. Neat, very closely set poles (ones a rooster couldn't get through) encircled the communal living space. Inside were well-built thatched and mud huts and tall storage racks neatly covering dried agricultural harvest and other items that needed to be kept off the ground. A few large melons sat in the shade, to be cooked and eaten when needed. The compound exuded a feeling of abundance, unlike any other I had visited.

Kxoma's wife, another Nisa, was waiting at the gate in the fence to welcome me. "My co-wife," I said. "It's so nice to see you. How have you been?" She returned my greeting.

"Have you been taking good care of my husband?" I asked.

"Eh, my co-wife," she said. "I have been taking good care of him for you."

I congratulated her on the prosperity of her surroundings and offered condolences on the death of her grown daughter. We talked about the illness that had killed the young woman, and about her three children, now in their grandmother's care. Yes, Nisa said, there was still much grief, but life was also quite busy.

Kxoma showed me, with pride, the work his group had been doing: fields still full of melons, stores of millet that had been harvested, corn kernels filling large barrels, for use in the coming months. Kxoma, like the others, took the food the government handed out, but he believed his group would have no trouble making it on their own. His people owned a large herd of goats, and Kxoma had one cow. Everyone worked hard, he said, clearly proud of his accomplishments as village leader.

〰〰〰 I went from compound to compound, most smaller and less elaborate than Kxoma's, asking who lived there, the approximate ages of the children, and other anthropological questions. Then at one of the compounds the people took me to see a sick child.

My heart sank when I saw him. He lay on his side, hardly moving. His eyes were glazed, and flies swarmed around his face, which was contorted and unresponsive. His father said he ate and drank almost nothing. There seemed no doubt that he was slipping toward death.

Seeing him lying there, I remembered another child. My thoughts went back twenty years. It was late in the afternoon when a woman we did not know came to Mel and me, her son in a leather pouch on her back. He was no toddler, an age to be carried this way; he was six, maybe even eight years old. When she took him from the pouch, we saw an emaciated child, thin, with bones protruding, his head large against his body. His eyes were unresponsive. His mother told us he had been sick for days. They had tried to cure him, but had failed. Yes, he had had diarrhea, and for a few days, maybe longer, he hadn't taken anything in his mouth.

Dehydration is one of the greatest killers of children in the third world, especially in hot climates. Often the simplest of medical interventions can save a life: an intravenous drip of an electrolyte solution. We had the solution to save this boy's life, but we did not have the equipment to get it into his veins. Mel tried forcing it into his mouth, but as he was unable to swallow, it poured uselessly down his chin. In desperation, Mel injected the solution into the boy's stomach, knowing that fluids were the only hope. The mother left the child in Mel's care, saying she would come back soon. Mel stayed with the child, giving him more injections, trying all he could. But the boy died, with Mel beside him, during the night.

We were left with so many questions. Why had the boy's mother waited so long? Had she not trusted us enough to bring him sooner? Or was the death of a child such a familiar occurrence that she had given up on him too soon?

Seeing the boy at Kxoma's village set off an internal chain reaction ending in near-panic. Why hadn't his parents asked me to take him to the clinic before? Baitsenke had driven there almost daily, whenever I thought people were in need of medical care. The boy's father, a gentle man, told me he had wanted to take his son to the clinic, but had been afraid because he had no money. "How could I live near the clinic and feed myself and the boy?" Then he added, "Perhaps tomorrow, when the truck goes, I'll take him."

"No," I insisted, "take him now. Tomorrow may be too late. I'll give you enough money. If you agree, pack your things now. Baitsenke will pick you up as soon as he can." The man eagerly agreed. He took the money and was explaining to others as I left.

I trekked the distance back to my camp. Of course, as soon as the news was out, everyone wanted a place in the truck. I rounded up those who had been promised a ride the next day, and, counting the two seats needed for the boy and his father, the truck was filled. Those who did not get seats protested. One man I hardly knew, who had been drinking heavily, argued with me endlessly. "I'm sorry for your disappointment," I said according to local etiquette. "Maybe another day."

I wrote a note for Baitsenke to carry to the health officer in Kangwa.

Dear Kangwa Health Officer,

I'm sorry to bother you on Sunday, but I visited one of the Basarwa villages at Dobe and saw this young boy with very great sickness. I was afraid he might not live until tomorrow. I have given his father money to buy food for himself and his son while he is helped at Kangwa.

Two other people have also come with the truck to see you: a woman with a swollen finger and an older man. The woman was seen last week and was not able to stay at Kangwa to continue her treatment. She isn't doing well, although you helped her considerably. If you can, please also see her today. I can only send the truck from Dobe every few days.

The older man was operated on in Maun, in the area of his stomach, about half a year ago. He stayed away a few months before he returned. It may have been his appendix; I do not know. He says the stitches hurt and are not healing well. If you would, please check out his pain as well.

Thank you for your generosity and your time in helping these people. Again, I am sorry to disturb you on Sunday.

Marjorie Shostak at Dobe

After the truck left, I headed back to Kxoma's village to finish my work. I wanted to ask Kxoma about his history of owning cattle. Since he was one of the most economically successful Bushmen around, I had been surprised to learn he had only one cow. No one other than Nisa had earned the sums of money that Kxoma had working for anthropologists. Of course, that had been years before. But if he hadn't amassed more cattle in the past fourteen years, what hope was there for others who were less enterprising?

Kxoma and I chose a spot where we could talk privately. We had barely begun, though, when I heard, in English, "Hello Marjorie. How are you?" Then, in !Kung, "Greetings, Kxoma." I turned, and there was Royal, the man I had met in Maun weeks before. He had finally given up on the Americans who had heard about him from Richard Lee. They had written asking him to take them to see Bushman trance dancing starting the first week in June. It was now July and they had not come, and he had not heard from them again. So here he was. Did I still want him to work with me?

I was delighted, of course. I had so many questions about the language: about tenses and tones and words that sounded the same but weren't, about words that expressed certain emotions, and about words for various stages of growth and development. Oh yes, this was a person I wanted to work with. But not right then. Right then I wanted to talk to Kxoma about cattle—as personal a question as asking someone about his finances—and I didn't want or need Royal there as translator.

I told Royal I would talk with him later. He nodded, and seemed to be finishing a conversation with Kxoma, but it went on and on. Finally, I politely asked him to leave.

Kxoma and I had just sat down again when a truck stopped outside the compound. An official from the Remote Area Development Organization got out and came to speak to us. We were both exceedingly polite. By the end of this conversation, it was time for me to leave to meet Megan. I walked one last time from Kxoma's village to my camp, gathered up Royal and a few others, and walked to the border.

Megan was waiting—on the other side of the fence, of course—when we arrived. She was traveling with a group of Bushmen who worked with her on the politics of land tenure and self-representation; she had been working with the Bushmen in Namibia for a number of years, one of a group of outsiders helping prepare the people for independence. After greetings, she and I walked a short distance away from the others and sat down face to face, or rather face to fence to face. She seemed somewhat distracted and tense. It was late, she explained, and people were waiting for her at her camp, which was still a few hours' drive away. She could stay with me about an hour.

That hour went quickly. I had so many questions. What might the upcoming elections mean for Bushman communities in Botswana and Namibia? Was there likely to be a military buildup along the border in Namibia? Would the Botswana Defense Force become more involved? Or was it possible that the transition would go smoothly?

Of prime concern to us was whether the new Namibian government would recognize the Bushmen's rights to their ancestral lands. Bushman lands had been lost before. In the 1960s, under the apartheid regime, more than half of !Kung land in Namibia had been handed over to the Herero. More recently, there had been talk of turning their remaining land into a game reserve for tourists. A small number of Bushmen would be allowed to stay in the reserve as long as they reconstructed their "quaint" customs of the past: no cows, goats, gardens, mud huts, clothing, utensils, or anything else associated with "civilization" could be in evidence. The rest of the people would be transported to a distant area that no one else wanted—so dry it could not support hunting and gathering, much less agriculture or pastoralism. In the end, it had taken the superhuman efforts of the anthropologist John Marshall to keep this plan from being implemented. Now, with the reins of power shifting to new hands, the issue was coming up again. Would

Bushman lands be used as political spoils, given as favors to long-time supporters of the now victorious resistance fighters?

And I wanted to know what Megan thought about the current tension at the border. She hadn't seemed hesitant about sending a messenger to me. Perhaps she didn't realize just how determined the Botswana Defense Force was to stop the flow of people across the border. They had every reason to be wary of the political outcome of an election in Namibia. If opposing parties challenged the vote, there might be civil war there. An open border would make it easy to foment trouble in Botswana—and the Bushmen, who had little political influence in either country, could be used as pawns in any struggle for power.

Until the impact of the elections could be assessed, Botswana had to remain on military alert. But closing the border to the Bushmen was a disaster. After the fence was erected in 1966, !Kung families had continued to cross the border at will. In 1974, when the fence was fortified and doubled in height, a stile had been set up near Dobe to facilitate their crossing. Then, without warning, shortly before I arrived, the Botswana government had closed the border in both directions. It caused hardship to the many local families with relatives in both countries.

Megan said there was a misunderstanding between the local Botswana representative, based in Kangwa, and her group. He had been stirring up trouble for them, even though their mission was peaceful. She told me that the Namibian political party most likely to win, SWAPO, intended the Bushmen no harm. Her group, she said, had asked the representative from Kangwa to meet with them at the border on Sunday afternoon. She stood up, ready to leave. "Try to come if you can." she urged. "The meeting should be very interesting. I'm hopeful we'll be able to work things out."

Then she was off. As her truck receded into the distance, I felt unbearably lonely. I had wanted much more from our conversation. I put the letter to Mel back in my pocket. Megan wouldn't be able to mail it after all, she had told me. I'd be home before her mail would go out.

〰〰〰 That night I wrote in my journal:

I visited with Old Tasa today, the matriarch of a huge family. We talked about children, hers and mine, and I almost started to cry. Later I talked with Mel's namesake, Tashay, who has been very sick, perhaps with tuberculosis. I mentioned my own illness and, again, a flood of feelings made my eyes water.

The emotional stream flows underneath. Where does it go when it is not pouring out, and why can I still feel happy? I must be more volatile than I'm aware of. Last night I had a gruesome nightmare about a museum with aquariums displaying dead children, their faces contorted, their skin pressed in places against the glass. I was furious that this was made public, especially to visiting children. I tried to reach management and other organizations to change it. I woke quaking with the images of those children.

As I write, my emotions churn. Megan, the dream, my passion for my children and Mel, and the ever-present low drone of fear for my health mix into a chaotic brew.

Then I sit back and look around me: a fire blazing, donkey bells ringing from all directions, the quarter moon near to setting, the cold air and the warmth of the fire commingling, the clear, fresh air, the hiss of the wood. Most of all, the deep quiet beyond. No cars, motors, planes, radios, television. Nothing to clutter my ears and my heart. No children making demands. No concerns about a husband and his needs. No telephones. Just the clarity of the air, like an ocean to the eyes—restful, wide, and enormously powerful.

I'm going to talk to Kxoma about killing a goat and doing a trance dance. I have strong feelings for him, akin to love. I'll ask Nisa as well, though at times I don't feel anywhere near as positive toward her.

It is obvious in retrospect, but it took time to see it: the longer I lived at Dobe, the more personal became my interest in the medicinal trance dance. There was the drama of the dance, and its fury, and the extremes of exertion displayed by the participants. There was also its spiritual expression, with healers bearing so much in their human effort to affect fate. Being at a dance was as awe-inspiring as being at the ocean or looking out at an expanse of mountains, but in this case the awe and humility were caused by human energy. And, if, with all this, I also held some hope of being physically healed—well, why not?

The next dance was one I negotiated. I had told Kxoma, in some detail, about my illness. "I have heard from others," he responded.

"I would like you to try and heal me, your wife," I said.

"Eh, yes. I am listening," he said politely.

"Because, if this illness does take my life, I would like to know you had tried to help me. If not, would we not both feel, 'If only Kxoma had tried . . . ?' And if it suits you, we'll do as we did in the past. I'll bring a goat for those who participate."

"Eh," he agreed, "but I fear my medicine is no longer strong."

That was all. We arranged to have the feast in his village. Kxoma would be the main healer.

The day of the dance was spent attending to the details. The goat was killed without fanfare, butchered, distributed, cooked in three-legged pots, and handed around. After dark, when the singing started in Kxoma's village, I was sitting among the women, clapping and singing.

But something seemed amiss. Kxoma remained in his hut for a long time, a kerosene lamp burning brightly inside. When he finally came out, he worked himself into a light trance and went around the circle laying on hands. He touched me briefly when it was my turn, as he did the others. I waited for a slight lingering, a word, or a touch that would tell me he would take care of me, as Nisa, a few nights before, had taken care of her niece Nai. His brief healings were only a start. I wanted the hands to stay and attend to me—to seek out evil, to argue with the gods, to gain insight, to wrestle with the fates, to be concerned about my future. After three or four times around the circle he came to me, apologetically, and told me he had finished. "I have little power," he said, "because sickness in my own body is robbing me of strength." Feeling robbed myself, I watched as he left the dimly lit gathering and walked back to his hut.

I felt desolate. And deserted. "My husband can't help me, or maybe he just doesn't care enough to try."

But while I bemoaned Kxoma, it turned out he was not indispensable. Kumsa-the-Hunter had arrived and had already entered a light trance. The women sang, weaving sound like a shawl around him. Kumsa's legs pounded the earth. His eyes, otherworldly, stared toward the fire. Soon his body glistened with sweat. He swayed, turning inward, following a familiar corridor of the spirit. His eyes closed, his neck strained upward, his short melodic phrases became ever shorter. Then he slumped down, unconscious.

Others tried to revive him, but the depth of his trance defied them. Finally they summoned Kxoma. The singing rose strong again as Kxoma came from his hut and entered trance. He dragged Kumsa, still unconscious, toward the fire. He rubbed Kumsa's body with his hands, with the sweat of his brow and underarms. He knelt and pulled Kumsa's back against his chest, rocking him, singing with words that weren't words. The women sang as a unit, their sound thick and comforting. Kumsa lay still. Then a tremor, a shaking, as his body began reuniting with life. The tremor grew from his middle—the center of medicinal power—and flowed down a leg or arm. The force gathered, collecting and discharging until there was no containing it and it broke out, like floodwater overpowering a dam. Just so, the rumbling that had gathered in Kumsa's middle grew to a roar and broke into the healer's shriek, "Kow-a-dili," exploding through his sinuous frame.

Though it was long past midnight, there were many for Kumsa to attend to. I sat beside Nisa and my namesake, clapping the simplest of rhythms, waiting my turn for his brief touch. The quarter moon moved slowly toward the west; it would set long before I left.

"Marjorie," Kxoma said the next day, "there is some talk we need to have." We went to an isolated spot in the sand, a place with some shade.

"I am listening, my husband."

"What are you going to pay me for the curing of the other night?"

"I offered your village a goat. I thought that covered it."

"The goat was small and eaten by so few, it wasn't much help."

"What are you thinking of?"

"Ten pula."

"All right, I agree."

In fact, I didn't agree. It wasn't the money—Kxoma would receive gifts worth far more than ten pula from me. It was his asking, just like everyone else. I believed I had been fair: a goat was considered a present of some largesse. And what of Kxoma's effort? The dance had hardly begun when he had finished.

"So," I thought, "I'm just another outsider to him. Just the white woman to get as much from as possible." These thoughts weren't new. Or unique. These thoughts in various guises are experienced universally by anthropologists. They arise on the first day of fieldwork and endure until the last. I had thought Kxoma was my friend, and I was devastated.

Perhaps what I really needed was to step back. Anthropology's number one tool of the trade, after all, is to interpret situations in their cultural context. I had been gone for fourteen years. I came and went as I pleased. Was I Kxoma's friend? Could he count on me? Also, he was poor, while I made a splash with money and goods and a truck and dispensed favors. Then I expected him to treat me as a peer. Also, weren't all these relationships exploitative? I wanted something from the !Kung, and I was willing to spend huge sums of money to travel to their country to get it. I collected their words, tabulated data, and gained prestige from the fieldwork. How could I expect them not to get what they could from me before I disappeared again?

I told Kxoma to wait while I got the money. The words of "professional wisdom" were strong as I walked to my hut, but they were hard to hold on to. As I handed him ten pula, the hurt slipped out. "I guess my heart isn't finished with this, it still has some talk."

This time it was he who said, "I am listening, my wife."

"I am surprised that you asked for money," I began slowly. "I thought you and I operated differently from the others, that we gave from our hearts. And I have never been stingy with you."

"I hear your distress. I didn't know you felt this way." He paused. "Next time I will make it up to you. I will not forget your words."

I was touched. Kxoma kept the money, but he also listened to me. I had no doubt that whenever I did come back, he would remember.

Past and Present

Kxoma's trance dance had not been enough. I asked Nisa about organizing a drum dance. She proposed that she work on me with Chuko, another female healer, and she graciously offered to charge me less than Chuko's fee of five pula. She would only charge three pula, "because you're helping me so much."

How ironic, I thought. I was buying her a fifty-pula donkey and giving her a sixty-pula trunk, among many other gifts. I was giving her husband forty pula worth of jerry cans and other items. Not to mention the six cows and one horse she already had. And she was taking off two pula because I was "helping her so much." I wasn't surprised; I was even touched to some degree by her offer. But I was also disappointed and hurt.

Later I wrote in my journal:

Our relationship really doesn't (or can't?) transcend my power over her, my ability to transform her life if, as she sees it, I choose to do so. She doesn't understand my loyalty and continues to badger me even though she has me squarely in her corner. I came back mainly for her. Of course I told her this. But how can she believe it? And what do I want from her anyway? What makes the money drop in her lap and makes me smile and say, "Ah, this is what I want"? Is it more talk? Fine. She'll talk as much as I want. But why is she getting only a donkey this time, when earlier she got cows?

Two pula means a lot to her.

That's the practical side, and perhaps it cannot recede into the background. But Nisa just seems to have so little compassion, at least for me. She's smart, and self-promoting, and able to ask for what she needs. But we never get beyond that. When she "sweet-talks" me, it's about how much I have done for her. She likes me because I have rewarded her for our work. She has no idea of what I feel. I don't even think she likes me in any real sense.

I sometimes wonder if I even like her. I'm attracted to her vigor and perseverance and wit. I am also touched by how caring she is toward her brother Dau, and the strong bond of love between her and Bo. During our interviews, she is direct and intimate, responding to my remarks with perspicacity. But her driving edge is hard to take.

〰〰〰 Tuma, my helper, lingered at my fire after the evening meal. He and Bo were engrossed in a story Kumsa-the-Hunter was telling. Pleased to have company, I joined them and offered tea. Kumsa talked in rhythmic phrases, at times repeated by Tuma and Bo. I picked up some words and even a sentence or two, but did not understand enough to remain attentive.

A two-thirds moon shone overhead. The Milky Way was lost in the moonlight. Scorpio and the Southern Cross stood firm, though, flanking the moon like loyal bodyguards.

The sound of beating hooves approached in the dark then receded, men coming back from the latest lion hunt. This time there were no processions, no yodeling. Perhaps it was too late at night. Or perhaps there was just no news. Two lions had been killed so far, but more were still at large. Everyone was afraid. The women had not gone gathering that morning.

I had asked the Tswana leader if I could go on a lion hunt with the men, perhaps following them in the truck. "No," he said, "too noisy." "What if I borrowed a horse and rode with the group?" "No," he said, "too dangerous." I was disappointed but relieved. The only time I had been on a horse out there, years before, it had bolted and tried to get rid of me by running under a low-hanging limb. Would I have climbed on a horse again, to be part of a great male venture? Probably. What could be more exciting than a lion hunt?

I tried to write in my journal. It had been a good day: I had finished the survey of the villages, so my mornings were now more relaxed. Tuma and I had been experimenting with yeast bread, which tasted pretty good.

But my concentration kept straying to the men's conversation. Tuma was telling a story about a woman and sex. I scribbled in my journal, trying to pretend I wasn't listening. Some young woman had refused him, but he got into her blankets anyway. "I sneaked up and entered her blankets," I heard him say. "She got up . . . when she went back into the blankets I took her."

Had he forced her to have sex? The phrase "enter her blankets" usually meant to have sex. But it could also mean that he just shared her blankets, without sex. And "took her" could also mean "touched her."

Then Kumsa was talking again. It seemed to be about his young wife and her refusal to sleep in his compound. Tuma was giving him advice. How I wished I understood the nuances of conversations better and not just words spoken for my benefit!

Later, as Kumsa got ready to leave, he said he wanted me to sew some beads for him to wear around his neck. As he walked away, he called me his woman. His talk with Tuma about his wife must not have gone well.

Time was passing. I had just seven more days in Dobe. Seven days, and perhaps a few more interviews with Nisa. It was difficult to tell how well the interviews were going. Some moments seemed vintage Nisa: her narrative flair was still compelling, and the stories were still priceless. But much of what was said seemed unimportant. Even our most recent interview, about trance medicine and her powers as a healer, had been uninspiring.

The end of my stay was in sight, and I wasn't entirely unhappy about it. I was feeling the strain of people asking for tobacco, favors, batteries, gifts, matches. The honeymoon was over. If I stayed another two months, it would only get harder. I'd react more strongly to the demands. With only a week to go, I was just doing my work as best I could, trying to accept the circumstances as they were. I felt I'd done pretty well so far.

But I knew I would probably be ready to leave when the time came. I wrote in my journal: "There is no magic cure for me here—although the environment is completely soothing. Going home does not mean I'll be sick again any more than staying here could ensure my being well. I'm also aware that if I do get sick again, I may not come back—ever. So I'm filling up as best I can."

I had arranged to conduct two "seminars," one with a group of men, the other with women. Some questions that interested me: What did they think about the hunting and gathering way of life? What did they want their children to know about traditional ways? Did they feel nostalgia? Or was it just "good riddance"?

When the men filed into the mud hut that morning, they were in good humor: hot tea with milk and sugar had already been served, and I had promised generous pay and a meal at the end of the meeting. They were six men I had known for twenty years, including Kxoma, Kumsa-the-Hunter, and Bo. Royal was our translator.

I began in English, speaking to Royal. "Can we start with . . . do they think . . . I don't really know how to do this . . . and who starts first . . . but maybe we should try to let everyone have a turn."

"We'll start with you?" Royal asked Kxoma, the most diplomatic of the group.

"Let Kumsa start," Kxoma suggested.

"The first question is," I said, still addressing Royal, "do they think things are better now than before, when they were living more in the bush?"

Royal spoke in !Kung: "She asked me to ask you . . . Wait, who is going to begin?"

"He is," came a few voices, using a term of respect to refer to Kumsa, the most traditional of the men.

Royal said, "Life today . . . is it good? Or that of the past, when you lived in the heart of the bush and the water pans, was that much better? She's asking which is better."

Kumsa-the-Hunter answered slowly, gathering his thoughts. "That of the past . . . that was wonderful! It was very good. Life in the bush . . . we worked there, doing all things. I mean while we were living in the heart of the bush. We lived there just very, very well. But life today, right here where we all are now, when I look at it . . . its livelihood for us is small."

Nisa's husband Bo disagreed. "Life in the past, living in the bush, it was terrible! There was no one to help you. Life got better once the others came here, giving us a small cow. We'd get food and drink milk. Today, life is very good!"

Kumsa responded, "Oh . . . don't talk like that. I refuse what you are saying."

One by one the others expressed their opinions. The third speaker, also a skilled hunter, agreed with Bo: "At first, when we lived in the bush, when we still worked the work of the bush, we were exhausted! Today, we can rest just a little. In the past, we'd have to think where we were going to go. 'I'm going to the bush,' we'd say, and walk and walk, and when we returned to the village we wouldn't have eaten anything.

That's why I agree that the life of the past was terrible. And things of today are better."

The fourth speaker was Debe, the youngest of the group, the husband of Nisa's niece Nai. His son herded cows for Nisa and for a wealthy Herero family. "Me, as I am here, I still haven't seen anything good in today's life. In the past, when people lived in the bush, they would hunt animals and eat and stay in the bush. And me, I still haven't seen what's good today. Not for myself."

Kumsa asked, "What about the cows you herd?"

"I don't own any cows," Debe answered. "The cows are other people's cows. I don't have even one. And I don't see a good life. A good life was the past. I'd like the truck to take us to the bush and people will hunt animals and we'll eat."

Tashay, a respected elder (and my husband's namesake), spoke next. "My thoughts about all this? Our fathers gave birth to us and fed us food of the bush and gave us *do*, and *gwea*,* and brought us up to be as we are today. And I would still like to be there. Because I, too, have not seen anything good for me here. I wish I were still there."

His voice got louder. "These people here, they talk about cows. Cows are the present. But I have no cows. Long ago, we had no cows, yet we had a good life. Our fathers gave us meat and brought us up as we are today."

Tashay said the Bushmen were given cows on loan—herding, grazing, and milking them for other people. "But it isn't your cow, it's someone else's. The person with his own cows sees a good life." But how could a Bushman get the money to buy cows? Tashay himself had worked for an anthropologist and had bought many cows, but all but one had died. His younger brother had bought one, also after working for an anthropologist. "And that white person, Marjorie here, she gave Bo cows. He bought cows and has many!"

Kxoma, the most articulate of the men, spoke next, the "sixthma," as he called himself, using the English word "sixth" with a !Kung modifier.

Me, I've been listening to what the others have been saying. The work of the bush, where we were living, that work was painful. That life, the

* *Do:* an abundant edible root. *Gwea:* a green vegetable of which both leaves and roots are eaten.

others say that their fathers brought them up. That part I know, and it was very good. Because they had no way to feed us if they sat in one place. They would barely get settled in one place before they were off again to the bush, because if they didn't get up and bring back meat, we'd die.

Now, today, with the black people that have come and worked with us, we are able to see a life of our own. We have a life now, and if one day the government chooses to help us, and gives us seeds to plant fields, then we can rest a little. It's not like the other way, where you sleep here one night and the next night somewhere else and the next somewhere else. That's a bad livelihood. And today, where we live now, it is a new way.

And that's why we're saying that the other way is a way that kills. You wouldn't know where you were going to sleep, and in the morning you'd wake up and you'd carry all your belongings on your shoulders. If you went off to hunt animals in Kangwa area, then you'd carry the meat on your body. Who says that was good?

All the men laughed at his question. One of them made a gagging sound. Kxoma went on:

It hurt! Today, I pack everything on a donkey. Long ago, people carried things on their shoulders. Where is the good in that? I don't see the good in the things that these others say were good. It wasn't good, to me. It was terrible! Today, I live where it is wonderful!

For someone who had cows, Kxoma said, it was really the good life, milking and drinking. For those without cows, he conceded, life was still not good.

All the men took care of cows. Bo and Nisa had six cows. Kxoma had one. Two of the men owned one or two and took care of others for Hereros. Kumsa owned two and cared for them himself. He would not take on any owned by Hereros. "I refuse the Herero," he said. "They've asked and asked, but I refuse them."

Those who herded for Hereros were not happy about the arrangements. Although the Bushmen drank milk from these cows, one of the men said, "What you own is yours. It's your meat, it's your food. If it's not yours, if it belongs to someone else and you just drink the milk, they can sell the animal and give you nothing. Because they do not pay us." Although he had been herding cows for many, many years, he complained, he had received only one calf, and that had been long, long ago.

Royal was amazed. Where he came from, he said, the Herero gave herders a calf at first, and then another calf every few rainy seasons. If the animal died, the meat was shared equally by the herder and the owner.

Here, the others contended, the Herero took advantage of them, paying Bushmen less than they paid others. "Except for Kxoma, whom they fear." The men believed fair payment for their services would be a blanket or some money. After a year or two they should be given a cow or a calf. Drinking milk from the cows was good, of course, but there should be more: "Just drinking milk doesn't give you a life."

I asked again about the past. What did they want their children to know about the past? Had it been hard and good? Or hard and bad?

One of the elders reminisced: "We would move from one place to another and eat *gwea* and *do* and eat *sha** and all different foods and they would hunt and kill animals and we'd eat."

"Was that good?" I asked. "Do you agree with Kxoma that the work was too much? That you slept in too many places?"

"Mama," he said, "it was wonderful if you lived around here. We made a very good living. But after the black people came here, it was no longer good."

He added, "Today, it is again possible to make a good living. But the past is gone. A whole new way of life has begun. That's why I feel we need the help of others, to help us buy cows and donkeys and goats. But today we end up eating only mealie meal. There's no sugar, no salt, and no milk. Mealie meal, when you eat it, makes you want meat. But the men of today are lazy, they don't hunt. That's why life today is terrible."

This discussion of life in the bush must have been strange to Royal, a !Kung man who had spent his childhood in school, learning to speak the languages of the Herero, Tswana, and "Europeans," as English-speakers were commonly called. He aspired to become a schoolteacher, and was likely to become one of the most influential men in the "new life." The "old life," however, he did not know as these six men did.

* *Sha:* an abundant root, one of the major plant foods in the !Kung diet.

And he probably carried a prejudice against it, as did the Herero and Tswana.

The next time he rephrased my question, he added flourishes of his own: "You've all heard this man speak. He said that, long ago, the things people did were very difficult. They'd kill a gemsbok near Kangwa and carry it on their shoulders, then stop and sleep somewhere. In the morning, they'd get up from there and pack their things and carry it all day until again, they'd stop to sleep. This elder has said that even carrying things like that, the life was good, because your fathers took care of you and you lived well. This other elder says it was not good. Which one do you agree with?"

Kumsa spoke. "I agree with the elder who says it was good."

Royal clarified: "You agree with him, and say that the past was good. And gathering food and living in the bush, where one day you sleep here, and another here, and another here . . . you say that was good?"

"Yes," Kumsa said without hesitation.

Royal sounded almost incredulous. "With all that carrying?"

"Yes."

"Where does the good come from?"

Again, Kumsa didn't hesitate. "We lived well. We ate *chon* and *klaru* and *nin** and all the different foods the adults would find. We'd live and eat and eat until we finished the food in an area. Then others would go looking for game elsewhere and see some. Then we'd travel to another area, far from there, where water was. And animals would be killed there."

The day after the men's seminar we were supposed to have the women's seminar, but Royal didn't show up. I fed the women and sent them home, then did a very satisfying two-hour interview with Nisa.

At last things about her life had started to fall into place in the interviews—her early contact with the outside world, and her experience with lovers compared to the experience of other women. She was so candid. The more I claimed I didn't understand and the more I asked to review a topic, the more frustrated she got. Then she dispensed with subtleties and hit the target right on. It was the best interview yet.

Then I brought up the drum dance. There hadn't been any "sponta-

* *Chon*: a grasslike plant with a small edible root. *Klaru*: an edible bulb. *Nin*: berries that are plentiful in summer and fall.

neous" dances since the second night, when Nisa had laid hands on me, and I didn't want to leave it at that. When I said this to Nisa, she repeated her offer to charge me only "three pula, because you are so good to me." I mumbled a minimal "Eh-hey."

I was trying to figure out how much to pay and to whom. I would have to negotiate separately with the other healer and the drummer. As for the singers, perhaps I'd sign up about eight of them. Everyone else would be welcome, but not for pay.

But I was afraid that, whatever I did, there'd be misunderstandings and hard feelings. I really didn't want to kill another animal. I kept hoping the participants would give the dance freely—and then I'd gladly give them triple what they would have been paid, in clothes, beads, cloth, food, shoes, items from my camp, and even money.

〰〰〰 Kxoma had asked me for a favor, actually a few favors. His dream, he had said, was to move his group to a new living site far from Dobe. In this unsettled, very beautiful area, he hoped they would dig a well, keep their goats and other animals, and start gardens. I knew a venture like this would take great determination, as well as multiple permissions and years of paperwork. Kxoma asked if I would take him to Kangwa and speak to the headman on his behalf. Then he asked if I would drive him and some others to see the place, almost two hours away. Most in his group had never been to the site. Finally, he asked, once I had visited and had helped him get permission, would I try to raise money to dig the well?

Of course, I said I would help as best I could. In fact I loved the idea of getting away from camp again and being in the bush—especially since Kxoma's dream site was in the opposite direction from where the lions were.

So the next day we piled into the truck, ten people from Kxoma's compound and I, for the trip to Kxoma's dreamland. Nisa did not go along; she said she needed to stay in Dobe to take care of her older brother.

We passed two trucks on the way, and two more passed by after we turned off the road to camp. Heavy traffic compared with the old days. Nevertheless, we saw plenty of wildlife on our way. First there were two puff adders in the road. We stopped the truck before we reached them, and everyone climbed out to look. One was huge, perhaps three feet long and thick in the middle. The other, resting beside it in the cool sand, was about a fourth its size. Jokes abounded because the huge one was female, the small one male. Then the men killed them, as they would any snake.

Riding on, we saw a large pack of wild dogs on the road, standing like statues, noble of bearing with exquisite lines and a sheen on spotted fur. The late afternoon light dappled them, contouring their long legs and large ears. These were dangerous animals: we stopped the truck, and the men readied their bows and arrows. Then the chase was on, the pack running, the truck following. Kxoma shot and missed. Another man shot and struck, but the dog ran off into the bush with the arrow, to die slowly of the poison.

We stopped about an hour and a half from Dobe and made camp under a spreading morula nut tree. It didn't feel as far from "civilization" as our first bush trip, but there weren't likely to be any lion tracks around, either.

After dark we all nestled around a huge fire. Kxoma and his wife talked quietly. I watched the moon rise.

It was good to be away from Dobe. I looked forward to the next day—maybe I'd feel as wonderful as I had during the first bush trip! Yet I was acutely aware of time. This was Friday night. I would leave in less than a week. In ten days I would be back with my family. Even this trip to the bush was rushed; we had to get back for Sunday's meeting with Megan and the Botswana government representative at the border. Monday Royal would leave, and before then I needed his help with the women's forum.

Kxoma planned to show me a cave in the hills the next morning. This time I would carry the snakebite anti-venom with me. I had read the instructions that came with the serum and was worried. They listed so many different poisonous snakes, and you had to know what bit you to know which anti-venom to use!

It was almost pleasing, in an odd way, to be scared, really scared, of something other than cancer, to admit that something outside my body could be as dangerous as the enemy inside it. Oh, how I hated the fear that had become my constant companion! How I hated knowing that my body had been transformed forever. How I hated the loss of my innocent belief that if I exercised and ate right my body would respond with health. And how could I ever accept a cosmic order that allowed me, a nursing mother, to foster cancer even as I enacted one of the most basic capacities of my female body?

I wrote in my journal:

Fear comes and goes, but when it goes it hides in the vulnerable nooks and crannies. Sometimes it is more, sometimes less, present, but it is never gone. It's like a rushing stream near my house, at first so loud that it obscures all other sound. With time, I no longer notice it. Until some trivial event flings open the windows and the roar is like a tidal wave, threatening my sanity and peace. Live there long enough, others say, and listening and not listening become the same.

I am not at that stage. When my fear is flung wide open, it deafens me. And though I try hard to keep it quiet, I know beyond doubt that it has been screaming all along. It's like this pain I have on the left side of my chest, which has been talking to me for days.

I am frightened. Fear fills my chest, and my heart pumps fast. There is a fork in the road ahead—one path leads to disease progression, the other to health. Which path is this pain on? If I have to choose death, I'd rather die from a puff adder's bite than self-destruct from within.

᚛᚛᚛᚛᚛ I woke before dawn and tossed about, unable to go back to sleep. Thinking, thinking, thinking. It was wonderfully still. A light flashed in the sky, yet the stars were out. Some distant cosmic event?

People stirred in their sleep, or snored. Two men talked quietly. Like me, they "txhudi"—sat hugging the fire—absorbing its warmth, blankets shielding their backs from the cool air.

Thinking. About the horrors of the past year. And about this trip: What was I going to do with it? Nisa's story had already been published. Yet the recent interviews were shedding new light on it. She had given me slightly different interpretations of some of what was in print. She now claimed that Besa had never married her, though in her earlier account the dissolution of their relationship had been described as a true union, a marriage. And she now said she had given birth three, not four, times. The births had been unclear in the original tapes, so that was not too surprising.

I was also realizing that in *Nisa* I had somewhat minimized her contact with outsiders. After first encountering the Herero in her teenage years, she had never again lived a traditional hunter-gatherer life. Although she always relied heavily on bush foods, the herding life of the Herero was never far away. Also, her grandfather had a gun, which led to a killing and retaliation within the group—all in the bush setting. It seemed that as early as the 1930s, when only a few Herero lived in the region, they lent guns to the Bushmen in exchange for meat. So, even in Nisa's grandfather's generation the outside world was not unknown.

Kxoma was in the lead as we left camp. He and three other men talked in relaxed tones, not in the cautious whispers of hunters seeking prey. Even though this was considered oryx country, they had not brought along their dogs—a decision they lamented at great length—so they had little expectation of making a kill.

After about an hour we reached the site. It was indistinguishable, to my eye, from the land we had just traversed: plentiful vegetation, open vistas, and virgin bushland. Kxoma pointed out the finer distinctions of the terrain: where the well would be dug, how the villages would be laid out, and the best places for gardens and corrals.

Our trek back to camp included a two-hour detour while the men tried to find a porcupine. Had I not actually witnessed a successful hunt years before, I would have thought it folly—and a colossal waste of energy—for humans to try to outwit a porcupine snug in its subterranean home. As on our earlier trip to the bush, the men found fresh urine in the sand at the entrance to the burrow. As before, they dug a hole in the mound, found nothing, and dug another hole.

At last they gave up—after digging a hole six feet deep—and we were off again. The men stopped beside dry vines or stalks and dug into the sand, but found few succulent roots or bulbs. Most had already been eaten by the porcupine or by mice. The little they did find, they gave to me to carry. After all, I was a woman. (An honor I loved, despite my amusement.)

Back at camp, one of the men killed a puff adder, which had hissed at him as he walked past. I made sure I knew where I had put the snakebite kit.

The men sat around camp, working on new quivers. They had cut pieces from the roots of a tree. They loosened the outer bark of each two-foot piece from its woody core, leaving intact a sturdy hollow tube—perfect in shape and size to hold arrows. The bottom was sealed with animal hide, secured by additional strips of hide banded around the tube. The top would be fitted with a removable cover. Arrows would eventually be inserted, a bow would be added, perhaps even fire sticks, and the entire unit might be used for hunting. More likely it would be sold in the crafts market.

Soon the women returned with their gatherings: pounds of sweet roots and bean pods. After a brief rest, they went off to collect more.

Kxoma took me to see the promised cave. It was huge and round and deep, its gaping blackness descending into the earth, frightening, mysterious. He said he had once gone down by rope with some anthropologists and they had been scared.

On the walk back to camp, Kxoma seemed happy. He told me he loved this area, and he kept showing me things he thought beautiful. "Marjorie, look at that rock ledge." "See that lichen?" "Those are wonderful trees."

〰〰〰 Back at camp I had a brainstorm: Why not do extensive interviews with a man, as I had done with women? There wasn't much time, but if I started now, perhaps I could collect enough information to sketch a life story. Perhaps I could raise money for the project and return. Perhaps there was even a sequel to *Nisa* in it—"The Life and Words of a !Kung Man."

And why shouldn't the man be Kxoma? He was articulate, he had a compelling personality, he had succeeded in bridging the past and the present, and he was a man of vision. The little I knew of his story was intriguing. He lived in the bush with his family. Then his father was killed by a lion. His mother remarried, and they moved from Namibia to Botswana, settling near cattle-keeping people.

"Kxoma," I suggested. "Let's talk into the tape recorder. You can send a message home to my son Adam, your namesake, and then I have some questions for you."

His statement to Adam was wonderful: "My little-name, I greet you and wish to see you. Tell your parents to bring you here so I can know you. I will take you with me and show you everything about our life. I will teach you to set traps, and we will learn the tracks of the animals. I am making a special present just for you that your mother will bring to you. I greet you, my namesake, and hope to see you some day."

But when we talked about his life, it was difficult. No matter what questions I asked, or how often I asked for more detail, he never elaborated on anything. The "interview" lasted a disappointing forty-five minutes. I was relieved when it was over.

〰〰〰 That night I sat in the truck with my flashlight on, writing in my journal. Outside, people talked quietly around the fire.

What a strange day it had been, so muted compared with the trip of two weeks earlier, when my heart had soared passionately in the wild bush country. Today had felt somewhat routine, especially when I waited for the men during the porcupine hunt. I had been glad the walk had not been too long. There had also been moments of great joy, though. It was the land that moved me—hills stretching upward, places thick with trees, sand collapsing underfoot from hidden mouse holes, bird sounds, and the comfort of immense quiet.

We would go back to Dobe in the morning, and the work I had yet to do was on my mind. This time, being in the bush felt like a holding pattern.

Until I looked around me. The light of the moon, not yet full, was magical. I could see a hill rising in the distance, shadowy, like the eerie gray the world takes on during an eclipse of the sun. A light breeze was blowing. All else was still. A lone cicada broke the silence and was answered by another. Then all was quiet again.

I would miss the land. That part of the honeymoon was not yet over: I was still in love. I especially loved this black and gray world created by the moon and its dark blue moon shadows.

Soldiers and Spies

Royal was at Dobe waiting for us. "I'm sorry I wasn't here for the seminar the other day," he said. "My aunt was sick at Kangwa and I had to visit her."

"Right, tell me another," I thought, marveling at the universality of human excuses. But I said, "Well, we still have time. Why don't we do it now?"

The women's seminar that followed—with six women, Royal, and me—was disappointing. One woman laughed and disrupted the conversation at every turn, apparently embarrassed at the topics we discussed and the candor of other women's responses. I wondered if the discussion would have been better if Nisa had participated. She had refused, saying, "I don't want to talk in a group. Just to you . . . alone!"

As a group, the women were even less sympathetic about the past than the men had been. Unanimously, they judged the present far superior.

At one point during the seminar, we heard a truck approaching the camp. A few minutes later a white Land Rover sped past. It didn't stop or even slow down.

It was time for the meeting at the border with Megan and the government representative from Kangwa. Many of the villagers, including Royal and Kxoma, climbed into the truck with me. I had promised that we would stop for firewood on the way back.

I hoped the meeting would resolve the differences between Megan's group and the Botswana government representative. Her work was important for the future of the !Kung in Namibia. The soon-to-be-elected Namibian government, it was understood, would be more likely to recognize Bushmen's rights to their traditional lands if the people had "proof" of residence. This meant tending domesticated animals and having a borehole for water. Megan and others in the !Kung San Foundation were helping the Bushmen reach this goal.

197

First, they encouraged the creation of a political organization to represent the people. Second, with money raised from outside sources, they relocated Bushmen living in "squatter" conditions to areas, or homelands, where their ancestors had lived. The people then organized villages on this old turf, dug boreholes, and brought in animals. About thirty of these settlements had already been established. As I saw it, Megan and her colleagues were heroes, helping to save a people and a culture that might otherwise be lost in a post-election land grab.

The one-mile track to the border always lifted my spirits. Usually it was just getting away from camp and watching the land turn from overgrazed to not grazed at all. Sometimes it was the peace the wind brought blowing my hair, or the cessation of demands on me, or the way the light hit patches of tall grass. It was also the way my most memorable trips to the bush had always begun.

And memorable this trip would also be. As our high-spirited group turned onto the last stretch of grassland before the border, I stopped the truck abruptly. In the middle of the open field, a few hundred yards from the road, stood a white Land Rover. Two white men I had never seen before and a Bushman I didn't know stood nearby, surrounded by a fully armed group of Botswana Defense Force militia.

Soldiers escorted the two white men toward us. One was just a boy, a teenager. "Are you Marjorie?" the older man asked. He looked terrified. He said his name was David, and the younger man was his son. "I brought a letter for you from Maun."

The letter was from Mel, the first news from him since I left Maun. I eyed it quickly. Everything at home was fine. Then I looked back at David.

"We've been looking for a Bushman named Royal," he said. "We got his name from Richard Lee, the anthropologist. He was supposed to meet us in Maun and take us to some Bushman villages."

"Royal is here, in the truck," I said. Royal raised his arm to identify himself. "But what is all this about?"

"It seems we crossed the border by mistake," David explained. When he and his son couldn't find Royal in Maun, they had rented a truck, located Kangwa on the map, and driven there. No one they met spoke English, so they just kept saying Royal's name. The Bushman now with them had seemed to understand; he had joined them in the truck to show them the way.

David looked toward the soldiers. "I told them all this, but they don't believe me."

"What do you mean, you crossed the border?" I asked.

"We thought the Bushman was taking us to Royal. We didn't know where we were. We came to a big fence, and parked the truck. We thought it was a game fence. We crossed it and started walking on the other side. Then these soldiers came out of nowhere, pointing guns at us." He looked at me pleadingly. "They know you—please help us. They think we're spies."

"That's enough," an officer interrupted him. "Take them back to the field." He turned to me, his voice stern. "Where are you going?"

I spoke carefully. "I understood there was to be a meeting at the border this afternoon. The representative from Kangwa and Megan Biesele, who works with the Bushmen in Namibia, were supposed to be there. I was invited to attend and had received permission from the BDF."

"Going to a meeting," he said suspiciously. "Then what are all these people doing in the truck?"

"The meeting was about the closing of the border. It's affecting the Bushmen's lives. They also wanted to attend." I paused, then added, "Is there a problem?"

"We'll see about that. Stay where you are," he commanded as he walked off toward the others.

We in the truck remained in stunned silence. The father had been taken somewhere out of our view. His teenaged son, alone, was being worked over by one of the soldiers. Beside every tree stood more soldiers in camouflage uniforms, ammunition belts crisscrossing their chests and backs, rifles at the ready.

We heard shouts across the field. "So, you didn't know it was a border?" Then, louder, "Do you expect us to believe that bullshit? You think we're fools?" The soldier pushed the boy's shoulders, forcing him backward, then grabbed between his legs. "Don't you have the balls to tell the truth? Do you even *have* balls? Why did you cross the border? What were you doing in Namibia?"

"Please," the boy begged. "It's the truth. We didn't know it was the border. It just looked like a fence. We were looking for Royal."

The soldier screamed, "The truth! The truth!" He slapped the boy's face, then pushed him backward again.

I turned away, unable to watch. Would they kill me for being a witness? What if they killed the boy? What if his father was already dead?

A soldier came to the truck window. "Drive ahead and turn around at the border. I'll walk ahead of you. Follow me. Don't go anywhere else."

I hoped Megan would help straighten things out. But at the border there was no Megan, no Kangwa representative, and no crowd of people waiting for a meeting. There was only a parked truck on the Namibian side with two Afrikaner men standing beside it, watching our approach.

I turned the truck around and stopped, as ordered. Suddenly another officer appeared at my window. "You should be ashamed of yourself!" he shouted. "Ashamed!" He slammed the side of the window frame.

"I have done nothing wrong," I countered, afraid but trying not to show it. "I was told there would be a meeting, and I had permission to attend."

The officer repeated the questions I had already answered. "What are these people doing in your truck?" "Why have you come to the border just now?" His manner was near the edge of violence. To him, it seemed, I was a conspirator. "You're taking these Bushmen to infiltrate the Namibian elections." "The father and son are part of it." "You're trying to disrupt Namibia. Maybe even Botswana." "What you're doing is wrong. Wrong!"

"Hey," one of the Afrikaners called from the other side of the fence. "What's going on? If this is about the closing of the border, it's downright disgusting."

All eyes turned to the heavyset man with a thick Afrikaans accent, who seemed not at all intimidated by the military display or the volatile emotions on the Botswana side of the fence. He walked closer, so undaunted and loose-tongued that I assumed he had been drinking. "You people in Botswana—you don't care a whit about the fate of the Bushmen, or the hardships you've caused them by closing the border."

"Bullshit!" the officer yelled. "You white people think you know everything. Why should you care about the Bushmen? You know nothing about them!"

"We care because their welfare is our job, just like yours," the man answered. As he and his companion walked back toward their truck, we heard, "Imagine their ignorance, closing the border on these people."

"Okay," the officer barked at me. "Turn back onto the road you came from. Follow me." Another truck joined us. I was relieved to see the father and son inside. In convoy, we drove to an abandoned Bushman village.

"Get out, all of you," the officer ordered.

I stepped slowly from the protection of the truck. Royal, Kxoma, and the others climbed out and stood near me. David, his son, and their Bushman companion were standing a short distance away. With soldiers watching our every move, I didn't dare speak to them.

Around us were the skeletal frames of half a dozen huts, the thatch removed to be reused in new residences. On all sides of the village, soldiers were staked out with guns in hand, their rounds of ammunition gleaming in the late afternoon light.

The questions were now flying hot and heavy at the father, who said he was a doctor from California, and his son. Their story did sound pretty far-fetched, even to me: they had left Maun without anyone who could translate for them; they had picked up a Bushman at Kangwa without communicating more than the word "Royal"; they had driven straight through my camp without stopping to ask questions, even though they were supposedly looking for me to deliver my letter; they had parked at the border and walked to the other side.

Assuming all this was true, the two men had taken risks that were stupid, as well as disrespectful to the country they were visiting. But the Bushman they had hired! Where could his thoughts have flown to? He had to have known the border was closed. Had he supposed the three of them would cross into Namibia and walk the thirty miles to the nearest !Kung camp? With no food, blankets, or camping gear? When, during whispered conversations, I was able to ask the others, "Is this man a dimwit?" and "Why didn't he bring them to my camp?" they answered, "Good questions . . . who knows?"

The fierce officer turned back to me. "You say someone gave you permission to attend a meeting. What was his name?"

His name? I drew a blank. When the soldiers visited my camp, I seldom asked questions, especially not questions as provoking as someone's name. And even if I had heard his name, given my unfamiliarity with the language, I wouldn't have remembered it unless I had also seen it written down. No, there was no way I could know it. Nor could I have picked the man out of a lineup. The brief conversation had seemed so ordinary at the time. "It was one of the soldiers who stopped at my camp," I said weakly.

"Which one?" the officer demanded. "What did he look like?"

Oh, this was bad. This was trouble. I had no idea. They would never believe me.

"The one with the narrow sunglasses," Royal spoke out in English. "That's who it was." Royal had been there. He remembered. I was rescued.

The officer asked Royal many questions in Setswana. Finally he turned to me and announced, "Your story and Royal's story are not the same. He says you were going for firewood. You said you were going to meet Megan Biesele."

"Yes, both are true," I responded, very carefully. "We were going to see Megan first. We were going to get firewood on our way back."

He spoke to Royal again, then turned to the others who had come with me. "How many of you were going to see Megan? Raise your hands."

Stillness fell over the men. Then, slowly, bravely, Kxoma raised his hand. Another hand went up, a man from Kxoma's village who followed his lead. Then a third man raised his hand. The officer made a show of writing down the men's names. Royal helped him spell out the clicks.

Just then a more senior officer arrived. I recognized him as the one who had visited my camp on my first morning at Dobe, the one whose fiancée worked for Dick and Verna. He nodded to me. His face was set hard, the professional soldier at his job. He spoke with the fierce one in Setswana, then came over to me. "Marjorie, I don't like this at all. You could be in very big trouble."

"I know." My legs were shaking. "But I've done nothing wrong."

"I'm not fully convinced. This is very serious. The soldier who gave you permission to go to the border was wrong."

Ah, I thought, at least they now believed I had had permission. Thanks to Royal.

"I don't want you on this road again," he added. "If you drive on this road, it will be considered an act of hostility and action will be taken against you. I will not be able to guarantee your safety."

"I have no need to be on this road again. I plan to leave later this week."

"Not even for firewood. You'll have to find it elsewhere."

"I will not come this way again. You have my word."

"What will you be doing until you leave?"

"I'll be at Dobe, and Kangwa."

"Okay. You are free to go. Don't forget how close you've come."

He turned to the father and son. "You two—you are lucky you are not dead, that we didn't shoot you. You are going to jail."

"Jail?" the father asked. "For how long?"

"Two weeks."

"Can I contact a lawyer?"

"You may contact no one."

"What about the American Embassy?"

"Isn't that the one encouraging the Bushmen to cross the border illegally?"

"What about my son? I'm responsible for this mess, not him. Put me in jail, but don't punish him." He looked in my direction. "Let him stay at Marjorie's camp. He won't go anywhere. Please, he's just a kid."

"No, you both go to jail."

"My other son is expecting me in Maun in the next few days. He'll start looking for me. May I contact him?"

"No one."

I was free to leave, yet these two seemed so pitiful, caught in a life-threatening mistake. "Get out of here while you can," I told myself, "before the soldiers change their minds." But I couldn't move. "Maybe the man is lying," I thought. "Maybe it wasn't just a mistake. Surely he couldn't have been that stupid." My mind was racing. But I still couldn't move.

Finally I turned to the senior officer and said, "I am grateful for your understanding, and I can see how problematic all this must appear. As I have stated, the first time I saw these two men was this afternoon. Yet, with your permission, I'd like to say a few words in their favor."

The officer didn't stop me. I told him that their story about Royal rang true. I knew Royal had been expecting some Americans, who had heard of him from an anthropologist named Richard Lee. When they were a month late in arriving, Royal had come to work for me.

"These men made many serious mistakes," I said, "but I think they did so innocently. They didn't seem to know where they were, or what they were doing. But the sensitivity at the border is new. I can see no reason, other than faulty judgment, for them to have crossed it."

I was shaking. David gave me a look of deep gratitude. But at what cost? The officer had already warned me how close to calamity I had come.

The officer didn't respond. There was a pause, then he told us to leave. As I climbed into the truck, I tried one last time. "If it helps," I offered, "I can take a note to this man's son when I get to Maun, to let him know about the delay."

The officer spoke without looking at me. "No need. I'll take them to my superior. They will be questioned, they will stay in jail one, at most two nights, and then they will be free to go."

Something—the softer tone of his voice, the easing of his posture—suggested that the Americans would, after all, be all right. I couldn't help wondering: had my words made the difference?

Back at Dobe, Kxoma and Royal and the others sat around my camp, talking it through. They said they were proud of me. "You didn't shake, you spoke well, and you defended the doctor and his son." Their support was wonderful. Out there with the soldiers, it had felt so easy to be shot. In speaking up for the two Americans, I had taken a big risk. It was easy to be proud of my courage, now that I knew the outcome. But had it made my situation worse, it would have been one of the most heroically stupid things I had ever done.

As it was, the soldiers had showed remarkable restraint. Imagine years of drill in attack and defense, then being posted in bush country near a border where nothing much happens. Still, you are accountable for anything that goes wrong. If you are complacent, you may be a fool. Better to be on your toes. An expert with weapons, you are among men all too eager to use them. Imagine the temptation to shoot. And you are handed the provocation on a silver platter: two white men illegally crossing a closed border, and a white woman (who has already aroused suspicion) driving Bushmen to the border to aid and abet a host of possible crimes. It was a testament to expert training and wise command that no one had been killed.

Meanwhile, it shouldn't have surprised me that there had been no meeting. I should have read the signs—no processions of dignitaries driving through our camp, no one knowing about the meeting but

Royal and me. It made perfect sense. Megan had requested the meeting; the Kangwa representative must have refused. Megan was outside the country, and the issue of the border, fifteen miles from his post, was not a high priority. Issues affecting the Bushmen rarely were.

༼༼༼༼༼ Hours later, writing in my journal by the light of the kerosene lamp, the moon, and the fire, I could still feel my fright. I wished I had some visitors that night, so as not to be alone. As though the day's fears weren't enough, there were rumors that the Afrikaners in Namibia were going to shoot at the Botswana army. There I was, a mile from the border, with conflict building on all sides. I felt like a perfect target.

I woke in the middle of the night, thinking about soldiers and invasions and about bullets finding me in the tent. Moon shadows played restlessly on the outside of the tent, teasing my fears. I turned in my blankets, looking for comfort. I worried about the father and son: how would they fare in jail? Images and voices filled my head: "Bullshit!" "The truth! The truth!" "You're in big trouble." Then, as I drifted back toward sleep, the images and sounds became distorted, bizarre. Pieces rearranged, feelings jumbled, words garbled and out of context. I slept.

༼༼༼༼༼ In the morning, with a group including Kxoma and Nisa, I left for Kangwa to talk to an official about Kxoma's plans, to take people to the clinic, and to find out what had happened to the two Americans.

We weren't very far from Dobe when the soldiers drove up. The Americans were with them, driving their own Land Rover. They had already stopped at my camp and were looking for me. "We wanted to drop off gifts for the Bushmen," David said. "We had planned to distribute them ourselves, but now of course that isn't possible." We transferred the goods—corn meal, clothes, sugar, and some medical supplies—from their truck to mine. I was eager to talk to them, but the full attention of the military was on us and I didn't dare. I did learn, however, that after one night in jail, they were free. They had been told to leave the area that afternoon and not come back.

An officer asked me where we were going. "To Kangwa, to the clinic," I answered.

"Where are you going after that?"

"Back to Dobe."

"Remember, you are not to go on the road to the border."

There was no danger that I would forget.

〰〰〰〰〰 At Kangwa, we searched for the official who would handle permits for Kxoma's new village site and its well. "He's not here," we were told.

"Where is he?" we asked.

"Not sure," was the reply.

"Is he here, in Kangwa?"

"Don't think so."

"When will he return?"

"Not sure."

We checked again before we left, but he was still not there. I promised Kxoma that when I got to Maun I would talk to the district commissioner.

We also met a group of soldiers who were stationed in Kangwa. Their top officer was surprisingly chatty. I mentioned the border incident and said, "I'm glad to be alive today."

He responded, "You have nothing to fear," with such reassurance, almost chuckling, that he—almost—put my worries to rest.

Nisa the Healer

On the drive back to Dobe, Nisa sat in the cab of the truck beside me. She said she wasn't feeling well—her back and legs were aching, and she was tired. She leaned gently against me, close and trusting. We planned the drum dance for the next night. "It's your last chance to lay on hands to help me," I said. "Because if I die . . ."

"Then I die, too," she said.

So here it was, two days before the end of my stay, and suddenly I felt close to her. She made demands always, and relented rarely, but she told things honestly and directly—as she saw them. It was a rare talent and great gift to me.

Packing to leave. Even though I wouldn't take much with me, the task was daunting. Organizing clothes and money to give as gifts, and almost everything else I owned to give away or to sell for pennies so I would not be accused of favoritism. It was my second-to-last day in Dobe. Tomorrow would be a madhouse. Everyone would want to see what everyone else was getting. People would come from miles around, people I had never seen before, to harangue me, to test my armor. "Marjorie, you're leaving and haven't given us anything. Only the Dobe people get things. What about the rest of us?"

"Marjorie," a man who had known Mel and me years before had said to me the day before, "I want to send something back with you for Mel." After a moment he added, "If only you would give me some beads, I could sew him a pouch." I glared at him. His older brother, sitting nearby, laughed and chided him: "A present for Mel has to come from you, not from Marjorie."

Leaving. After the encounter with the soldiers, I felt ready. The stakes had gotten too high. There was too much anger on both sides of the border. In any case, I had essentially finished what I had come to do: Nisa and I had done nine interviews (with one more to come) and had covered most of what I wanted; I'd gotten a sense of how the others were doing; I'd immersed myself in the language and culture; and I'd had the intense pleasure of spending time in the bush. Of course, I'd also had a delicious distance from my family—and now I longed for them. Mel's letter, letting me know that they were doing well, had filled me with delight.

But I was also afraid to leave. Here, somehow, in spite of the soldiers, I felt protected. Even the weather felt healing—perhaps a little too warm during the day and a little chilly at night, but clear, clean, crisp, and sweet. At home, I felt vulnerable. Whatever facilitated the growth of cancer was still there.

The moon shone brightly overhead. The fire burned small. Glowing timbers released delicate, tender sounds. The deep orange light fanned outward as it met the darkness. I stoked the fire. Bright flames darted momentarily in all directions, warming my legs and face, even as the night cold made me shiver.

The smell of the firewood was sweet and distinct: at the first scent, I had known I was back in Dobe. Even when smoke got in my eyes, there was a gentleness about it, an annoyance easily forgiven, as with the misdeeds of a naughty child. There were other familiar smells in the village, too: meat roasting over the coals and mongongo nuts under the coals, the hot ash bubbling as the nuts baked beneath; the nuts, cooled slightly and freshly cracked; water roots just pulled from the warm earth. And there were people-smells: of perspiration that dried quickly, of aromatic powder applied generously, of fats rubbed on the skin to counter the dry, hot air.

I wrote in my journal, unwilling to stop and go to sleep. Was it the last night I would sit like this? There might be time the next night, but there would be so many last-minute details to attend to. Baitsenke had said we would have to leave by ten in the morning to get to Maun by nightfall.

A few nights more, and I'd be with my family. The thought excited me. It scared me. Would I drown? Would I find this voice again, the one in my journal, the one that had sustained me, like a good companion and supportive friend? Should I take a paraffin lamp into the backyard after the children were asleep and write—with traffic and planes, smog and pollution, with extreme cold and humid heat, with the buzz of city life all around?

I didn't want to give up these nights, writing, being by myself. No traffic, no mosquitoes, no phone calls, no obligations, and few thoughts about sickness. The environment and the people nourished me. The demands were immediate and relatively easy to manage. At nightfall, work stopped. I'd even indulged a fantasy of setting up a small cattle farm with a group of Bushmen.

I wanted to linger in this night, to touch it as a lover would her beloved. Donkey bells rang in the distance. A jackal called its descending cry and was answered by another. The air was filled with moonshine falling unfettered in a cloudless sky. The stark world of daylight was now soft and blue, as if passed through a filter, making it otherworldly and strange. Trees and bushes, in leaf or bare, pressed against the translucent backdrop. The immense sky absorbed this fringed horizon with grace, its own grandeur undiminished.

I turned off the lamp and wrote by moonlight. I was a junkie on an incredible high, unwilling to stop writing. If I went to sleep, whatever came next would be there when I woke. As long as I kept writing, I could hold on to this moment.

Without the lamp, the world of sound widened. Moon shadows sneaked under every object. Magic was in the air, with bells all around. Did donkeys not sleep at night, or was it dreams that stirred them? Beyond the donkeys were birds, and beyond them was quiet—enveloping circles, with me in the center. What a privilege to be in this place, my truck and tent proclaiming my temporary sovereignty over this piece of earth. Me, under the moonlight, alive, savoring the desert air.

Hunting and gathering was the way of life of people who lived long before us, people just like ourselves. Those hunter-gatherer ancestors left behind someone who left behind someone who eventually left behind our grandparents and parents who gave us life. We would not be here without that unbroken chain.

Their way of life was so well adapted to their needs that it thrived for tens of thousands of years. In terms of time, hunting and gathering has been the most successful way of earning a living that people have ever devised. It is the world in which our modern bodies were shaped, the world that is most familiar to our bodies even today.

Agriculture is a relative newcomer to human experience. When it arose, it was able to support large aggregations of people, but it also limited the range of nutrients typical in a wild-food diet. Food deficiencies, famine, and epidemic diseases increased exponentially, fast becoming the greatest threats to the human lineage.

And life as we know it today, in the technological fast lane? It is new and untested. Will it last as long as agriculture, for ten thousand years? Or the forty thousand years of hunting and gathering?

The people of Dobe were the children of that ancient way of life, and they were choosing to move on. Most cultures, given the choice, had done so. Many of the people I spoke to recalled the traditional past as a life of struggle. For them, the allure of the "modern" was great. A few, though, saw the past as having had balance and beauty.

Nothing stands still. I support the Bushmen in the road they have chosen. In many ways their life has become easier, with the government providing schools, medicine, occasional food relief, and help with agriculture and animal husbandry.

But the gains of moving forward often come with losses. I have been touched most by what has been left behind. It was not for everyone. But walking the wild trail with men carrying bows and quivers, whose hands talked a silent language of nature, and who knew the world around them as a storehouse of survival; and gathering food with women who were as familiar with the environment as they were with their children, who combined childcare and productive work and still joked and laughed and supported one another, who gave me presents of roots and berries so I wouldn't return empty handed—sharing in these activities swelled me with joy and pride. "Marjorie," an inner voice shouted whenever I returned to the bush, "look where you are!"

I woke at dawn to a fierce wind. A cold front had moved in during the night. I desperately wanted more sleep, but my gut and bladder forced me outside. Half frozen, I returned to my tent, grabbed another sweater, folded my blankets in half for extra warmth, and lay awake. My last full day in Dobe, and the weather was uninviting, punishing. The tent shuddered, buffeted by the wind. Was the tent restless, ready to leave? How would I get through this day?

The soldiers showed up early, as usual. By the time they left, fifty or more people were milling around my camp. By midmorning I had distributed the last of the tobacco and the few items of children's clothing I dared give out in public. Still the people sat. And sat. Many left around two o'clock, disappointed. After that came the buying of my things, for a fraction of their cost. People seemed happy to pay.

After everyone left I visited Nisa and Bo. We hugged the fire, the wind whirling sand into our faces and hair. "Is the drum dance still on in this weather?" I asked. I reminded them that I had agreed to pay six women to sing, two drummers, and two healers.

There was a pause. Then Bo said, "Besa says he wants you to pay him for the use of his drum."

"Pay him . . . pay him?" By repeating the words, might I perhaps squeeze a different meaning from them? How many times had I driven Besa to the clinic because of the festering boil on his thigh? Just the day before, I had picked him up at his hut and transported him—door to door—to the clinic and back. I knew walking was painful for him. And what of the highly coveted present I had given him? "It's from Mel and me," I had said, handing him a thick winter sweater. "For our friendship in the past, and for our continued friendship today." And, of course, my hand was always open to him with tobacco and other goods.

"Pay him?" I asked myself again. I can't say I am proud of what I did next. The month of demands, disappointments, and insults finally over-flowed. I turned to Nisa and Bo, measuring my words, trying to quell the inner storm. "Working out the details of this dance has been very difficult," I said. "And now Besa has asked me to pay for the drum. It has ruined my heart, and I can't continue with the dance this way. I have helped people here in every way I could. If they see fit to 'give' me this dance, that will be wonderful. But I won't pay anyone. If the dance happens, I will be generous with gifts to those who participate. If the dance doesn't happen, that will be all right, too. After all, I am leaving tomorrow."

Nisa and Bo listened sympathetically. They always seemed willing to accept fault in others, especially others from families living on the far side of Dobe.

"Nisa," I asked. "Do you understand? I'm asking you to participate in the dance without pay. You know I have never been stingy with you."

"If that's how you want it, I accept," she answered.

"Bo," I said. "I have to talk to Besa about the drum, and to the women I hired, too. But I can't do it alone. Someone has to help me, to speak for me. Are you willing to be that person?"

Asking Bo in this way was one of my best moves in the field. It had taken years of learning about !Kung culture to figure it out. If I had fol-lowed the passion of the moment, I would have tromped up to Besa in his village—White Woman on the War Path—and pursued the argument myself. However it might have ended, I would probably not have gained the use of the drum. But asking Bo to speak for me—that was how the people themselves settled differences, especially when strong emotions were involved. However unfavorable a position was, if someone held it, at least one other person—usually a close relative—could be counted on for support.

"I will try to help," Bo said. He seemed somewhat reluctant, but the format was set and he could not have easily refused.

Bo and I walked together to Besa's camp, shouting to hear each other in the wind, rehearsing what he would say. With Bo beside me, my anger softened. His presence gave me the courage to confront Besa. Together, we were strong. It was as if he and Nisa were family I could count on.

Besa was stretched out on a blanket, still unable to walk. He was wearing the sweater I had given him, bundled against the wind and cold. The late afternoon sun cast long shadows on the ground. He looked up as we approached, shading his eyes from the glare.

We exchanged greetings.

"We've come to talk about Marjorie's thinking," Bo began. "She heard that you were asking for money to use your drum. Her heart is miserable about this."

The two men talked. Bo spoke well, but never said anything substantial. Besa retained a dispassionate, even slightly amused stance, maintaining that he had every right to charge money. They didn't argue, but neither did they resolve anything.

I thanked Bo and said I would speak for myself. "I understand that you want to charge me for the use of your drum," I said to Besa. "And as Bo has explained, that makes my heart feel pain. I thought that we had a friendship of many years and that we were people who helped each other. But this—charging for use of the drum—this is new. Today is the first time I've seen this and the first time I've heard of this. Perhaps this would be appropriate for a stranger. But I am Hwantla and we have known each other from my first days here, when I was a young woman and you were a teenager."

He challenged me: "That you have never seen it before doesn't make it wrong for today."

"I see," I said. "Now I fully understand. Before I didn't. Then shouldn't I have charged you for your trips to the clinic in the truck?"

"Well," he said defensively, "if you had wanted to charge me for riding in the truck, you would have had to negotiate that in advance. You can't tell me afterward that there is a fee."

"You are right," I said. "I will not charge you. But I wouldn't have charged you under any circumstances, not before, not after—even if I had already learned the 'new' way. Because I thought we were people who helped each other, and who liked each other."

"This has nothing to do with liking. It has to do with money."

"Well, I don't see it that way," I said. "I see that I have helped you with the clinic and with gifts and tobacco. And although all those things also have to do with money, I did them because I thought we understood each other. But today I see that your heart is far away from me. I am no different to you than my driver, Baitsenke, who doesn't know your language, and who doesn't do anything for anybody. I do not accept your proposal and will not pay for the drum. If the other drum owner also refuses, there will be no dance."

I stepped away, holding back tears, and asked Bo to say the appropriate parting words. As Bo spoke, Besa seemed cool and detached. I stopped listening, content that at least I had said what I felt. Their words floated past me, until Besa called, "Marjorie . . ."

"Yes?" I realized he must have been speaking to me while my mind wandered.

"I said, 'So use the drum if you want it.'"

"Really? That's it?"

"Mm."

"Thanks. Perhaps we do help one another after all."

Bo and I stopped at two more villages, explaining the new rules. No, I wasn't going to pay for the dance. I thought perhaps I had earned their support. I also had never been stingy to those who helped me. Would the singers come anyway? Yes, they replied. And what about the two drummers? Yes, they'd be there.

By late afternoon, the wind was whipping loose anything not weighted down. Baitsenke drove off to find firewood. People began gathering at my camp. Nisa arrived with Chuko, the second healer, and the drummers. Then the singers showed up, about ten women and a few young girls, dressed for the occasion: some with newly sewn skirts and tops, others with decorative beaded shapes rimming their foreheads. Most wore hats for warmth; all had blankets wrapped around them, and some of the blankets enclosed a small child as well.

As the sun set and the cold settled in, the dance began in earnest. "Wo u oh, wo uoh u o," one woman sang in the dimming light, her voice jumping the large intervals with ease. "Wo u oh," came the response, as other women complemented the melody and added their own variations. Their clapping hands—splayed wide to catch the explosive pocket of palm-to-palm air—glowed in the light of the fire. Multiple rhythms created a texture of sound as rich and luxurious as seamless brocade.

Besa's drum, decorated with wood-burned images of mountains and houses, was played by a man from Kxoma's village. It entered with a single beat, "I am here!" The second drummer, a young man still in his teens, responded, "So am I!" And the group was off—an expert ensemble whose sound traveled out beyond us into the cold dark air. From without, the ensemble was a perfectly balanced organism, pulsating and alive. From within, it provided the context for those with healing powers to move from the realm of the everyday into the extraordinary.

Nisa seemed quick to feel the change in her thought patterns, and focused her gaze into the darkness. She sang and clapped, swaying slightly. Sweat glistened on her face; her body trembled; her upper torso shimmied; then she was on the ground, sitting slumped to one side beside the fire, eyes closed. Chuko, also in trance, laid hands on Nisa to help revive her.

The music swelled again as the two women went around the circle laying on hands. They attended to everyone, even babies and young children. Nisa came to me often, sometimes with Chuko. They worked on me together—rubbing my sides, pulling out whatever sickness they could "see"—and they worked on me separately. I loved the touch and the attention, and visualized the seeds of disease flying out of me as they laid on hands.

They made a number of rounds, always coming back to me. Once, toward the end, Nisa tried to carry my weight on her shoulders, moving me as she moved. I felt huge and awkward. She soon stopped, and the two healers repeatedly tapped my waist, a symbol of transferring n/um, the healing power, from them to me. When they were with me, I savored the moments, never wanting them to leave. When they returned from working on others, I yearned to lose my own bound-in-reality self and be swept away by the moment, much as they—in trance—were.

I closed my eyes as their hands touched me, hoping to feel the cure they were trying to effect. Would it come as warm light, as a cleansing, as a feeling of peace, or perhaps as pure knowledge—experiences I had read about in accounts of exceptional recoveries from illness? Or would it be mundane and not immediately discernible? Or would it be nothing at all?

What actually took place that night, I can never be sure. I do know that the poking and touching and dragging and shaking made it difficult for me to experience anything beyond my immediate senses. Nor was there a !Kung cultural norm to experience laying on of hands as much else. Curing was seen as the work of the healer, not of the recipient. Healing dances were usually quite casual events, and people often maintained conversations with others while being cured.

After perhaps two hours, Nisa and Chuko said they had finished. Although the wind had died down, the cold was bitter. Later that night, standing water would freeze.

"We saw a little sickness in your chest," Nisa told me. "We took it out and now it is gone. We also fired your insides with *n/um*. It should keep you well until you come back."

Then everyone left, to return to the warmth of their own fires and huts, and my camp was quiet.

If the weather had not been so foul, who knows how long the dance would have lasted. It might even have been an all-nighter, like many dances in the "old days" within my memory. But as it was, I was given what I had asked for. Women from all the camps showed up, some I had known for years and others I had just met. The drummers played passionately, with few breaks and no complaints. Nisa and Chuko were sensitive guides who attended to my fears and worked hard to help me. And I, Marjorie-Hwantla, was acknowledged, my psychic pain made public. Evidently "the talk" in the villages had been that I was to be supported.

Then I was alone once again, with the moon, the fire, the clear cold air, and just the faintest hint of distant bells. Baitsenke and I planned to leave by ten the next morning. I felt ready. Just about everything had been given away or sold. I had one last stash for the people who had participated in the dance. And I wanted to talk privately with Nisa once more in the early morning before I left.

I had already said my goodbyes to the beauty of this place. It was so bitterly cold that I was already feeling somewhat removed.

Last Goodbyes

At noon the next day Baitsenke and I passed the last of the Bushman villages dotting the riverbed that remained dry except in the wettest of rainy seasons, when, for a few days at a time, it became a raging river.

Baitsenke was glad to let me drive through the sixty-five-mile water-less region that linked Kangwa and Dobe to the outside world. In places the track was more like a rut, with deep sand that could stall the most expert of drivers in the dry season, and thick mud that mired the same drivers in the wet season. The hard-packed sections had so many ridges that we averaged under fifteen miles an hour. Even then, we bumped around in the cab so much we wondered if the springs would hold out. The midday sun cast few shadows, equalizing all it touched with a dull hue. The scenery that had so captured me a month earlier now seemed repetitive—a blessing to my overwhelmed senses. Saying the last goodbyes and leaving Dobe had been wrenching.

The icy night had been another restless one for me. I opened the tent flap at five-thirty and was startled by a beam of white light bursting upon my eyes. It was the full moon, readying to set. The cold was so intense that I retreated under the covers for another half-hour. Then there were gifts to dispense—to the drummers, the healers, and the singers. Others came around too, but I had little left. I dropped some things at Kumsa-the-Hunter's camp and then woke Nisa for our last interview.

It didn't begin well. Nisa too had slept poorly, she said, woken often by dreams of my leaving.

"Nisa," I asked. "Before we start this last interview, is there anything you would like to say into the tape recorder to Susanna, my eldest daughter and your namesake?"

Her words are only in my memory now, but they went something like, "Greetings, my little-name. Send me blankets. Send me money. When you come, bring me beads." And on she went.

I winced and glared at her. How could she? Then I noticed that the volume control on the tape recorder had been set so low that it could have only barely recorded her voice. Without thought, I rewound the tape to the beginning, pleased to have an excuse to be rid of her words. Before asking her to start again, I said, "It's probably better not to ask your namesake for a list of things. She's young and won't understand."

Thinking about this exchange later, as I drove the truck toward Maun, I was reminded of my first interview with Nisa, twenty years before, when I could not accept her story about her brother's birth. This time it was our last interview, and although her response was believable enough, it was equally unacceptable to me. The protective mother in me stomped all over the anthropologist's measured cool. I had never liked Nisa's demands on me, and I rose up to censor them for my daughter. I did not attempt to come up with a generous explanation for her words. I did not even leave the evidence on tape, to return to at another time with cooler ears.

I turned on the tape recorder again. With roosters crowing in the background, I asked, as though for the first time, "Would you like to greet your namesake?"

This time Nisa was on cue. "I greet Nisa, my little-name. Please help me by visiting here. I would be very grateful for that. I send you my greetings. Another year, when you come, I will see you." Then she said to me, in a different tone, "I'm finished with that."

We talked about her dreams. While I was away on Kxoma's bush trip, she had dreamed that she heard the sound of a truck and said, "My little niece Hwantla is coming back." The next morning she wondered why she had had that dream, because I hadn't yet returned. Bo asked her, "Why are you dreaming about Hwantla? She's away." And Nisa answered, "Because I like her. I like Hwantla and that's why I dreamed about her." Not much later, the truck did sound. "Yes, my niece is coming back," Nisa said. "Others took her and slept out in the bush with her and made me feel pain."

She recalled two other dreams, both from the night just ended. The first was about healing medicine. She dreamed that I was in *thada*—a trance state in which the entire body trembles and the mind loses focus. "I dreamed that you were doing *thada*. You did it and did it and did it! I thought, 'If Hwantla is doing this, maybe the healing force Chuko and I put into her last night took hold. Mine is inside her!' For you kept shaking and doing *thada*. I prayed, 'Eh, thank you. I am grateful.'"

In the other dream, she called out to me. "Hwantla . . . Hey,

Hwantla, are you going away and leaving me behind?" And I said, "Oh, Auntie. Yes, today I am leaving so I can take good care of Little Nisa." She said, "Be sure to greet Little Nisa for me." And I said, "Of course I will." Then the dream took a sad turn. "Hwantla is refusing me," Nisa called out, and went into her hut and cried. "My niece is leaving."

When Nisa woke from this dream, she said, she told Bo she was unhappy: "I'm just going to stay in the blankets." That was why she was not yet up when I came to interview her. While Bo was fixing the fire, he saw me approaching. "That one, she's coming," he told Nisa. Nisa called out, "Eh-hey, my daughter," and got up to meet me.

⟪⟪⟪⟪⟪⟪ Changing the subject, no longer talking about dreams, Nisa turned to me. "Mother," she said. "You are fine. Your body is well. It is very good."

I asked, "Did you and Chuko see something?"

"Yes. I saw the talk . . . I heard the talk from far away, where you live. I heard what was being said about your sickness. This is what I was told: 'Hwantla has been living far away, and she didn't return because the government here made it too difficult. They didn't allow her to go see you, her aunt. That is why we wanted to kill her.'"

This logic reflected the !Kung belief that people who are not well treated or cared for are vulnerable to sickness and death. They say that the gods take such people because no one else wants them. The connection between sickness, healing, and other people's actions is reflected in our own culture, too, in the belief that sick people who are prayed for heal better and faster than those for whom no one prays.

Nisa continued to quote what she had heard the gods say while she was in trance. "But now that she has returned to you, Nisa, now that your young niece has come back, we're leaving and are finished with her. We won't kill her. She will go and live in her country for a while and then will return to see you. That way, she will do very well. Because we want you to be together and to see each other. If she goes and lives for a long time, if she doesn't quickly come back to see you—that's very bad. That's why we said we wanted to kill her before. But your child, we will not kill her. Eh-hey!"

Then she quoted what she had told the gods:

Yes, let her be. She lives over there and works and gives me things. She finds a little something and sets it aside. Finds something else, and sets that aside. Because I am old now. She saves money for me and gets me things. That's why, when she comes here, she takes very good care of me! Next time, she will clothe me well so I am beautiful! I'll be like a young woman! When she lives there, that's what she does—she works to help me.

Now don't you take her from me! Don't trick me and take Hwantla from me. Hwantla is mine. She helps me and supports me. I pray to you, tomorrow when she leaves, let her go in wonderful health. And when she goes and lives, let her live and live well. And work well.

Thank you, thank you, thank you. I am grateful.

Nisa paused, then went on: "And those where you live who said such terrible things—that sickness would enter you and kill you—they were being deceitful. They were tricking you. Tricking you. Because they won't do anything to you." She paused again. "That's why I say, 'Stay well,' because you are going to be fine."

I asked, "Who did you speak with?"

"I spoke with the chief, God."

"Did you see him last night?"

"Mother, yes, I saw him. And he was pleased with me. And pleased with you. When I took you and carried you, he was very pleased. He said, 'Very good, you're doing the right thing carrying her.' He spoke to me and I was thankful. God was pleased, very strongly pleased. And said, 'She is yours, your child. Yes. And I won't do anything to her. Work well with her.' That's what God himself told me."

"Very good," I praised her.

"Eh, mother," Nisa said.

〰〰〰 I thought about the interview as I maneuvered the truck through a long stretch of soft sand. Nisa's dreams moved me, especially when she cried because I was leaving. They reflected an intense involvement with me, something she rarely discussed. It was as though only through her dreams could she air these feelings. Meanwhile, I kept being put off by her manner and her constant demands—which made me feel I didn't count, except in the most materialistic of ways.

The engine strained in four-wheel drive. I downshifted to first gear. The going was slow. I smiled when I thought of her explanation for my health problems: that the gods had been angry with me for not having returned to my "aunt" sooner. And of her defense of me, telling the gods that I did not deserve punishment because I had stayed away to work so I could buy her things.

When I first heard her reasoning, I had resented her. Here was the trance experience I had longed for, here was Nisa the experienced healer "curing" me, and the "psychological insight" she gained in trance reflected more about her own needs than about mine.

But there was certainly some truth in my working to help her. *Nisa* had been published six years after I returned from my previous field trip, and a few years later I had sent money for cows. Two years after that I had sent money for a branding iron. A few years more, and I had raised enough money to be there myself. And why was that so important? I remembered "Miss Chirpy," who had visited me in the hospital after my mastectomy, and her question about what I could no longer put off if my life was to end prematurely. And what had been my response? Return to Africa, of course—and to Nisa.

The truck pulled clear of the sand and, by comparison, started sailing on the next stretch, with its hard crests and ridges. I put my foot on the clutch and moved out of four-wheel drive, then managed a short distance in second gear before the bumps forced me back into first.

〰〰〰〰 "Nisa, what do you think of our work?" I had asked, hoping she might reflect about our relationship. She didn't speak. "I mean what do you think of our talk? Has it been good? What do you think about it?"

"Our work is good."

"Because I pay you well? Or is our talk good in other ways?"

"For you, maybe it hasn't been good. For me, it's been good."

"No, for me, it has also been good. I mean in your heart. Does the talk make you happy?"

"The talk makes me happy. Because I see money, a lot of money. And by working, I can get the things I need."

"I know the money is good. But for now, let's set that aside. What about the talk itself—does it make your heart feel good or, at times, your heart feel bad?"

"Listen," she said, steering her answer in a different direction from the one I had intended. "If the talk made me feel bad, then I would do what the others do—hide those things from you. I wouldn't talk about the people who have died—my daughter, my son, my daughter—all of whom have made me feel pain. Or my mother and my father, whose deaths also gave me pain. I wouldn't mention them if it still hurt. I would hide them, as the other women do. But it doesn't hurt my heart now. They died long ago and are gone. And so I just talk about it."

"Is there anything that has made you feel pain that you haven't wanted to talk to me about?" I asked.

"No, nothing."

I was silent, gathering my thoughts.

"What is it?" she asked. "Should those things still be making me feel pain?"

"No, that's not it. I have not been asking my questions well."

"Yes. Then it's your thoughts you are speaking about, and your heart, not mine. My heart is washed and clean."

She seemed riled. I agreed, not wanting to offend. "Yes, so is mine. That is good."

But she wasn't finished. "Look, it's the same as yesterday, when you said that if you paid me, your heart would feel pain. That was your heart, not mine. And just now, I said that talking about the people who died did not cause me pain. That's my heart."

Not sure where she was taking this, I agreed. "Eh."

"You said yesterday that if you paid me, you'd feel pain. Isn't that right?"

"Yes," I answered. "Because I was afraid that my aunt thought only about my helping her, and that she wouldn't also help me."

"Me?"

"Yes, I wanted you to help me with something. Because when we work, I pay you well. But this time I wanted you to give me something. That's why I didn't want to pay."

"Eh," Nisa said.

"Because," I persisted, "when I saw your heart, I didn't know what you thought. When you saw me, did you think, 'Hwantla is someone who gives money,' and that's it?"

"Didn't I tell you," she asked impatiently, "about the healing? Didn't I tell you that even if you didn't pay me it was fine? That I didn't feel pain? And that if you just traded me something for it, it would do? Isn't that what I said?"

"Eh," I answered, accepting defeat.

"And today, even though you've given presents to other people, I don't feel pain."

"Yes," I said, grateful for whatever small token she sent my way. "I have been generous with you and have given you many things."

"Eh-hey. And as I am today, even a sweater . . . I don't have one to wear. But I don't say, 'Why doesn't my child give me a sweater?' I don't say that. Nor do I complain that my husband has no pants and why doesn't my niece . . ."

"The pants I had were very small," I responded defensively, not hiding my irritation. "And Bo is much bigger than I am. I gave what I had to the young men."

She asked if I had paid the other healer and two other women she depended on in her daily life. "I didn't pay them, but I gave them presents," I answered. Nisa was just making sure. Had I overlooked them, their resentment would have been difficult for her.

We moved on to talk about the days, weeks, and years ahead. By now I had confirmed that I would give her a donkey. With the donkey, she said, she would be able to gather food even when she wasn't strong. For now, she still had food from our gathering trip. "When I finish eating that, I'll go gathering again. I won't just lie around and rest. Even when Richard Lee was here, I asked him to tell you to come and take me to the bush. He took my tongue and carried it to my daughter. And here you are! And you took me for mongongos and kama ko berries. And here I am, eating those foods. I am very grateful for that! For even after you leave, I'll still have this food to keep me alive."

Then, with self-mocking humor, she added, "And I will think, 'Eh, Hwantla . . . did you come and help me gather food and then leave?'"

She declared that if other white people came she wouldn't work for them. We laughed about it. She said, "I'm telling you, Hwantla, I'm telling you." Even if Richard Lee returned, she'd go to him only if a messenger told her he had a letter from Marjorie. "Otherwise, I will remain silent. Even after you have gone home, you won't hear that I've worked with others."

I laughed, touched by her concern, then told her she should work with anyone she chose. She became serious. "Of course, if I have the strength, I will work. But what other white person will treat me the way you have? Mother! No one will treat me as you have. That's why I say that if another white person comes, I'll just stay where I am."

I asked who gave her support. She repeated the names of two women—my namesake, Hwantla, and the wife of Kantla, the one steady lover in her life—who both lived nearby.

"How about you and your husband?" I asked. "Do you think things will go well between you?"

"The two of us are doing well. When you first leave, we will miss you greatly. After a while, we will try to clear our hearts, so that we don't feel too much pain."

"I also mean, just the two of you. Will you be happy together and love each other?"

"Eh," Nisa responded, "we get along well and our hearts go out to each other."

I asked about Bo's recent visit to the clinic. "Oh, my niece! My niece!" Nisa cried affectionately. Her face lit up as she told me his new medicine was helping. It "was giving him strength," he had told her, and the place with the stitches was less painful.

I teased her, "Maybe now, in the night, you will have some food to eat."

Nisa laughed in surprise at my double-entendre.* She pointed to me, took my hand, and commented on my cleverness. "My little-name asks and I tell!"

Then she whispered, as though we were conspirators, "Yes, at night . . . he still hasn't done anything. He's still not finished with the pills. He wants to take them all, and then, when the medicine is finished, he will look for some food to eat."

"And is there any food left?" I asked, laughing again.

"What! There's food!" She laughed too. "Yo, my daughter! Mother!"

"And that other man, Kantla?"

"That one, his body . . . he says he has no more food. He says he's old. His body is doing that to him. But mine, it still is strong."

ༀༀༀༀ This had to be a short interview. Everything was packed and Baitsenke was waiting, watching the time. "Before we finish," I said, "is there anything you would like to ask me?"

"Mother, what would I ask you about?"

---

* The !Kung use food and eating as metaphors for sex.

"I mean, are there any questions you have about me, like about how I live, or anything else?"

Nisa paused, "I want to ask you . . . I am going to ask you . . ."

"Go ahead."

"I want to ask you about something, but maybe you'll be upset with me."

"What would upset me?"

"Will you yell at me if I ask you about something? Do you . . . what is it I want to ask you? You, who are a child, and me, an older woman. One thing you have is Tashay—Mel—and I'm going to ask you. Have you ever stolen away from him?"

"Me?"

"Yes."

"No, I still haven't had a lover. In my thoughts, maybe, but not with my body."

"What I'm asking," she continued, perhaps not pleased with my answer, perhaps just not sure I had understood, "that which belongs to Mel, that which you hold onto down there . . . the food that belongs to Mel. Have you held onto it well? Have you given it to another man?"

"Have I given it to another man? Is that what you are asking?"

"That's what I'm asking you," she answered with a nervous laugh.

"I still haven't done that. My husband and I are the only two who share it. And no one else."

"Eh," Nisa responded.

Was she disappointed? I modified my answer. "But I think about it. When I see another man who is perhaps very attractive, maybe he looks at me and I look at him . . . sometimes I think about it."

"You're someone who likes handsome men?" she asked.

"Eh, yes."

"You like good-looking men. And refuse those who are not?"

"Eh," I answered, worried that I had said something wrong.

She lit her pipe and inhaled deeply. I waited for her pronouncement. Finally she exhaled and said, "Then you are like me. That's what I'm like. I refuse an unattractive man. That which is mine, I won't give to a man who doesn't appeal to me. An attractive man will have it. Because that is my own little thing. Now, hold onto yours very well and give it to Mel."

"Yes." I laughed with her.

"And Mel will give you a small child . . . a child named Bo." I gathered she hadn't approved of our naming our son after Kxoma.

"No, I'm finished with having babies."

"You can drink medicine, and then Mel will give you little Bo. You've got a Nisa and now you need a Bo. Why not?"

"Because I'm done with having children," I repeated.

She didn't believe me and accused me of using cleverness. "You're tricking me."

"No, I'm not tricking you. I can't have any more children. I am too old."

"My daughter. You're not old. But the two of us are the same in that way. Last night, when I was speaking with God, I asked him to take good care of me and to take good care of you. Then we will be able to be together again. Mother, that's what I said. And he agreed."

"That's very good. I, too, want to come back so the two of us can be together again."

〰〰〰〰 Knowing it was time to leave, I said, "Is there anything else you'd like to ask me?"

"There's nothing else I want to ask . . . except . . . where you are going, to your home, do you have lovers?"

"I don't have lovers," I laughed, thinking we had already finished that topic.

"You don't have any lovers?"

"Mm."

"Me, here," she said, "you say you don't have lovers. But me, I have lovers. And when you go-o-o-o-o-o and another day you come back, I'll give you that talk, what I have lived and done."

"I will like that."

"You will return with Mel and with Little Nisa?"

"I hope so."

"When you come with Mel I'll greet him . . . then I'll take him as my lover." She laughed. "Would you not kill me? You'd kill me!"

"Yes, I'd kill you."

"You'd kill me."

"Of course." We both laughed.

"You don't take your daughter's husband because he is your in-law. I won't steal Mel from you. He gave birth to Little Nisa and I wouldn't steal from my daughter. That's just the way we talk. I just really like you and your husband."

We were having a good time, teasing each other and just being together. With our spirits high, I said, "Well, I guess this is it. It's time for me to leave." I turned off the tape recorder and we stood up. She pulled me to her cheek and gave me a loose hug, which I returned.

We walked back to the sandy area that had been my camp. Chuko, the other healer, was waiting there. She greeted me warmly, repeating Nisa's reassurance that they had seen just a little sickness inside me and had taken it out. "You are all right now. Nisa and I put the healing energy into you, to keep you well. But remember, Hwantla," she added, "don't eat that fish in cans."

She had said something similar the night before, but I hadn't been sure what she meant. "Which ones?" I asked. "The ones that look like small fish, sardines and kippers, or the ones that have just the meat, tuna fish?"

"I don't know the difference," she answered. "Just don't eat fish in those cans."

"I will remember," I said. "And thank you for working on me so well last night, working on me with your healing energy."

I found Bo among the stragglers at my camp area and said goodbye. I whispered to Nisa that I hoped the donkey would be helpful, and that she and Bo would be healthy. We hugged once again.

Then, at close to ten o'clock, Baitsenke and I drove away.

Epilogue

It is two o'clock in the morning. A fire smolders and burns in the fireplace before me, and the air carries its pungent aroma, so different from the scent of fires in Dobe. I am at home in Atlanta, Georgia, six years after my trip to Nisa. My husband and my three children, now aged seventeen, fourteen, and nine, sleep quietly upstairs. It is bitterly cold outside, with temperatures in the teens and a wind chill factor that makes it even colder. The moon, full a few nights ago, is high in the blue-black dome above, ragged on one side, in its cycle of decline.

I wish with all that is powerful within me that I could close this book with a fairytale ending. I wish I could say that I had been physically as well as emotionally healed by my return to Nisa and to Africa; that the voice that screamed "Africa!" so passionately before I left had found answers to the questions about mortality that had driven me back to the bush.

It's true that the trip was good for me. I felt happy there in a way I had not felt since my diagnosis. Also, although cancer was no less a threat in the bush, for one month I had to leave that worry behind. I reasoned that those four weeks would not make a life-or-death differ-

233

ence. I practiced "hands clasped together on top of the desk"—as my elementary school teachers used to command to ensure that our young hands, and bodies, stayed out of trouble. I stopped exploring my body for suspicious pains, suspicious areas. Rare baths at night with one bucket of hot water and sleeping in several layers of clothing helped as well.

So with cancer pushed to the background, what was in front? Nisa was. During the fourteen years since I had seen her, I had given birth to three children and had published my book based on her narrative. She had bought cows with money I sent and had moved with her husband to Dobe. Despite the length of our separation, Nisa had remained present in my inner life. She and I had discussed many issues over the years—all in my head, of course.

It was not only that I had listened to and translated her interviews, repeatedly, for years. Nor was it that we had become the best of friends or like close family. It was simply that she and I had shared the most straightforward connection I had ever had with anyone, before or since. And after years of immersing myself in her culture—both in the field and, at home, in my work—I found many !Kung customs and beliefs so reasonable that I had adopted them for myself.

My first childbirth was modeled on !Kung women's experience. After twenty-two hours of difficult labor, I continued to refuse all medication. How else would I have understood the stories !Kung women had shared with me? How else could I have pared myself down to the essential female I was, touching eons of female existence that joined maternal bravery with new life struggling to emerge? I was determined to meet one of the most important people in my life—my child—for the first time without dulling the experience with medication. Much of what came later was also influenced by the !Kung: nursing on demand, sharing a "family bed," aiming for a birth spacing of three and a half years. And interpreting children's behavior as essentially senseless: "When they get older, they won't act that way anymore," I would say, echoing the !Kung.

When it came to friendships, marriage, attitudes toward sex, productive work, child care, divorce, leisure time, the !Kung were my yardstick. "What would they say?" I'd ask myself. A !Kung phrase would come to mind, and I would smile and say quietly, "Eh-hey, my people." Or it would be Nisa's voice and I'd think, "Eh-hey, my aunt."

It was as if the !Kung culture and my talks with Nisa touched something beyond reason in me. As though, at the not so tender age of twenty-four years, I had imprinted on the people, on Nisa, on their way of life. Even though I didn't like everything Nisa said, nor did I like everything about her, my heart had been captured.

𝕂𝕂𝕂𝕂𝕂𝕂 When I was translating the tapes for the first book, I laughed with Nisa, I waxed poetic when she did. But how often I wished she had been nobler, more selfless, more philosophical. In editing her narrative, I was often tempted to adjust what she said, to leave out less attractive incidents. But I resisted temptation. "Let her speak for herself," I reasoned. "What value will there be if she sounds like me?" So I left in the violence of the men in her life, her infidelities, her cover-ups, the murder of her daughter, her father's temper, and her mother's discontent.

Publishing the book was an extraordinary experience for me. I gained respect, started teaching at the college level, lectured to a wide range of people, and appeared on radio and television. My goal was always to make the exotic familiar. I'd speak about traditional !Kung life and show slides, then say, "But enough of the anthropologist's voice. Let's hear about !Kung life from Nisa." I usually chose to read the most appealing excerpts, because I wanted to present an accessible view of !Kung culture. Reactions varied. Some who read the book were reinforced in their belief that members of this socioeconomically simple, or "primitive," culture were less advanced as people than those living in industrialized nations. Most readers, however, were struck by how similar the human struggle was, no matter what society one lived in.

Some of the most moving feedback of all came from Blanca Muratorio, an anthropologist from the University of British Columbia who had worked for several years with an indigenous woman in the Ecuadorian Amazon, a Napo Quichua woman of about Nisa's age named Francisca. Blanca Muratorio sent me an excerpt from her field diary, dated July 2, 1990:

Francisca saw a copy of *Nisa* on top of my working table. She immediately noticed, with admiration, Nisa's beads and face decoration. "Who is she? Where is she from?" she asked. I told her Nisa was a storyteller like herself, someone for whom dreams were very important . . .

Francisca wanted to know more. I opened the book and tried to translate for her the starting quote from *Nisa,* * thinking to myself: How can
I convey meaning from !Kung to English, to Spanish, to Quichua? I
translated Nisa's words. I think Francisca understood exactly what Nisa
meant. She smiled and said: "She shouldn't be sad. In my dreams I can
travel far. From the top of the hills I can see . . . I will hear that nice
woman's voice in the winds."

〰〰〰 Returning to Africa also had much to do with the land, its
great sparseness and isolation, and the integrity of an environment only
minimally disrupted by human manipulation. It had always been too
dry to be part of the competition. If I had been seeking beautiful landscape alone, the Dobe area of Botswana would not have been my first
choice. Rough in terrain, with few vistas and even fewer game animals,
it had to be known well to be appreciated.

Had to be known well to be appreciated: a description that also fits
Nisa, along with complex and difficult. But she probably would say
much the same about me. Each of us wanted certain things from the
other, and neither of us got as much as we hoped for. That we both got
some of what we wanted made it extremely valuable.

And the mortal questions? Those which had screamed "Africa!" so
loudly that I left young children to search out the answers? Well, Cosmic Answers was probably off somewhere with Cosmic Woman, because I never found either of them. Nor did I find Nisa-the-Mentor,
Nisa-the-Guide, or Nisa-the-Earth-Mother. Instead, I found Nisa-the-
Human. Imagine that!

But the trip was one of the greatest experiences of my life. In the
black of the night—with journal in hand, and fire ablaze, with blankets
wrapped around my legs and scarf protecting my head from the cold,
with mice cleaning freshly washed tin dishes laid out to dry, and with
voices wafting close and then gone, marking the ephemeral existence of
village life beyond, in the dark, with worlds upon worlds of exploding
stars quiet in the dome above—I heard the beat of my own heart.

〰〰〰 Since that trip in 1989, I have longed to return. In 1993 I
made the arrangements and bought a ticket to Botswana. Then my

---

* The book begins with this quotation from Nisa: "I'll break open the story and tell you
what is there. Then, like the others that have fallen out onto the sand, I will finish with
it, and the wind will take it away."

oncologist called. I had taken the standard blood test three weeks before, and on that day he had told me, "Marjorie, I consider you to be free of disease at this time." I was so thrilled I wrote it down.

But on the phone he said, "One of your tumor markers has risen. Come in and let's redo it. I can't in good conscience let you go off to Africa without checking this out." That was two and a half years ago, when a new growth was found in my liver. Metastatic disease: the most frightening words I have ever heard—more frightening, even, than "cancer." I canceled that trip and have not been back to Africa since. If I had my health, I'd go at the first opportunity. But the intense yearning waned after the last trip, and arises rarely, even as the reality of my mortality has been honed to a sharp point.

Now, when I ask myself what I have yet to do if my life ends prematurely, the inner voice no longer screams "Africa!" Instead it whispers: "Just look around you. The answers are here, wherever you are . . . Stay close to your family and friends . . . Write your story." In my earlier years, if I had been told, "There are two flowers which contain the answers you seek. One is in your backyard. The other is in Africa," there is no doubt that the one in Africa would have drawn me to it. Then, the process of finding answers was as important as the answers themselves. And just think of all the excitement I'd experience along the way.

Now, with my energies being marshaled to stay alive, I am grateful there is a flower in my backyard. I need all the help I can get. Living with metastatic disease is the hardest challenge I have ever faced. Terror so often overwhelms me. It is as though I am walking on a flimsy rope bridge strung high across a deep ravine. The terrain is lush primeval rainforest. If I look down, I am immobilized by fear. If I yearn only for the far bank, which a rare few reach, I miss what I do have: my breath and my senses and the miracle of being alive.

As I walk the bridge, I am not resigned to death. I am determined to use every ounce of my power to hold on, to keep from falling, to notice the changes in the light, to hear the sounds of the forest, and to hope against hope that, while I take one step after another, a technological breakthrough will come along to help me in my fight against cancer. A helicopter will appear and lower a rope, then set me gently back on solid ground. But until then, I will not let go. However fragile it may be, the rope bridge needs only to be strong enough.

Marjorie Shostak died on October 6, 1996.

Nisa learned of her death in November 1997. This was her response:

Strong. Hwantla held me strongly. We held each other as if we were one. Hwantla, I greet you in the sand where you are sleeping now. Sleep well. I don't know why the spirits have taken you away. All the cows you gave me have died—now I know why.

Tashay is not alone in his sorrow.

Hwantla, the spirits that took you away should not let you get lost on the way. They should take you directly to where they wanted you to go, so that your family will live well and stay well.

The great God took my daughter Hwantla and made me blind. Hwantla was like my eyes, and when God took her away, I became blind. I don't know if I will ever see again, because my daughter has been taken away.

Acknowledgments

The words "fought cancer" are often said, but never with more justification than in the last eight years of Marjorie Shostak's life. Her love of life was intense, but her desire to remain as a force for good in her three children's lives, to see them grow and change another hour, another day, was nothing less than fierce. This book, beautifully crafted to highlight Nisa and her people, only hints at that struggle.

Few things could compete with her family as reasons to live, but Nisa and her continuing story were next on the list. After completing her initial six months of chemotherapy, Marjorie began preparations to go to the Kalahari. It was to be a great and healing adventure, despite the bittersweet ambiguities of the two women's strange and wonderful transcultural friendship.

I cannot pretend to understand the bonds between women, but I could watch in awe as Marjorie's friends rallied to her side in the years thereafter. Always under the shadow of a grave threat to her life, constantly searching for more knowledge, better treatments, she found solace in the effort to write this book. The manuscript she left at the time of her death in 1996, along with many journal entries and letters, was a treasure trove, but not yet a book. Preoccupied as I was with Marjorie's own foremost preoccupation—the happiness of our three children—I could not take on the task of bringing this book to life, of completing it, of persuading a publisher to show it to the world. My own complex emotions presented a thousand obstacles to doing this job well.

But once again, Marjorie was gifted and blessed in her friendships.

The women who, along with Marjorie and Nisa, made this book a reality did so naturally and with powerful but quiet motivation. They did not expect acknowledgment, but they deserve that and more. Marjorie's best friends, Lois Kasper and Sarah Steinhardt, had been at her and my side while she was dying, and in the midst of their own grief afterwards they began immediately to gather manuscript pages, sift through computer disks, and contact Marjorie's agent, Elaine Markson, and publishers who had expressed interest in the book.

Lois, to whose memory this book is dedicated, was already ill with the same disease that had killed Marjorie. Her prognosis was not good. Yet she took on as a major task of her own life that of continuing her friend's life work. They had been pals since second grade, and at Marjorie's funeral Lois lifted the mourners' hearts with a story they both loved to tell, about how they had sung a duet on the stage in elementary school but had to stand back to back to keep from giggling. And so, in a similar way, they echoed each other's emotions for forty-five years, as they courted, married, managed frustrating husbands, and pursued complex careers. They talked endlessly about all three of Marjorie's trips to Africa, beginning in 1969. This was the moment the women's movement was born, and Lois helped Marjorie keep up with the revolution at home even while Marjorie posted bulletins from Africa, reporting on how near–Stone Age women courted, married, and managed frustrating husbands—in ways at once immensely odd and startlingly familiar. The two of them laughed together until the end of Marjorie's life, and Lois was still making others laugh almost until the day she died. She lived to see the book completed and "in press." She smiled as friends and relatives read it to her at her bedside in her last weeks and days. And she died knowing that this mission of hers, to complete her friend's last work, had beautifully succeeded. I have dedicated this book to Lois's memory, as I believe Marjorie would have wanted me to do.

The book's other champion was Sarah Steinhardt, Marjorie's great *Atlanta* friend and our younger daughter's Big Name in the !Kung naming system. Sarah was with Marjorie almost daily during her eight-year struggle with cancer. She and her husband took our family in for weeks when we came home from the second chemotherapy session to find our house in flames. She followed intimately Marjorie's thinking about her last encounter with Nisa and what kind of book should come out of it. Through her own struggles with illness, divorce, and a challenging career in music and teaching, she never flagged in her support for Marjorie while she was alive nor in her devotion to this project after her death. Together she and Lois urged it along month by month, goaded agents, changed publishers, insisted on the very best that they could do for Nisa and Marjorie. And when Lois became too ill to go on with it,

Sarah pushed it to completion, letting Lois know by telephone and e-mail that their dream was indeed coming true.

I strongly hesitate to mention anyone else because there were so many, and I am guaranteed here a sin of omission that will hurt someone I leave out. But there are some who must be mentioned. Betty Castellani, director of the DeKalb Hospital Cancer Center, is a Presbyterian minister whose calling it is to counsel cancer patients and their families. She faces daily what almost all of us shrink from, and she sustained Marjorie through the last four years of her life. Kathy Mote, our nanny throughout all those years and since, is a second mother to our children. She learned, through constant association with Marjorie, to become as good a substitute as anyone could be. Maureen O'Toole is a psychotherapist who befriended Marjorie and became a major support. She could be called at midnight and would be there in minutes, holding Marjorie in her arms, speaking soothing words, massaging her neck. Shlomit Ritz Finkelstein was a source of strength throughout those years. Polly Wiessner, a leading ethnographer of the !Kung, was at Marjorie's side when she lived in Germany to seek a novel cancer treatment. Later, Polly was the one who told Nisa of Marjorie's death and wrote down Nisa's response. Millie Broughton, Marjorie's clinical psychologist, went far beyond professional responsibility. Among her many doctors, Boyd Eaton, Julian Lokey, Richard Leff, and Sidney Stapleton stand out as exceptional.

On the last night of Marjorie's life, Lois, Sarah, Maureen, Betty, and Kathy were all there with me, a passionate grieving seminar of women making end-of-life decisions that they knew I lacked the strength to make myself. In the small hours of that morning, when the very wishes that Marjorie could no longer express were all that mattered, they helped me reason through those wishes. Never was a husband more blessed in his wife's friends.

Our three children, Susanna, Adam, and Sarah, are at this writing 21, 18, and 13. They have survived the greatest loss that a child can experience, after growing up under the shadow of cancer. Their love, strength, and good humor, not just their needs, helped sustain Marjorie throughout her illness, as they have done for me since. Marjorie's parents, Jerome and Edna Shostak, as well as her sister Lucy, all struggling with their own grief, helped in many important ways. During her last weeks they were often at her bedside, and her mother slept beside her in the hospital toward the end.

This project was given a great boost when Brenda Bynum, a distinguished stage actress, director, and teacher in Atlanta, proposed to Marjorie that they mount a play about her last trip to see Nisa. The result, which owes much to Brenda's genius, was a powerful two-woman play, "My Heart is Still Shaking," performed by Brenda and Carol Mitchell-Leon. It tells in less detail the story told in this book, and its performances helped keep the book alive in Marjorie's mind during a most difficult time.

It is indeed lucky that the book finally landed on the desk of Elizabeth Knoll at Harvard University Press. Elizabeth gave it an exceptionally high priority in her busy schedule; she approached it and carried it through as a true labor of love. But the pivotal role at the Press was played by Camille Smith, and it is her participation especially that made the book's connection with Harvard so fortunate. Camille was the manuscript editor of *Nisa* itself, back in 1980 and 1981, and her contribution to that book was great. But when it came to this one, an unfinished manuscript with sheaves of associated letters and journals only mildly to moderately in order, I doubt that this excellent result could have been achieved with anyone else. Not only because of her thorough familiarity with Marjorie and Nisa, but because of her formidable editorial skill, Camille's work was vital. Since she had gone over the manuscript of *Nisa* so many times with Marjorie, discussed every matter of translation, every subtlety of cultural interpretation, only Camille could have edited this book as if Marjorie were still alive and looking over her shoulder.

For a full account of all who played a role in the initial publication of *Nisa*, I hope the reader will consult the acknowledgments written by Marjorie for that book. Without their help, this one could not have existed either. I must mention just a few of them here: Elaine Markson, Marjorie's agent, the first publishing professional to believe in her; Eric Wanner, her first editor at Harvard Press; Irven DeVore and Richard Lee, her anthropological mentors; and others who studied the !Kung, including Nancy Howell, Megan Biesele, Polly Wiessner, John Yellen, Patricia Draper, Henry Harpending, Richard Katz, Verna St. Denis, Nancy DeVore, Lorna Marshall, and John Marshall. As indicated in the text, some of these colleagues also played a role in this project. Last but not least, this book owes its greatest debt to the !Kung people, whose hospitality made it possible, and especially to Nisa herself. Her proud and personal voice proclaimed through Marjorie, to all who would listen, that all women share enough common hopes and dreams, enough obstacles to those dreams, enough humor, and enough pain to be sisters at heart, and to laugh and mourn together across even the widest cultural gaps.

Index